CANNABIS

A Study of its History, Prohibition and Use

Rupert Simmington

Written and Compiled by Rupert Simmington

A Pull No Punches Publication – July 2019

Cover Photo – Cannabis Sativa

ISBN: 9781077454897

ACKNOWLEDGEMENT

Most of the information contained in this book is in the public domain. It would not have been possible had it not been for the work carried out by the Indian Hemp Drugs Commission of 1893, the Le Dain Commission of 1970 and the Shafer Commission of 1972.

My thanks also to those who worked on the Wooten Report of 1968, the La Guardia report of 1944 and especially everyone who contributed to the Panama Canal Zone Military Investigations, who entertained me with their report on the use of marihuana by American Troops.

I would also like to acknowledge the comprehensive studies carried out by the Transnational Institute, the Advisory Council on Drug Abuse in the UK, the Institute of Economics Affairs, the Global Drug Policy Observatory, the United Nations Office of Drugs and Crime and the International Narcotics Control Board.

My admiration goes to the parents of Alfie Dingley, Billy Caldwell and Teagan Appleby. In particular, Alfie's mother Hannah, who fought tooth and nail to provide her son with the cannabis-based medicine that he so desperately needed. Her campaign ultimately forced the UK Government to introduce legislation, enabling thousands of others to receive similar treatment.

I would like to express my respect for the great people of NORML, who have campaigned tirelessly for years to bring about sensible, logical legislation, and who continue to offer free advice for those arrested for cannabis offences.

My respect also goes to those working for the United Patients Alliance and the Multiple Sclerosis Society, who offer support for everyone using cannabis for medicinal purposes.

There is no doubt that this remarkable plant has an important role to play in 21st century medicine, our only challenge is to find even more ways to use it and, to insist that governments allow us to do so.

CONTENTS

FOREWORD

Fifty years ago, on May 19th, 1969, Timothy Leary finally brought an end to the Marihuana Tax Act of 1937, when the U.S Supreme Court overturned his conviction for the illegal possession of marihuana.

Leary had been sentenced to 30-years imprisonment and fined $40,000 for less than a quarter of an ounce of dope.

In a unanimous decision, penned by Justice John Marshall Harlan II, the court concluded that the Marihuana Tax Act of 1937 was unconstitutional, and as a result, Timothy Leary's conviction was overturned.

After leaving the court a free man, Leary announced his intention of running for the Governorship of California, under the slogan;

"Come together, Join the party"

Things have changed a lot since then and the cannabis plant, which for so long was demonised in the western world, is now enjoying an almost celebrity status, especially among the more enlightened members of the international medical community.

The use of cannabis for medicinal purposes can be traced back to at least a thousand years before Christ and even in Victorian times, enlightened European practitioners realised that it had enormous potential.

As Michael Donovan, an Irish apothecarist who, in 1829, wrote, The State of Pharmacy in Ireland, stated;

"I content myself with expressing my belief that Indian hemp will one day or another, occupy one of the highest places amongst the means of combatting disease".

BHANG, GANJA, CHARAS – A SPIRITUAL TRINITY

The cannabis plant played a vital role in ancient China, where it was grown to produce fibre for ropes, cloth and paper and for its seeds, to produce animal feed and oil for lamps. Although there is evidence that they also used it for medicinal purposes, they were not the first to identify its psychoactive properties. In all probability, that tradition began with tribes living in remote regions of the Himalayas, an area which now includes parts of Iran, Afghanistan, Pakistan, India, Nepal, Tibet, Russia and China.

From there, it came out of the mountains and via the silk road, spread to Turkey and Europe, where it was grown for rope and clothing. Arab traders took it to Africa and African slaves took it to Brazil and South America, while indentured Indian workers carried it to Jamaica and other islands in the Caribbean.

It has played an important role in Indian culture for thousands of years. Its use in Ayurvedic medicine can be traced back to at least 1,000 years before Christ, but its role in spiritual rituals goes back even further. In India, cannabis has always been associated with Shiva, and because of this, Hindus consider the plant to be sacred. Shiva temples can be found all over the country, where devotees and priests smoke ganja every day of the week, as people leave gifts of cannabis, as an act of devotion.

There are three forms of cannabis used in India;

A) *Bhang* is an edible preparation made from cannabis leaves, although in a few areas, flowering tops of the female plant are also added. It is generally sold in liquid form, mixed with either water or milk but sweets and fried dishes, which contain bhang paste, are also very popular.

B) *Ganja* is what American's call marijuana, weed, herb or grass. This is the dried flower tops from the female plant, which in India is generally smoked in conical-shaped, clay pipes known as chillums.

C) *Charas* is solidified, sticky resin, which the plant exudes as a protective coating, sheltering the flowers from intense sunlight and periods of drought. The resin can be extracted from the plant in a number of different ways. In India and Nepal, it is done by rubbing the plants by hand, while they are still growing in the fields.

The most common form of cannabis resin is hashish, produced in Turkey, Lebanon and Morocco, which is prepared from dry, dead plants, which are sieved to produce a very fine powder. In the case of Lebanon, the powder is put into small cotton pouches, tied up tight and then pressed into bars, by first steaming and then pressing them.

Although the word hashish has its roots in Arabic, Muslim tribesmen in the Himalayan regions of Afghanistan and Pakistan who have their own dialect call it chars. Phonetically, it sounds very similar to charas and this is borne out by the fact that in India a charas lover is called a charasi while in Afghanistan, he is known as a charsi.

This has recently led to a fiery debate among the old school smokers, particularly in England. Some are of the opinion that the word charas should only be applied to the hand-rubbed variety made in India and parts of Nepal and that everything else is hashish, while others point to the fact that as far as the Afghanis and Pakistanis are concerned, they have been making chars for at least 300 years.

The word "charas" has its roots in both Sanskrit and Persian, linguists have pointed out that it is connected to the word for a type of primitive bag used by beggars and wanderers.

Afghan tribesmen dry the female tops of the plants for several weeks and then sieve them using a fine cloth. They fill leather bags with the moist powder and leave it to cure for about 4 months. In the early spring, they place the bags in sunlight in order to warm them up and then they beat them with sticks, to release the oil in the resin and they continue to work it until it is a solid, oily black mass.

This method is far more effective; hand-rubbed charas is a very slow laborious process, completely unsuitable for any form of commercial production. It also contains a fairly high, water content, and subsequently is prone to mould if it's not stored properly.

Chars on the other hand is extremely stable in any climate, and therefore perfect for inter-community trading, between the various tribes who inhabit these remote regions of the Himalayas.

The one thing that India, Nepal, Afghanistan and Pakistan have in common, is that the resin they produce has all come from Himalayan varieties of the plant, so to be fair to everyone, perhaps the word charas, should be applied to all cannabis resin produced in the Himalayas.

That would only leave one problem, how to distinguish between a resin that has been produced by sieving dried plants from one which has been prepared by rubbing the plant with one's hands?

I would be more than happy to refer to the latter as "nasher", a word much favoured by charas smokers in the Parvati Valley. However, since I am a member of the Old School Indian Brigade, I shall continue to use the word charas, when describing a resin that has been gently rubbed from the plant by hand and all other resins by their country of origin, and now that has been cleared up, it's time to move on.

Hinduism evolved from the Vedic period, around 4000 years ago, when Aryans, Indo-Europeans, began to settle on the banks of the Indus River, which was populated by people belonging to the Harappa culture. It was the integration of these two groups which produced the Vedic Age, which used Sanskrit, a language that had been introduced by the Aryans, to compile India's ancient Vedic texts known as Vedas. These consist of chants, prayers, medicinal texts as well as rituals concerning family life, and the structure of society as a whole.

Many of the concepts laid out during this period, including the caste system, the designation of the cow as a sacred animal and the belief in reincarnation, became key elements of the Hindu faith. Hinduism is based on the Trimurti, the Hindu trinity of Brahma, Vishnu and Shiva. Brahma is considered to be the creator, Vishnu the preserver and Shiva the destroyer. Destruction is viewed as an essential component, since it is only through destruction that creation can once again take place. It is a cyclic system, which explains why Hindus believe in reincarnation, where life is the prelude to death, which is in itself, merely a prelude to life.

The three main Gods manifest themselves in different ways; Vishnu for instance often manifests himself as Krishna or Rama, while Shiva manifests himself as Natraj, the cosmic dancer or Hanuman, the Monkey God. Shiva's consort, Parvati, also appears as Kali, the Goddess of Death or Durga, a demon that fights against evil. Their children are Ganesh, the God of Wisdom and Skanda, the God of War. Vishnu's consort is Lakshmi, the Goddess of Wealth who is highly venerated in Bombay, the commercial capital of India.

Hinduism presents many challenges for the western mind. The thousands of deities that make up its spiritual pantheon, often appear to have no rhyme or reason, but on closer inspection and with many years of study, one is able to see that they are all part of the Trimurti family.

Shaivites are devotees of Shiva, who practice an ancient form of Hinduism known as Shaivism. They believe that Shiva is the source of everything, who performs the five distinct functions as the one who creates, preserves, conceals, reveals and destroys everything. The river Ganges, which flows from Shiva's head, is considered to be the purifying, liberating consciousness of all divine knowledge and whoever bathes in it, becomes shivam, meaning pure or enlightened.

Shiva is often depicted holding a trident or *trishul*, and this represents his power to destroy the three obstacles to enlightenment, namely egoism, attachment and delusion.

Sadhus are a religious sect, who adhere to the practice of sadhana, a path of spiritual discipline. It is a Sanskrit word, meaning to practise and there are around 5 million of them in India today, where they play an important role in society.

Many wander around the country living in forests, caves and Shiva temples, surviving on offerings, spending their time meditating and smoking chillums which they fill with ganja or charas. Whenever a group of them congregate, chillum smoking becomes a ritualistic, religious act, which aids meditation and contemplation, stimulating communication with powers of a divine nature.

They believe that by renouncing physical attachment to material wealth, abstaining from sexual practices and devotion to Shiva, their karma and that of the communities that they pass through, is purified. This is one of the fundamental reasons why people donate gifts of food and why they are revered. In Hindu epics like the Mahabharata and the Ramayana, sadhus are depicted as saints, seers, sages and holy men, who are considered to be chaste, virtuous and noble.

There are many forms of sadhus, some like the Shaiva sadhus follow Shiva, while Vaishnava sadhus follow Vishnu. These two groups consist of many sub-groups, like the Naga Sadhus, easily recognisable by their thick dreadlocks, who appear naked holding a sword or a club, who, in ancient times, protected Hindu pilgrims from Mughal warriors.

For more than 2,000 years, bhang has been used by millions of Indians of all classes during the spring festival of Holi, which marks the end of winter and the beginning of spring. It is for many the most popular festival of all, an explosion of colour and music, where people dance in the streets, throwing coloured water and powder at each other as they yell;

"*Bura na mano, Holi hai*";

This can be interpreted as;

"*It's OK, it's only Holi*".

It is a festival of love, when people forgive and forget the problems committed in the previous year and it is seen as a time to mend broken relationships. Like all Indian festivals, Holi has a deep religious significance, illustrating the power of faith and its ability to overcome evil.

One of the principle stories that relate to Holi, depicts the son of Hiranyakashipu, a demon king who had acquired special powers. These prevented him from being killed by an animal or human, neither indoors nor out, neither during the day nor at night, neither on land nor at sea, by weapons that were neither thrown nor held by hand.

He became so arrogant, he believed he was a God and demanded that everyone should worship him. His son, Prahlada disagreed and continued to worship Vishnu which infuriated his family, and in order to teach him a lesson, his evil aunt, Holika, invited Prahlada to sit on top of a fire with her.

She wore a magic cloak which was said to protect her from the flames, but the cloak wrapped itself around her nephew instead, protecting him, while she was consumed by the fire. The Holika bonfire that is always lit on the first day of the festival, commemorates this event.

Vishnu then took the form of Narasimba, a half-human, half-lion, which was neither human nor animal and he waited until dusk, which is neither day nor night. He then sat on a doorstep, which was neither indoors nor outdoors and placed King Hiranyakashipu on his lap, which was neither land nor sea and then disembowelled the evil king using his claws, which were neither a handheld weapon nor one that was thrown.

Some of the biggest celebrations take place in Varanasi, formerly known as Benares. It is a city that is synonymous with Shiva and one of the holiest places in India. Pilgrims come here every day of the week to bathe in the sacred waters, which washes away their sins, and devout Hindus are cremated there, or have their ashes scattered in the waters.

Shiva is the Lord of Bhang and during the Holi festival, devotees prepare drinks and snacks all along the banks of the river. Thandai, a delicious milkshake made from bhang, crushed almonds, pistachios and sugar, is given out free, along with bhang pakoras and little sweets called gollies, a sweet intoxicating green halva, made from bhang, ghee and sugar.

Dussehra, or Vijaya Dashami, is the last day of the Navaratri Festival which is celebrated all over India. It commemorates the victory of Rama over Ravana, which forms the basis of the Ramayana, one of the most loved and important works of Indian literature, written thousands of year ago.

The story is very similar to Helen of Troy. Ravana, the wicked King of Lanka, stole Rama's wife Sita but with Hanuman's help, Rama got his wife back.

Hanuman the Monkey God, an incarnation of Shiva, set fire to his tail and jumped around the countryside burning everything in his path as he shouted, "burn Lanka, burn". It is another illustration of the power of good over evil and in many parts of India, it also celebrates the victory of the Goddess Durga, who killed the evil demon Mahishasur.

Local actors and street performers wander around towns and villages performing excerpts from this ancient book to commemorate the event. It is street theatre at its best, and the colourful costumes and strange looking characters are an impressive sight.

In Bengal, male family members carry an image of Durga to the river, and after washing her, they return to the home where they and their guests participate in the drinking of bhang tea and little sweetmeats containing bhang paste.

A similar religious custom takes place in Orissa, at the Jagannath Temple in Puri, where, every year, the temple priests prepare bhang drinks and sweets which they and their congregation consume, during a festival which honours Ganesh, the son of Shiva and Parvati.

Shiva of course has many festivals dedicated to him, and they don't come any bigger than Maha Shivratri which means, the Great Shiva Night. This festival not only celebrates his wedding to Parvati, it also commemorates his unselfish act which saved the world.

Legend recalls that when the oceans erupted, a bottle of poison appeared which was so toxic, a single drop was said to be enough to destroy the whole world. Shiva drank the poison and as he waited for it to take effect, all the Gods spent the night dancing and singing in order to keep him awake. Shiva's neck was said to have turned blue, but he survived the ordeal by drinking bhang, which cooled the poison's fire and the universe was saved. An ancient text, called the Shivmahimna Stotra recalled the event;

"When the poison came up through the churning of the ocean by the gods and demons, they were all aghast with fear as if the untimely end of all creation was imminent. In your kindness, you drank all the poison that still makes your throat blue".

Shaivites stay awake all night, smoking chillums filled with ganja, chanting mantras or prayers, to commemorate the event.

In the north of India, it is Shiva's wedding to Parvati that is the focus of attention during Maha Shivratri. The lingam, a phallic symbol which is found in every Shiva temple, which sits in a yoni, representing the female sexual organ, is decorated with flowers and dairy products. Milk, yoghurt, bhang and other offerings are poured over the lingam every few hours, while the temple priests and sadhus, drink bhang and smoke chillums filled with ganja or charas, to symbolise their connection with Shiva.

Others believe that this is the night when Shiva performed the dance of creation, preservation and destruction, when he took the form of Natraj, the cosmic dancer.

His devotees drink bhang, smoke chillums and then perform a dance routine, while others chant and sing prayers. Certain Hindu temples around the country celebrate this event by holding classical dance festivals. It is a colourful, vibrant and exciting aspect of Hindu worship, which continues today at temples in Konark, Khajuraho, and Petakatal.

During one of my many visits to India, I went to Rameswaram, situated at the very bottom of the country. The town sits on a small island in the Gulf of Mannar, and a little ferry carried pilgrims there from the mainland.

It is one of the holiest places in India, especially to the followers of Shiva. Legend has it that Rama paid homage here before the battle of Lanka, described in great detail in the Indian epic, the Ramayana.

The Ramanathaswarmy temple, dedicated to Shiva, was built in the 12th century, the interior is breath-taking, and it is without doubt, one of the gems of India. Highly decorated corridors containing beautifully carved, wooden sculptures, painted in bright colours, stretch out in all directions. The inner sanctum contains larger than life statues of Hanuman and Rama, paying homage to Shiva and Parvati who are seated in front of a stone lingam, with an intricately carved head of a cobra behind it.

Only Hindus are allowed into this sacred place, but a local sadhu that I stayed with in town, took me in and we smoked a few chillums of charas there. It was an unforgettable experience for me, I had smoked many chillums in Shiva temples all over India, but never in one as beautiful, or as holy as that one.

The Kulu valley in the Himalayas is often described as the "Valley of The Gods" because the small isolated villages, scattered all over the region have their own stone temples.

Within these are images of ancient earth spirits, demons known as devatas which play an integral part of village life, not only worshipped but also chastised when things are going badly.

When Shiva and his wife Parvati were walking there one day, Parvati dropped a jar she was holding that contained the spirits of pagan gods that Shiva had given her as a present. As the jar fell to the ground it broke, the spirits escaped and began to dance around the valley. Parvati thought they looked cute and she begged her husband to leave them in peace.

Another story associated with Shiva and Parvati, concerns the hot water springs in the village of Manikaren, some of which are located within the Sikh temple.

Parvati was bathing there one day and left her earrings on the bank of the river and when she returned, she was dismayed to see that they were gone. Shiva was very angry and demanded the spirit responsible to return them. A demon serpent had hidden them in his nostrils and when he heard Shiva's voice, he trembled so much that the earrings flew into the air and landed at Parvati's feet. At the same time boiling hot water sprouted out of the ground, and it has been gushing out ever since.

Sadhus and Shaivites have been known to walk from the bottom of India to this holy place, sometimes taking more than 10 years to complete the journey.

Charas that has been hand-rubbed in the Parvati Valley, which runs parallel to the Kulu Valley, is considered to be a holy sacrament and therefore, venerated by sadhus and Shaivites.

The most important place in the Parvati Valley is Khirganga. There is no temple there, no town, and not even a village and it is a long, hard walk up the mountain to get there. There are hot springs and a small cave to sleep in, but it is considered to be an extremely holy place. The reason is, on a good day, if the climatic conditions allow it and if one is extremely lucky, it is possible to get a glimpse of Mount Kailash, the home of Shiva, and a sacred mountain to four religions.

One of the rituals when smoking a chillum is to chant;

"*Kailash Patti*".

Which translates as;

"Kailash, where the cannabis seed was planted".

Lord Shiva lives at the top of Mount Kailash, where he spends his time making love to his wife Parvati, meditating and smoking cha*ras*. For a Hindu to visit this sacred mountain and to bathe in its view, is to attain release from the clutches of ignorance and delusion. The ancient origins of Hinduism, Jainism and Buddhism suggest that it was the location of the mythical mountain of Meru, the "Axis Mundi", the centre of the earth and a place of power and mystery.

Unfortunately, very few have had the opportunity of visiting it, because this pyramid shaped mountain, rising up more than 22,000 feet, is situated in a remote region of Tibet. There are no roads and even with a rugged 4-wheel-drive vehicle, it is a long and dangerous journey, which can take more than three weeks.

Mount Kailash was already famous long before the Indian epics, the Mahabharata and the Ramayana were written, and many believe it was a holy place of an earlier civilisation that has long disappeared. Ancient astronaut theorists have described it as an ancient power source, an actual pyramid that inspired every pyramid that followed it, although nobody will ever be allowed to investigate its summit because it is forbidden to climb it, at least for now anyway.

It is therefore one of the holiest places on planet earth and one that is the least visited, with less than a few thousand pilgrims making the journey every year.

Buddhists call it *Kang Rinpoche* meaning "*The Precious One of Glacial Snow*" and they regard it as the home of Demchog and his consort Dorje Phagmo. Jains call it Astapada and they sincerely believe it was where Rishaba, the first of the 24 Tirthankaras, attained his enlightenment. The Bon's, a pre-Buddhist shamanistic religion call it Tise, the seat of the Sky Goddess Sipaimen and the site of a legendary battle, when the forces of the Buddhist Sage Milarepa, defeated the Bon Shaman, Naro Bong-chung.

Khirganga offers a rare opportunity for sadhus to get a glimpse of this sacred mountain and many will stay there for weeks if necessary, until climatic conditions allow them to have a view of Shiva's home.

There are some beautiful Shiva temples situated around the Kulu Valley, in particular the grey sandstone temple of Gauri Shankar, another incarnation of Shiva, who was responsible for inventing the chillum, hence the chant when lighting one;

"Boom Shankar".

The temple, which sits on a paved square, also has a fine statue of Nandi, the celestial bull, who faces the entrance to ward off evil spirits.

One of the many stories associated with Shiva and one that demonstrates his status, concerns a fight between Brahma and Vishnu. They began to argue about who was the greatest and as the battle became more intense, the other gods called on Shiva to intervene. He turned himself into a column of fire and placed himself between them so they could no longer fight.

Brahma took the form of a swan and tried to fly to the top of the flame and as he flew upwards, he came across a flower that was slowly floating down. Brahma asked the flower where it had come from and the flower told him that it had been placed on the top of the flame as an offering. Brahma took the flower as proof that he had reached the top.

Shiva knew that Brahma was lying and as a punishment, he told Brahma that nobody would ever worship him, because liars did not deserve to be venerated. It is interesting to note that there is only one temple in the whole of India that is dedicated to Brahma, and that is the Pushkar temple in Rajasthan. Shiva also punished the flower and told it that it would never be worthy to be used as an offering, because it too, had lied.

Sikhs have a long history with the cannabis plant and there is a lovely story, concerning Guru Gobind Singh, the founder of the Sikh religion. He was involved in a battle with a hill tribe who used a huge war elephant, which carried an enormous sword in its trunk. A man was given bhang to drink and told to stop the elephant by looking in its eyes and commanding it to stop.

After drinking the bhang, the brave soldier rushed towards the war beast and the elephant was so scared, it stopped dead in its tracks. The hill tribe fled in fear, the battle was won and Guru Gobind Singh was so impressed, he called his servant and told him to prepare a bhang drink for him, so that he too, may be fortified by its power. From that day, Sikhs drank bhang before a battle and even though they are no longer at war, the custom persists today and even though they are forbidden to use alcohol or tobacco, bhang is not only tolerated, it is revered.

The importance of bhang in Indian culture was beautifully summed up by Mr J.M Campbell, an elderly tax collector for the British Government who lived in Bombay in the 19th century;

"*To forbid or even seriously to restrict the use of so holy and gracious a herb as the hemp, would cause widespread suffering and annoyance and to the large bands of worshipped ascetics, deep-seated anger. It would rob the people of a solace in discomfort, of a cure in sickness, of a guardian whose gracious protection saves them from the attacks of evil influences, and whose mighty power makes the devotee of the Victorious, overcoming the demons of hunger and thirst, of panic, fear of the glamour of Maya or matter, and of madness, able to rest to look on the Eternal, till the Eternal, possessing him body and soul, frees him from the haunting of self and receives him into the ocean of Being*".

I can only endorse what Mr Campbell said, and I think it proves beyond doubt, that there were a few British living in India, who understood the importance of social and religious values of the indigenous population, it is only a pity that there were not more like him.

One thing I would like to stress before finishing this section, is to emphasise the spiritual significance of bhang drinking and ganja and charas smoking, because this is the aspect that is sacred, not only for sadhus, Shaivites, rishis, babas and temple priests, but to all Hindus.

In the village of Bauri in Gaya there is a large hollow stone. Local legends say that it is the bowl of a famous folk hero called Lorik, who used it to mix his bhang, before going into battle. Other epic poems from the 12th century, contain stories about brave warriors drinking bhang before performing magnificent feats of courage.

Within this context, the cannabis plant is not a narcotic and it is not a drug, but a mythical, sacred stimulant, and one which demands the greatest respect of all those who use it. Mr Campbell was well aware of this, as he so eloquently said;

"*He who scandalises the user of bhang shall suffer the torments of hell so long as the sun endures. He who drinks bhang foolishly or for pleasure without religious rites is as guilty as the sinner of a hundred thousand sins. He who drinks wisely and according to rule, be he ever so low, even though his body is smeared with human excrement and urine, is Shiva. No god or man is as good as the religious drinker of bhang*".

The use of cannabis for spiritual purposes, is seen in all its glory at the Kumbh Mela, the largest gathering of people the world has ever seen, where sadhus, Shaivites, and Indian pilgrims of all castes bathe in a sacred river. This event takes place every 12 years in 4 different cities, all of which are located on the banks of holy rivers.

Haridwar on the banks of the river Ganges, Trimbac-Nashik on the banks of the river Godavari and Ujjain on the banks of the river Shipra. The greatest Kumbh Mela of all is at Allahabad, which sits on the confluence of two sacred rivers, the Ganges and the Yamuna.

It is perhaps the most important pilgrimage a Hindu can make, and millions attend them whenever they are held. The 2013 Kumbh Mela in Allahabad attracted 120 million people during the two-month festival, with more than 30 million arriving on the first day, prompting the world's press to describe it as the, "greatest show on earth".

There is a strict code for the order of bathing, where the naked Naga Sadhus, their bodies daubed in ash and cow dung, take preference over ordinary pilgrims who are forced to wait their turn, before plunging into the sacred waters. At the 1974 Kumbh Mela, held in Haridwar, a favourite among Shaivites, because it is the place where the Ganges emerges from the Himalayas, a street was covered in hot coals. Shiva's devotees walked down it, barefoot, smoking chillums as they went, chanting mantras to Shiva, as ordinary pilgrims looked on in disbelief. It is a festival that has been written about for centuries by many foreign travellers including Mark Twain, who saw the event in 1895, which he described as;

"It is wonderful, the power of a faith like that, that can make multitudes upon multitudes of the old and weak and the young and frail enter without hesitation or complaint upon such incredible journeys and endure the resultant miseries without repining".

Mark Twain was clearly impressed, as he wrote;

"It is done in love, or it is done in fear; I do not know which it is. No matter what the impulse is, the act born of it is beyond imagination, marvellous to our kind of people, the cold whites".

The most important aspect of the festival is what Indians call "darshan", the absorption of a spiritual sight, by being in its presence. For this reason, millions of sadhus and ascetics of all kinds attend the event, since it provides ordinary pilgrims with the opportunity to consult them on a wide range of topics.

This festival, perhaps more than anything, illustrates the importance of the sadhu's role in Indian society, which values spirituality, above everything else.

GANJA AND THE RASTAFARI FAITH

India is not the only country with a religious connection to cannabis. Jamaica is known all over the world for reggae music and Rastas, ganja smoking followers of the Rastafari faith, which began to develop in the 1930's, after Haile Selassie was crowned Emperor of Ethiopia on November 2nd, 1930.

Marcus Garvey, a Jamaican born political activist, who founded the UNIA (Universal Negro Improvement Association) in 1914, believed that all descendants of African slaves should return to Africa and build a new nation, free from colonial rule.

In 1916 he moved to New York, where he got a job working in a printing shop and at night, he preached his message on street corners, urging others to follow his example. He gave his first public lecture at St Marks Church, in which he criticised the slave-trade, the exploitation of the black race and the hypocrisy of the American system, which claimed that all men were equal.

Later that year, he began to travel around the country in order to deliver his message to a wider audience and the following year, with the support of others who shared his beliefs, he opened a branch of the UNIA in Harlem. On August 17th, 1918 he launched a newspaper called Negro World, which he used to encourage more people to join the UNIA which, by 1919 had more than 2 million members.

In 1921, an evangelical Baptist preacher, by the name of James Morris Webb, joined Garvey's association. Webb had written a book called, *The Black Man – The Father of Civilisation*, which had been published two years earlier. The book, in many ways, played an important role in the foundation of the Rastafari faith, since it examines the Bible from a black perspective.

Reverend Webb presents a very strong argument which states that most of the key figures featured in the Bible, were black, a hypothesis which was, at the time, even more controversial than it is today, although extremely logical none the less.

The foreword explains his view that the woodwork on Solomon's Temple was carried out by Sidonians, a black tribe descended from Canaan, son of Ham whose father was Noah. Webb believed that King Solomon himself must have been a black man because his mother was a Hittite, a tribe that was descended from Heth, the son of Canaan. He points out that Jesus was born of the tribe of Judah and therefore must have also been a descendant of Canaan and therefore could not have been white.

Webb reminded his readers that according to biblical scriptures, Nimrod founded Babylon, Menes was the first King of Egypt and they were both descendants of Ham.

It was James Webb who coined the phrase;

"Look to Africa, when a black King shall be crowned, for the day of deliverance is at hand".

This was a quote that Garvey often used and one that has been incorrectly attributed to him. There is no doubt that Webb was extremely proud of his black heritage, and this was a view that Garvey shared with a passion and one which was at the very core of his teachings.

Ganja was already widely used in the country and had been since the early 19th century. It was introduced by Indian indentured workers, 40,000 of whom were taken there by the East India Company, as labourers, servants, managers and bookkeepers, who worked on the plantations and in the homes, offices, shops and factories, belonging to the white colonists. They took cannabis seeds with them, primarily to produce bhang for religious purposes, but its use as a recreational stimulant, soon became part of Jamaican culture, especially among the poorer classes.

When the International Opium Treaty was signed in the Hague in 1912, the Colonial Government of Jamaica decided to adopt the treaty and incorporate it within Jamaican law.

The Council of Evangelical Churches, supported by white colonial planters and traders, urged the government to include ganja as a prohibited substance. Their chief argument at the time was that cannabis had already been banned in the British colonies of Mauritius in 1840, and in Singapore in 1870, and as a result, the Jamaican Legislative Council introduced the Ganja Law in 1913. This gave the authorities unrestricted power, to arrest without cause and to impose severe prison sentences and floggings on anyone who was viewed as a threat to colonial rule.

Poor, working class Jamaicans viewed it as a racist law, introduced by white colonists, to repress any notion of rebellion, freedom and independence.

The post-slavery era saw a huge rise in revivalist teachings. Methodists, Baptists, Congregationalists and Evangelists began to replace the traditional Protestant teachings, and this was particularly true in Jamaica. At the end of the 19th century, there was a huge rise in the number of people attending prayer meetings, where people would pray directly to the Holy Spirit, rather than to Jesus.

Life was hard, the Jamaican economy was an agricultural one, that relied on the export of bananas, coffee, nuts and sugar, along with rum, pineapples and other tropical fruits. Its wealth and its land was owned and controlled by a minority of white colonists, who viewed the black man as nothing more than a tool, a beast of burden, whose role was merely to provide labour from which the planter derived his wealth.

The vast majority of its population were descendants of slaves, brought over from Africa to work on the plantations. When the Great War ended in 1918, many black Jamaicans, returning from the horrors of war, demanded better wages, more humane living conditions and union representation.

Indians were not the only indentured workers that were brought over by the East India Company, Chinese workers had also been exported to Jamaica by British colonists.

They introduced opium to the country, which the local, ganja smoking labourers disliked immensely, causing a lot of friction between the two communities.

This spilled over in 1918, when riots broke out after a story appeared in *The Gleaner*, claiming that a group of Chinese had beaten a local man to death. The riots quickly spread to other parts of St Catherine and the parishes of St Anne, St Mary and Clarendon, where Chinese shops were looted and then burned to the ground.

As Bob Marley wrote,

"A hungry man is an angry man".

Jamaicans were both hungry and angry and it was the Chinese who bore the brunt of their frustration.

Ganja was viewed as the source of all social discontent and the white planters, supported by the church, began to demand tougher legislation and as a result, the Dangerous Drug Law was introduced in 1924. This imposed a £100 fine for anyone caught in possession of ganja, with mandatory imprisonment for those who couldn't pay. A wave of police brutality swept across the country as they raided houses, closed down social clubs and harassed anyone who was connected with ganja smoking.

When Haile Selassie was crowned Emperor of Ethiopia in 1930, Leonard Percival Howell, a Jamaican by birth, was in New York. He had joined Garvey's Universal Negro Improvement Association in Harlem and although Garvey had already returned to Jamaica, Howell adopted many of his beliefs, which encouraged black consciousness and the rejection of white, Anglo-Saxon ideals, which had enslaved and exploited the black man.

Howell began preaching his message on the street corners of Harlem, which attracted the attention of the local authorities. He was seen as a political threat and as a result, he was deported in 1932 and returned to Jamaica, where he decided to pronounce Haile Selassie as the new messiah.

Joseph Hibbert had already started a movement in 1931, when he returned from Costa Rica, where he had been working as a farm hand for 20 years.

As a child he had been a member of the Ethiopian Baptist Church, which had been founded in Jamaica in the 18th century by George Lisle, an emancipated slave who became the first American missionary when he arrived in Jamaica in 1782.

When Hibbert returned to Jamaica, he began to preach the beliefs of the Ethiopian Coptic faith and as a result of studying an Ethiopian translation of the Bible, he had already identified Haile Selassie as the new messiah.

The Oriental Orthodox faith is very different to that practised by the Catholic church, who, like the Protestants, believe in the two natures of Christ, who is seen to have a divine nature, as well as a human one.

Oriental Orthodox Churches believe in the unified nature of Christ, a view which was first put forward by Cyril of Alexandria. He was a central character in the Christian movement in the 4th century, who believed in the single nature of the Word of God, where the divine and human nature of Christ becomes a single entity. This view, known as miaphysitism, believes that since Jesus Christ is both divine and human, his essence is, in nature, the same as God the Father.

At the Council of Chalcedon in 451 AD, 500 Bishops from Alexandria, Antioch and Jerusalem, refused to accept the Catholic Church's view of dyophysitism, (two natures of Christ), and this caused the first major split within the Christian faith.

Ethiopia established Coptic Orthodox Christianity as its national religion in 333 AD, it was a founding member of the World Council of Churches and its beliefs and manner of worship has remained unchanged.

Saint John Chrysostom, Archbishop of Constantinople at the end of the 4th century, spoke highly of the Ethiopians in Jerusalem, who had no difficulty understanding the Christian teachings. Socrates of Constantinople was adamant that Ethiopia was one of the regions visited by Mathew the Apostle, a fact that is not disputed by the Catholic Church, so Ethiopia has a religious history that stretches back to the beginning of Christianity.

One of their sacred texts is the *Kêbra Nagast*, "The Glory of the Kings". This remarkable book tells the story of the Queen of Sheba and her only son Menyelek, who had been fathered by King Solomon.

It is an incredible tale, which traces the journey of the Ark of the Covenant or the Ark of Law as the Ethiopians call it, from Jerusalem to Ethiopia. Many believe it was written around the 6th century, by a Coptic priest, because the biblical references in the book, conform to traditional Coptic beliefs that were prevalent at the time. The book first came to the attention of western scholars, when an Arabic translation of it was discovered in the 14th century.

For Ethiopians, the *Kêbra Nagast* represents tangible proof, that they are descendants from the tribes of Israel, and that their Kings can trace their Solomonic line, all the way back to King David and King Solomon himself.

Most western scholars disagree, but what cannot be denied, is the fact that Ethiopians believe it, and some would merely point to the Book of Psalms;

"Ethiopia had stretched out her hands to God, and He went to her, with the Ark, to preside over Menyelek's Kingdom, which was established in accordance with the commands that He had given to Moses and the prophets and priests of Israel".

When Haile Selassie was crowned, the head priest, His Holiness Abuna Kyrilos, the Ethiopian Archbishop, proclaimed;

"Ye princes and ministers, ye nobles and chiefs of the army, ye soldiers and people of Ethiopia, and ye doctors and chiefs of the clergy, ye professors and priests, look ye upon our Emperor Haile Selassie the First, descended from the dynasty of Menelik the First, who was born of Solomon and of the Queen of Sheba. A dynasty perpetuated without interruption from that time to King Sehale Selassie and to our times".

It's a great story, and like many ancient myths and legends, that have now been shown to be based on actual, rather than imaginary events, this one has all the hallmarks of a genuine revelation.

The Ethiopians continue to be the custodians of the Ark, which is kept in the church of Our Lady Mary of Zion. Only one priest is allowed to enter the inner sanctum where the Ark is kept, and it is a job that he has for life. Nobody has ever been allowed to see it, which explains why nobody believes it, but the fact remains that the Ethiopians believe it and that they continue to protect it.

Holy relics have been around for thousands of years, churches claim to have bones of Holy Saints and pieces of wood from the cross that Christ was crucified on, so it's a good bet that the Ark would have ended up somewhere safe, why not Ethiopia?

Henry Dunkley was another Jamaican preacher who had arrived at the same conclusion as Hibbert. Dunkley had spent years working as a seaman for the United Fruit Company, but when he returned to Jamaica in 1933, he founded a church group, on the site of the old King of Kings Ethiopian Mission.

Robert Hinds had also studied the Ethiopian version of the Bible and it wasn't long before he, Hibbert, Dunkley and Howell, started a new form of revivalism with a political, social twist. In 1933, they began to travel around the countryside, spreading the word that the Black Messiah had been crowned. Their teachings, which were very critical of slavery, encouraged Jamaicans to think of Ethiopia as their home and Haile Selassie as their King.

Howell in particular, endorsed Black Supremacy, which he believed was the most effective weapon against white colonial rule, criticising white church leaders for perpetrating lies that he said were designed to subdue and subjugate the black race. In January 1934, he and Robert Hinds were arrested and charged with sedition.

During the trial that took place in March of that year, Howell proclaimed Haile Selassie as the new, Black Messiah, who had returned to earth to free his people. He was sentenced to two years imprisonment by Robert William Lyall-Grant, Jamaica's Chief Justice and it marked the beginning of his struggle against colonial rule, which lasted his entire life, throughout which he continued to promote the Rastafari faith.

Those early preachers were the founders of the Rastafari faith, which they promoted by reciting passages from the Bible, to illustrate their belief that Haile Selassie's coronation, signalled the beginning of the End of Days.

The word Rastafari is an amalgamation of Haile Selassie's name prior to his coronation, Ras Tafari Makonnen. Ras is the Ethiopian word for Prince, so Rastafari can be interpreted as, one who follows Prince Tafari. Ethiopians believe that he is a direct descendant of King Solomon and King David, and Howell and his fellow preachers, quoted biblical passages to explain their beliefs, Psalms 68:31;

"Princes shall come out of Egypt; Ethiopia shall soon stretch out her hands unto God".

Two of the many titles bestowed on Haile Selassie when he was crowned, was King of Kings and Lord of Lords, which they saw as a fulfilment of Revelations 19:16;

"And he hath on his vesture and on his thigh a name written, King of Kings and Lord of Lords".

Howell was particularly attracted to passages in Revelations that deal with the Book of Seals, Revelations 5:2-5;

"And I saw a strong angel proclaiming with a loud voice, who is worthy to open the book and to break the seals thereof. And no man in heaven, nor in earth, neither under the earth, was able to open the book, neither to look thereon. And I wept much, because no man was found worthy to open and to read the book. And one of the elders saith unto me, Weep not: behold the Lion of the tribe of Judah, the Root of David, hath prevailed to open the book and to break the seven seals thereof".

When Italy invaded Ethiopia in 1936, Haile Selassie appealed to the League of Nations and their failure to act, was seen as proof of the Babylonian conspiracy, against the black race. Haile Selassie, his family, priests and advisors fled to England, where he set up his government in exile, in a large residence in Bath, called Fairfield House. He was politicly very active during the five years he lived there, addressing the League of Nations, where he condemned war in all its forms, corresponded with world leaders and gained the support of Britain, for a free Ethiopia. *Time Magazine* made him internationally famous, when his photograph appeared on the front cover, in recognition of his nomination as the "man of the year".

1938 marked a year of civil unrest in Jamaica, the *Daily Gleaner* published a story on May 3rd, under the headline;

"4 dead, 9 in hospital, 89 in Jail. Police forced to shoot down rioters in Westmoreland. Dollar-a-day demand ends in death".

It was an act of desperation on the part of Jamaican workers, who were unable to feed their families as a result of low wages, excessive taxation, high rents and the spiralling cost of basic foodstuffs.

Jamaican dockers, working on the wharves in Kingston went on strike, refusing to load bananas belonging to the United Fruit Company, an American multi-national conglomerate, owned in part by Allen Dulles, Director of the CIA, who cared little for the plight of Jamaican workers. A correspondent of the *Daily Herald* who visited Jamaica, best summed up the living conditions of black Jamaicans, when he wrote;

"I entered the wooden houses, little more than huge dog kennels, of men who are expected to live on ninepence to two shillings a day wages. Families of six were living in one room, eating one poor meal a day and supplementing it with a few odd coconuts blown from the trees".

In 1941, allied soldiers with the support of local freedom fighters, drove the Italians out of Ethiopia and Haile Selassie returned to the capital, Addis Ababa. The Rastas viewed this as proof of his divinity, and from that moment, the movement gradually expanded all across Jamaica. They began to set up communes, where they grew their own food, practised their faith and lived according to their own code.

Mortimo Planno was an interesting character. He was born in Cuba to a Jamaican mother and a Cuban father and the family moved back to Jamaica in the early 1930's when he was still a child. He became a prominent teacher of the Rastafari faith during the 1950's and was one of the founding members of the Rastafari Movement Association.

In 1961, he was part of a Jamaican delegation that went to Addis Ababa to meet His Imperial Majesty, Haile Selassie. The Minority Report, prepared by Planno and two others, stated;

"Later in the afternoon the Rases were invited to visit His Holiness Abuna Basilios, the Archbishop of the Ethiopian Orthodox Church at his residence. The other delegates came along too. We discussed H.I.M. Emperor Haile Selassie, being the returned Messiah. His Holiness the Abuna told us at the conclusion of the discussion that the Bible can be interpreted that way. We had tea and honey with him".

Haile Selassie himself, never claimed to be the Messiah and Ethiopians don't worship him as such, but that didn't prevent others from believing that he was.

As the Rastafari faith grew, discussions within the community soon revealed different aspects and these were dealt with by the formation of Mansions, which although differed from one another, were all considered to be Houses of the Rastafari Faith.

After their visit to Ethiopia, many Rastafari teachers made a concerted effort to present the Ethiopian Orthodox teachings, which proclaims Jesus Christ to be the Messiah.

As a rule, Rastas follow a very strict code. They eat only pure foods that do not contain colourings, preservatives or additives of any kind. Rastas are vegetarians, although some eat fish, but they all refrain from alcohol, tobacco, caffeine and drugs that they view as poisons that pollute their bodies, given to them by Jah, the Jamaican abbreviation of Jehovah, who they regard as God.

They wear their hair long, in dreadlocks, or dreads, which they regard as a symbol of rejection of vanity, but they also have a biblical significance as well; Numbers 6:5;

"*During the entire time of his dedication, he is not to allow a razor to pass over his head until the days of his holy consecration to the Lord have been fulfilled. He is to let the locks on his head grow long*".

Dreadlocks are also worn by the Naga Sadhus, who, like the Rastas, reject vanity, ego and pride, which Shiva regards as obstacles to spiritual development. Rastas, like sadhus, consider ganja to be a holy sacrament which they smoke in groups known as reasonings or groundings, where they exchange views and ideas much in the same way as sadhus do. They view ganja as the wisdom weed, that cleanses the body, frees the mind and purifies the spirit and they justify its use by another passage from the Bible; Revelations, 22:2;

"*In the midst of the street, and on either side of the river, was there the tree of life, which bare twelve manner of fruits, and yielded her fruit every month: and the leaves of the tree were for the healing of nations*".

Another verse, in the Book of Psalms, could easily depict the way that sadhus in India smoke their chillums, which they light by placing a piece of glowing charcoal on the top of the mixture; the Book of Psalms 18:8;

"*There went up a smoke out of his nostrils and fire out of his mouth devoured: coals were kindled by it*".

Rastas regard themselves as one of the lost tribes of Israel and Ethiopia, as their spiritual home, the promised land of Zion. Although Babylon is associated with the captivity of the Jews, Rastas use it as a term for white, western societies, that exploited, persecuted and enslaved their African descendants.

They consider it to be the home of the devil, responsible for the corruption of the Bible and as a result, they reject many western beliefs, considering them to be lies, propagated to maintain white supremacy. They cherish much of what is written in the Old Testament, especially Revelations, which they regard as being the true message of Jah.

The 1950's also saw the birth of Ska music and many of the musicians were Rastas, who used well known stories from the Bible, as a basis of their lyrics. Songs about King Solomon and his many wives was a popular subject, so was the story of Samson and Delila.

On April 21st, 1966 Haile Selassie arrived in Jamaica. Leonard Howell was unable to be among the many thousands that greeted him at the airport, because he was once again in prison, but I have no doubt that he celebrated the event from his prison cell.

Mortimo Planno greeted him as he stepped off the plane, together with Joseph Hibbert and several other important Rastafari elders. Haile Selassie was overwhelmed by the rock star adulation of the thousands of happy, ganja smoking Rastas, who had all gone to the airport to see the King of Kings and Lord of Lords.

His arrival in Jamaica is celebrated every year by Rastas and their other official holidays include November 2nd, which commemorates Selassie's Coronation, July 23rd, Selassie's birthday, September 11th, the Ethiopian New Year and August 17th the birthday of Marcus Garvey, who is regarded by the Rastas as a modern-day prophet.

It is easy to portray the Rastas as a dope smoking, reggae playing, rebellious tribe, rather than a religious sect, but their faith is based on ancient religious beliefs and while they may conflict with main-stream Catholicism, that is no reason to dismiss them.

DAGGA SMOKING IN SOUTH AFRICA IN THE 19TH CENTURY

Cannabis is not indigenous to Africa, it was introduced by Arab traders, but it was the African's love of tobacco that was the cause of its popularity from a recreational point of view. Smoking pipes filled with a mixture of tobacco and "dagga", the African name for marihuana, became an integral part of a large number of tribes, some of which used it for medical and spiritual purposes.

One of the first Europeans to write about cannabis use in Africa, was a Dominican priest by the name of Joao dos Santos who wrote a book in 1609, based on his observations during his travels. He said that the locals chewed the leaves of the plant to such an extent, that they became intoxicated, as if they had drunk a large quantity of wine.

In 1658, the Governor of the Dutch colony, the Cape of Good Hope, described the use of cannabis by the Hottentot tribe, who he described as;

"They are not a pure tribe, but rather the offspring of Egyptian soldiers, who had deserted their posts in Ethiopia around 650 BC, and Bushmen women".

The Hottentots were a proud, rich but peaceful people, cattle herders by trade but dagga smokers at heart. They were no match for the well-armed, ambitious Boers (Dutch settlers), who quickly took over large areas of their grazing land and turned it into farms.

Some of the Boers were fascinated by the Hottentot custom of ritual dagga smoking, who constructed water-pipes, filling horns with water, that were attached to wood or stone bowls, filled with a mixture of dagga and tobacco. One Dutch farmer described the event as follows;

"At the start of a typical native "smoke-in", a quantity of water was put into the horn, the mouth was applied to the large orifice of the horn, and the smoke, after being drawn through the water, was inhaled quickly three or four times and then exhaled, in a violent fit of coughing, causing tears to stream down the cheeks. This was considered the height of ecstasy to the smoker. The process continued until the fumes of the dagga produced a kind of intoxication or delirium and the devotee commenced to recite or sing, with great rapidity and vehemence, the praises of himself or his chief, during the intervals of coughing or smoking".

Small groups, without the use of a conventional pipe, resorted to making earth pipes, by connecting tunnels to a central hole, which was filled with dagga and then set alight. The smokers would have to lie flat on their face, with their mouths over the hole, through which they inhaled the fumes. These were all the rage in the 1960's in California, but we have tribes like the Hottentots, the Bushmen and the Bantus to thank for this innovative, natural way of smoking.

Zulus were very fond of smoking dagga, especially prior to going into battle, like the Sikhs in India, they used it as a stimulant, increasing their ability to run and fight.

When they weren't fighting, the Zulus held spitting contests, where the players would smoke huge amounts of dagga, which has a tendency to dry one's mouth, thus making it very difficult to spit, which made the game even more challenging.

The players had to spit out lumps of saliva, forming little blobs to create a complete circle around their opponent. The winner was the first to achieve this, due to the fact, that the circle symbolised his opponent caught in a bubble, surrounded by the troops of his enemy.

The English Explorer, G. Thompson, noted that African's were so addicted to dagga smoking, white colonial settlers grew fields of it to encourage the locals to stay and work. In 1818, he wrote;

"The white man grows it as an inducement to retain the wild Bushmen in their service whom they have made captives at an early age. Most of these people being extremely addicted to the smoking of dagga".

By the time that explorers like Livingston and Stanley and opportunists like Cecil Rhodes arrived, the custom of dagga smoking had swept across the entire continent. Just as the Europeans, who drank away their sorrows, through the use of wine, beer, gin, whisky or brandy, Africans were achieving a similar result from smoking dagga.

Some of the whites, particularly missionaries, were very much opposed to the custom, but this had little effect on the general population, who had been smoking it for generations and who by now, had embraced it as part of their culture.

It was largely ignored by the early Dutch settlers, they were not concerned with the cultural aspects of the natives and they considered it to be an entirely African thing and therefore, of little importance. The problems began in 1843, when Natal became part of the Cape Colony. Its main objective was to increase sugar production, but the abolition of slavery had reduced the number of workers, so 6000 low-paid, indentured Indian labourers were brought in, to work in the sugar fields.

They must have been very happy when they realised that ganja was widely available in the native communities and white planters soon realised, that their Indian "coolies" were getting stoned every night, as a way of relaxing after a long, hard day in the sugar fields.

Many white farmers didn't like it, they thought dagga smoking made them weak and lazy and although they tried to prevent it, there was very little they could do. In the post-slavery era, they were forced to accept the fact that without low-paid workers, sugar production would grind to a halt.

By 1870, European settlers were in control over most of South Africa. Many of the Indian indentured workers remained in the country after their term of service was completed, and they set up shops, started small farms or took jobs in the cities, much in the same way as they had in Jamaica.

More coolies were brought in from India, the dagga smoking continued, and the whites decided to put a stop to it by introducing a law;

"Prohibiting the smoking, use, or possession by the sale, barter, or gift to any coolies whatsoever, of any portion of the hemp plant (Cannabis sativa)".

It had very little success, dagga for the African natives was a part of life and the fact that it was not part of the white man's world didn't bother them in the slightest.

The Indian workers, most of whom were from the south of the country and therefore very dark, were treated the same as Africans, who were more than happy to supply their Indian brothers with as much dagga as they wanted.

In 1887, Supreme Court Judge, Walter Wragg, headed a commission to investigate the cultivation and use of dagga in the Cape Colony. The Wragg Commission concluded that the custom of dagga smoking posed a serious problem to white South Africans and as a result, measures were taken to prohibit the cultivation, sale and use of cannabis.

European settlers completely under-estimated the situation, the law had very little effect, armed confrontation was out of the question, since the whites were a very small minority and the dagga smoking culture continued, just as it always had. It was after all an African thing, Africans cultivated it and Africans smoked it, so it was nothing to do with the white man and there was very little that he could do about it.

After the Boers were defeated, the British unified the Cape Colonies in 1910, when the area became the Union of South Africa. White settlers once again began to demand prohibition of the use of dagga, which they claimed made the workers lazy, and prone to bouts violence. The British Office of Native Affairs was against such a move, they regarded its use as a social custom, they also felt that prohibiting it would cause so much resentment, it would probably lead to rebellious behaviour.

White owners of the gold mines in the Transvaal were against the miners smoking it, but it was tolerated in the coal mines. Fruit growers in the Cape allowed its use in the workers compounds, because the white fruit growers believed that it encouraged harmony and stability amongst the native workers, which improved production. With so many different opinions, it was difficult for the white authorities to come up with a solution that would keep everyone happy.

A compromise was reached. The Office of Native Affairs said that it would pass a new law, which would give urban law enforcement the power to prohibit its use in white areas and workplaces, but it stated that it would be one that would oppose drastic or ill-advised actions in tribal areas. It was in essence, a racist law, and perhaps the only one which favoured the African native.

The Office of Native Affairs considered it to be the obvious solution, dagga smoking was an African thing, so only whites would be prohibited from using it. As the white urban townships grew, tribes like the Hottentots began to grow dagga on their tribal lands and for some, it became a lucrative business.

Even white townships had large African populations, not only as domestic servants, but also for the commercial sector. Many were dagga smokers and although the whites had tried to stamp it out, it was only when poor, young white youths discovered it, that dagga smoking became a problem, when it became readily available to bored, white youths.

In 1924, the Department of Public Health published a document titled; *A Memorandum on Dagga Smoking and its Evils*.

A Probation Officer was quoted as saying;

"There is a considerable amount of dagga smoking among European males, of the poor white and delinquent type, but I have never met an instance of the habit amongst intelligent or educated Europeans. All the European smokers I have met have acquired the habit during adolescence, though most have dropped it again in early manhood. It is sometimes acquired in boyhood from association with natives, while herding stock or in similar occupations in the country".

It was not a favourable report as far as white dagga smokers were concerned;

"The type of youth from whom the dagga smoker is recruited, is generally of a low standard of intelligence, the deteriorating effects of the drug react upon this nidus to confirm the habit early, and to drag the smoker to the lowest depths".

Use of it by that time must have been fairly widespread among the white lower classes, as the memorandum stated;

"The attraction of the drug is greatest for those living dull and monotonous lives, such as in barracks, compounds, prisons, reformatories, hostels and also for the degenerate or mentally unstable. The latter are especially prone to become addicts once they have experienced the drug".

A Cape Town police officer highlighted the extent and effects of dagga smoking among white teenagers;

"In certain quarters of the town and in certain schools, "gangs" of lads between the ages of 10 and 16 years, daily smoke three or more cigarettes containing dagga. The evil effects of the drug quickly show themselves in these immature youths by their emotional instability while under the influence of the drug and the dull, lack-lustre look that stamps their faces when the effects have passed off".

The South African authorities were determined to stamp it out and their opportunity arrived at the Geneva Opium convention the following year, but more about that later.

MEDICAL RESEARCH IN INDIA IN THE 19th CENTURY

Contrary to popular perception, it was the Dutch, not the British who were the first Europeans to arrive in India, after Vasco da Gamma, the Portuguese navigator, discovered a sea route around the Cape of Good Hope in 1497, arriving in what is now the Indian State of Goa.

Garcia de Orta, a Dutch physician and a keen botanist, wrote about the medicinal properties of cannabis in his book, *Colloquies on the Simples and Drugs and Medicinal Matters in India*, which was published in 1534.

During the course of his observations, he noted that it was used to combat fatigue, restore appetite and to rejuvenate the bodies of those who were engaged in heavy, manual labour. His book reveals that its use was widespread throughout the entire population, stating;

"*I believe that it is so generally used and by such a number of people, that there is no mystery about it*".

Cristobal Acosta confirmed his findings in his book, *A Tract about the Drugs and Medicines of the East Indies*, which was published 15 years later.

Cannabis was already widely used in Ayurvedic medicine and there are numerous references to it in the Atharva Veda, an ancient Vedic text written more than 3,000 years ago, which many regard as the Ayurvedic bible.

In the Sushruta Samhita, written in the 6th century B.C, it recommends this medicinal plant for the treatment of catarrh, phlegm and diarrhoea and other books of the period, praise its ability to stimulate the digestive system and encourage a healthy appetite. Other texts of the period mention its use as a painkiller, while others describe it as having a calming effect on both the mind and the body.

When the British East India Company took control of India, at the end of the 18th century, they imposed a tax on the cultivation, sale and use on all cannabis products, which caused enormous resentment among the local population.

It was during this time that Doctor William Brooke O'Shaughnessy arrived in India. Born in Limerick, Ireland in 1809, he began studying medicine at Trinity College Dublin, before moving to Edinburgh University, where he studied medicine, chemistry, anatomy and forensic toxicology, before graduating in 1829.

Like many of his generation, in 1833 he was employed by the British East India Company as an assistant surgeon in Calcutta. This marked the beginning of a love affair with India, that remained with him for the rest of his life.

He became aware that cannabis was used in Ayurvedic medicine, and that it had been for thousands of years. When he realised that its medicinal properties were virtually unknown in Europe, he decided to begin his own experiments, using the recipes that were given to him by local practitioners.

In 1839 he presented his initial research to students and scholars at the Medical and Physical Society in Calcutta. His work focused on the use of cannabis for the treatment of cholera, rabies, rheumatism and tetanus.

A patient that was suffering from rabies died, but he noticed that the man's pain had been greatly reduced, stating;

"*The awful malady was stripped of its horrors; if not less fatal than before, it was reduced to less than the scale of suffering that precedes death from most ordinary diseases*".

Another patient that he treated was a baby of less than two months old who suffered from terrible convulsions, which subsided greatly after being treated with cannabis, prompting him to write;

"*My profession has gained an anti-convulsive remedy of the greatest value*".

He continued his work for a number of years and after returning to England in 1841, he published several works including, *The Bengal Dispensatory* and *The Bengal Pharmacopoeia.* This had a section devoted entirely to cannabis, which extended to more than 25 pages. His studies were described by James Mills in the *Cannabis Britannica* as;

"*The most comprehensive assessment of the properties of cannabis, undertaken at that time*".

O'Shaughnessy's research, which was subsequently re-published in British and European medical journals, led to an increase in cannabis research. Sir Russell Reynolds, Queen Victoria's personal physician, prescribed the Queen with a cannabis preparation as an effective treatment for menstrual pains. A review of O'Shaughnessy's work appeared in the *Lancet* in 1840 which stated;

"*The labours of Dr O'Shaughnessy, as a scientific chemist, are already known in the most favourable manner to our readers. Unlike the greater number of chemists, he combines practice with theory and directs his scientific discoveries to the advancement of medicine as a healing art*".

He returned to India in 1852 and was promoted to the rank of Surgeon-Major in 1861 and was later the Professor of Chemistry at the medical college of Calcutta. In later years he focused his efforts on the development of a telegraph system and was appointed Director-General of Telegraphs in India.

Within a year, under his supervision, a telegraph line stretching more than 800 miles connected Calcutta with Agra and within another two years, it was extended, linking Calcutta with Bombay and Madras, covering nearly 4,000 miles. It was an incredible feat of engineering for which he was awarded a knighthood. Sir William retired in 1861 and died peacefully at his home in Southsea on January 10th, 1899. While some would argue that he was one of the first, holistic practitioners, very few would disagree that he was indeed, the grandfather of medical cannabis research.

One of the many who followed in his footsteps was Michael Donovan, an Irish apothecarist and chemist who worked in Dublin. He wrote a number of important works, including, *The State of Pharmacy in Ireland*, which was published in 1829. After reading O'Shaughnessy's research, he began working with cannabis preparations, which were sent to him by his mentor from Calcutta. In 1845 he published an article in the Dublin Journal of Science; *On the Physical and Medicinal Qualities of Indian Hemp*, describing O'Shaughnessy as;

"He brought to light a medicine that possessed a kind of energy which belongs to no other therapeutic agent known to man".

Like the Dutch physician, Garcia da Orta, Donovan noticed that many of his patients developed great appetites shortly after ingesting a cannabis preparation, prompting him to write with great joy;

"I have witnessed this effect so often, that it suggests the idea of using it as a remedy worthy of a trial, in that most intractable symptom or disease, anorexia".

Donovan was one of the first to experiment with cannabis tinctures, which he prepared by using charas. In 1851, he published an important book, *Observations on the Resin of Indian Hemp*, which contained a large number of case studies. Like many of his colleagues at that time, he envisaged a great future for cannabis use as a medicine, writing;

"I content myself with expressing my belief that Indian hemp will one day or another, occupy one of the highest places amongst the means of combatting disease".

Mr Donovan, like his illustrious predecessor, was clearly a very enlightened man who epitomised everything that was great about the Victorian age, when knowledge was cherished, and new discoveries were being made on a regular basis.

THE INDIAN HEMP DRUGS COMMISSION 1893 – 1894

In 1858, when the East India Company's rule came to an end and Queen Victoria was crowned Empress of India, the British Government realised that they could increase their revenues by raising the tax on bhang, charas and ganja.

In 1893, following a series of questions that were raised in the House of Commons, relating to the safety of hemp drugs, the British Government ordered a Royal Commission, for the purpose of making a comprehensive study of the effects of its production and use, in the Indian province of Bengal.

Lord Kimberly proposed that the report should include the whole of the country, in order to provide a comprehensive assessment of cannabis use in India and as a result, the Indian Hemp Drugs Commission was established in July 1893.

The Honourable W. Mackworth Young MA, the Financial Commissioner of the Punjab, was appointed President and Mr H.J McIntosh, the Under-Secretary to the Government of Bengal, acted as his Secretary.

Other members included, Surgeon-Major C.J.H Warden, a Professor of Chemistry who was the Officiating Medical Storekeeper to the Indian Government in Calcutta, Mr A.H.L Fraser M.A, a Commissioner of the Central Province of Chhattisgarh and Mr H.T Ommanney, a Government tax collector who was based in Bombay. Three respected Indian natives, Raja Soshi Sikhareswar Roy of Bengal, Kanwar Harnam Singh from the Punjab, and Lala Nihal Chand, from the North-Western Provinces, were also included.

The final report, consisting of 7 volumes containing more than 3,000 pages, remains one of the most comprehensive and detailed study of cannabis ever carried out. It not only investigated the physical, mental and moral effects of cannabis use, it also examined the methods of cultivation, processing, regulation, taxation as well as the medicinal and religious uses of bhang, ganja and charas, providing a fascinating insight into life in British India at the end of the 19th century.

During the course of the study, nearly 1,200 witnesses gave evidence. These included 467 civil servants, 144 cultivators, 335 medical practitioners, 34 missionaries, 75 people who were involved in the cannabis trade as well as a wide cross-section from Indian society, including Maharajas, sadhus and temple priests.

The investigation, which took 12 months to complete, evaluated the physical effects of chronic cannabis use, including possible links with insanity, crime, mental illness, and its effects on society as a whole. Witnesses gave evidence at 86 hearings in 30 cities, covering eight Indian provinces, which included parts of Burma.

In order to acquire the information that the Commission required to carry out their study, witnesses were presented with a series of questions, to determine any risk to public health. Their response was noted and written down and they form the bulk of the report which provides a valuable insight, into the use of bhang, ganja and charas during the Victorian era.

Witnesses were questioned if further clarification or explanations were deemed to be necessary, and it was duly noted in the report in what form the testimony was given, whether written or oral. Some of the many questions that were directed to the witnesses, are as follows;

Does the habitual moderate use of any of these drugs produce any noxious effects, physical, mental or moral? Does it impair the constitution in any way?

Does it injure the digestion or cause loss of appetite? Does it cause dysentery, bronchitis or asthma? Does it impair the moral sense or induce laziness or habits of immorality or debauchery?

Does it deaden the Intellect or produce insanity? If it produces insanity, then of what type and is it temporary or permanent? If temporary, may the symptoms be re-induced by the use of the drug after liberation from restraint?

In such cases of the alleged connection between insanity and the use of hemp as are known to you, are you of the opinion that the use of the drug, by persons suffering from mental anxiety or brain disease to obtain relief, has been sufficiently considered in explaining that connection?

Do you think there is any evidence to indicate that insanity may often lead to indulgence in the use of hemp drugs, by a person who is deficient in self-control through weakened intellect?

Are any large proportion of bad characters habitual moderate consumers of any of these drugs? What connection, if any, has the moderate use with crime in general or with crime of any special character? Does excessive indulgence in any of these drugs incite premeditated crime, violent or otherwise?

Do you know of any case in which it has led to temporary homicidal frenzy?

It is clear by the number of questions that were asked, concerning the mental effects of cannabis use, that the commission was particularly concerned about any possible link to insanity and psychotic behaviour. This was probably due to the fact that there were over two hundred lunatic asylums in India at that time.

Many of these were visited by members of the Commission during the course of their investigation, who were keen to see if they were adopting methods that were unknown in Britain.

Treatment of mentally ill patients was very different in the Victorian age, when straitjackets and restraints were often deployed as a means of controlling patients, who were more often than not, used as guinea pigs. Inquiries were made into the running of 24 asylums and the Commission were very critical of much of the evidence that was presented, stating;

"They have known nothing of the effects of the drugs at all, though the consumption is so extensive, except that cases of insanity have been brought to them attributed with apparent authority to hemp drugs. They have generalized from this limited and one-sided experience. They have concluded that hemp drugs produce insanity in every case, or in the great majority of cases, of consumption. They have had no idea that in the vast majority of cases this result does not follow the use. They have accordingly without sufficient inquiry assisted, by the statistics they have supplied and by the opinions they have expressed, in stereotyping the popular opinion and giving it authority and permanence".

In 1892, 2,344 patients were admitted to lunatic asylums and after examining 222 cases, allegedly caused by the use of ganja or charas, they concluded that 61 may have been caused as a result of cannabis use. 12 were dismissed very quickly and a further 10 were deemed to be unsatisfactory, since the hospital had no knowledge whatsoever of prior medical history and even among the other cases, there was very little evidence to support the doctor's diagnosis.

Another cause of concern was the practice by some users, to smoke a mixture of datura and ganja. Datura is a poisonous plant sometimes known as jimson weed, devil's weed or devil's trumpets, on account of the shape of their flowers. Curiously, it is also associated with Shiva and as such, sadhus and Shaivites are known to smoke it on certain occasions, in very small amounts, but poor people in particular, often mixed it with ganja. It is an extremely dangerous plant, which causes hallucinations, psychosis and death if taken internally.

Having studied the cases and consulted numerous medical experts, the Commission's conclusion was;

"The fact of the existence of the hemp habit is easy enough to ascertain, but that it is the cause, or one of the causes of the insanity, or that it even preceded the insanity, is much more difficult to establish".

Brigade-Surgeon-Lieutenant-Colonel D.D. Cunningham, a highly respected surgeon as well as a Fellow of the Royal Society, carried out 3 experiments, at the Biological Laboratory at the Zoological Gardens in Calcutta.

His first involved a 16-pound, male rhesus monkey, who was placed in a chamber, into which ganja smoke was pumped in. It was estimated that the monkey inhaled the smoke 181 times during an eight-month period, which was considered to be comparable with a normal, chronic user.

An autopsy revealed no brain malfunction of any kind.

The second experiment examined the effects of eating charas, and two smaller cynomolgus monkeys were used.

A suitable amount, calculated on a weight ratio between the monkeys and human users, was mixed with milk. After 62 days, with no apparent difference in the monkey's behaviour, the dosage was increased by 400%, but after three days, the monkeys refused to drink it, although again, they appeared to be perfectly normal. Since it was felt that no further useful data could be gained, the monkeys were released and left to play in peace.

His third investigation evaluated the effects of datura smoking on a large rhesus monkey, who was placed in the chamber, in which datura smoke was pumped in every day for six-weeks. There is no information regarding the dosage used, but it must have been a horrible experience for the animal concerned.

A post-mortem examination of the central nervous system revealed the following effects;

"On opening the cranium, the dura-mater was found to be somewhat thickened and, especially in the neighbourhood of the superior longitudinal sinus, very conspicuously congested. The cerebral substance was abnormally soft and so friable as to render any immediate removal of the membranes impossible".

The brain had basically turned to mush, the membranes were so soft and flimsy, it was impossible to remove them in one piece, due to the amount of blood that had accumulated in the brain. My heart goes out to that poor animal, who had to endure 60 days of hell, using a drug that would have fried his brains as easily as eggs on a skillet.

The surgeon explained the result of his tests;

"In so far as a single experiment goes, the results in this case would seem to show that the habitual inhalation of the smoke of datura, even when only practised for a relatively brief period, is sufficient to establish serious morbid changes in the cerebral nervous centres. It therein differs from the habitual inhalation of the smoke of ganja, extending over a much more prolonged period".

"This clearly indicates the necessity of distinguishing between cases in which ganja and datura is substituted for it, as otherwise, certain prejudicial effects which are really due to the use of the latter drug, may be erroneously credited to the former one".

The Commission concluded;

"So far as the information from all sources before the Commission is concerned, there is no evidence of any brain lesions being directly caused by hemp drugs, as they have been found to be caused by alcohol and datura; and there is evidence that the coarse brain lesions produced by alcohol and datura are not produced by hemp drugs".

The Commission felt that some of the patients only claimed to be ganja addicts, in order to stay out of prison. This was a view that was expressed by the following;

"It is not expedient nor is it just, that intoxication from hemp drugs should secure immunity from punishment which is not allowed to alcohol".

In areas where malaria was prevalent, witnesses said that bhang was considered to be very beneficial and those who were involved in heavy, manual labour, used it as an additional dietary supplement, which helped to combat fatigue. Assistant Surgeon Devendra Nath Roy, who had 20-years' experience working in the North-Western Provinces, Rajputana and Bengal, said;

"Those of my patients, who admitted having been habitual ganja smokers, suffered from dysentery or diarrhoea, but they have been exposed to conditions which produce these ailments. Hence, I do not draw any conclusion as to ganja being a primary cause of those diseases".

The question of diet was brought up by a number of witnesses, including a native practitioner, Kedereswar Achariva, who was of a similar opinion;

"Those ganja smokers who cannot command abundant wholesome food suffer from dysentery, but it is difficult to determine how far it is due to ganja or to improper food. As to asthma, I have not seen any typical case originating from ganja smoking. I know that a chronic catarrhal condition of the air passages with a certain amount of spasm is the misfortune of many old ganja smokers".

Surgeon-Captain Prain, a man with more than 30-years of experience stated;

"I do not believe that the habitual moderate use of any of these drugs produces any noxious effects, physical, mental or moral. I think perhaps that the use of bhang does injure the digestion and impair appetite even when used moderately, but I am convinced that it neither causes dysentery, bronchitis or asthma".

Having questioned a large number of witnesses, the Commission arrived at the following conclusion;

"In the case of bhang, there is nothing in the physiological action of the drug which could in any way set up an acute inflammation of the large intestine resulting in ulceration. As regards ganja or charas smoking inducing dysentery, even assuming that the products of the destructive distillation of the drugs directly reached the intestines, there is evidence that those products, when condensed and injected into a cat's stomach, failed to induce any inflammatory process".

"The connection therefore between hemp drug smoking and dysentery, appears even remoter than in the case of bhang drinking and that disease, and cannot be accepted by any stretch of the imagination, as even a possible direct cause of dysentery".

Surgeon-Lieutenant-Colonel Bovil, an elderly gentleman who had been in service for 21 years, concluded with his colleague, but added;

"I have noted hoarseness of the voice probably due to some laryngeal irritation among ganja smokers".

The Commission considered that the evidence showed that moderate use of ganja or charas was not appreciably harmful and that moderate use of bhang was quite harmless. It noted that as in excessive cigarette smoking, considerable bronchial irritation and chronic catarrhal laryngitis may be caused by excessive ganja or charas smoking.

After hearing testimony from a number of officials and members of law enforcement, they examined 81 case records of violent crimes committed during the previous 20 years that were alleged to have been the result of cannabis use.

Five of those cases were immediately dismissed, probably due to the lack of court records or insufficient evidence and after examining the remaining cases, the Commission stated;

"The connection between drugs and crime is only established in four cases. It is astonishing to find detective and misleading are the recollections which man witnesses and retains, even of cases with which they have had special opportunities of being well acquainted. It is instructive to see how preconceived notion, based on rumour and tradition, tend to preserve the impression of certain particulars, while the impression of far more important features of the case, are completely forgotten".

Their view on the possible link between cannabis and crime was expressed as;

"In respect to his relations to society however, even the excessive consumer of hemp drugs is ordinarily inoffensive. His excesses may indeed bring him to degraded poverty, which may lead him to dishonest practices; and occasionally, but apparently very rarely indeed, excessive indulgence in hemp drugs may lead to violent crime. For all practical purposes, it may be laid down that there is little or no connection between the use of hemp drugs and crime".

Regarding general health matters, the Commission concluded;

"In regard to the physical effects, the Commission have come to the conclusion that the moderate use of hemp drugs is practically attended by no evils at all".

"There may be exceptional cases in which, owing to the idiosyncrasies of constitution, the drugs, in even moderate use may be injurious".

"There are also many cases where, in a specially "malarious" climate, or in circumstances of hard work and exposure, the people attribute beneficial effects to the habitual moderate use of these drugs; and there is evidence to show that the popular impression may have some basis in fact".

The commission then turned its attention to the religious and social aspects of cannabis use in India;

"It is sufficient to say that the custom is now a general one, and that where the Holi festival is observed, there the practice of consuming bhang during its observance is common. On other occasions, such as the Diwali festival, marriages, and family festivities, there is evidence to show that among certain classes, the consumption of bhang is common".

Witnesses from the Punjab, a region predominantly inhabited by Sikhs, explained the religious significance. Sodhi Iswar Singh, an Assistant Commissioner stated;

"As far as I know, bhang is pounded by Sikhs on the day of Dussehra, and it is ordinarily binding upon every Sikh to drink it as a sacred draught by mixing water with it".

Mr Jacob, a local vicar, gave a brief account of a strange social custom;

"At Chanda, the Chamar caste use ganja dust in the preparation of a beverage called gulabpani, which is drunk at a ceremony called dadhi, the first shaving of the beard, when no liquor is permitted".

Some of the local customs regarding the dead, appear to have their roots in ancient Sanskrit texts, which refer to the use of smoke as a way of combatting evil spirits, much in the same way that Chinese practitioners use herbs in moxibustion. A Witness from Satpura, in the Central Provinces stated;

"In the funeral ceremony amongst the Gonds, ganja is placed over the chest of the dead body and when the funeral party returns home, a little of the ganja is burnt in the house of the dead person, the smoke of which is supposed to reach the spirit of the dead".

Sadhus also appeared before the committee, informing them of their customs and beliefs;

"Somewhat similar accounts varying in detail are given by many witnesses coming from different parts of the province, of whom some also refer to the habit which ganja smokers have of invoking the deity before placing the pipe to their lips".

In respect of its use as a sacred object, the Commission concluded by stating;

"The custom of worshipping the hemp plant, although not so prevalent as that of offering hemp to Shiva and other deities of the Hindus, would nevertheless appear from the statements of the witnesses, to exist to some extent in some provinces of India. The reason why this fact is not generally known, may perhaps be gathered from such statements as that of Pandit Dharma Joshi, who says that such worship is performed in secret. There may be another cause of the denial, on the part of the larger majority of Hindu witnesses, of any knowledge of the existence of a custom of worshipping the hemp plant, in that the educated Hindu will not admit that he worships the material object of his adoration, but the deity as represented by it".

One of the duties of the Commission was to determine if the cannabis trade should be liable to further regulations or to prohibit its use entirely. They reproduced several paragraphs from Mill's Political Economy, which they believed, contained a clear guide to the principles that should be used, in order to determine whether hemp drugs should be prohibited by Government;

"To be prevented from what one is inclined to, or from acting contrary to one's own judgement of what is desirable, is not only always irksome, but always tends, pro tanto, to starve the development of some portion of the bodily or mental faculties, either sensitive or active; and, unless the conscience of the individual goes freely with the legal restraint, it partakes either in a great or small degree, of the degradation of slavery".

"Scarcely any degree of utility short of absolute necessity will justify a prohibitory regulation, unless it can also be made to recommend itself to the general conscience; unless persons of ordinary good intentions either believe already, or can be induced to believe, that the thing prohibited is a thing which they ought not to wish to do".

There had been a previous inquiry in Bengal in 1798, which examined the possible prohibition of a large number of intoxicants including opium, bhang, ganja, charas, alcohol and tobacco. It decided that taxation would not only raise much needed revenue, it would also deter abuse and that was the route that was chosen. Following another inquiry in 1873, the tax on cannabis was increased, to further deter it's use and to raise more revenue, as the government noted at the time;

"In India, the practice of ganja smoking has existed from time immemorial and among certain sects of Hindus, ascetics, and religious mendicants, hemp intoxication is habitually indulged in. It would be impossible to supress the growth of the plant but although we consider it impracticable to enforce the absolute prohibition, we fully recognise it as our duty, to restrict its consumption as far as practicable".

Some were concerned that if the tax on ganja was too high, poor people would resort to smoking datura, as one officer noted;

"Even if the absolute prohibition of the use of the drug could be enforced, the result might be to induce the use of still more noxious drugs. India abounds with plants growing wild from which drugs can be procured which are more deleterious in their effects than ganja. One such plant is datura (stramonium) the seeds of which are already used to intensify the narcotic effects of bhang, a liquid preparation of hemp leaves; and we apprehend that if the use of ganja were suppressed altogether, datura might be largely resorted to by the poorer classes as a means of satisfying their craving for stimulants".

It was against this historical backdrop of taxation, that the Commission considered its position in respect of possible prohibition. They also took into account the example set by Turkey, who had already prohibited the use of cannabis. A letter from the Grand Vizir to the Ministry of Commerce in Constantinople stated;

"From the reports furnished by the Imperial Medical Council, it appeared that the use of hashish in the preparations of medicines was extremely rare, and that, being a narcotic, its use must of necessity be injurious, and that consequently the suppression of the cultivation of hashish could not fail to prove highly advantageous".

Egypt had prohibited its cultivation, use and importation in 1868 but in March 1884, a new law was passed, allowing confiscated hashish to be sold for export and the proceeds split between informers and customs officers who had taken part in the seizures. This was a decision taken by the Director-General of the Egyptian Customs Services, who said;

"This measure was rendered necessary, by the absence of any fund from which rewards could be distributed; while, on the other hand, the profits of smuggling being very great, large sums were paid by the smugglers to ensure the silence or complicity of the Customs officers, coastguards and others".

Greece had banned its smoking in the cafes of Athens and Piraeus, a thriving port which was at the heart of the Greek hashish trade, which shipped huge amounts to Egypt and Turkey. The British Caribbean colony of Trinidad had prohibited its use in 1885 but, unable to prevent the cultivation of it, they resorted to issuing expensive licences, as a deterrent. Even that had been a disaster, when some residents moved to Venezuela where they began growing it in large quantities before shipping it back to Trinidad.

A Surgeon-Major, who had previously been posted there, produced a report by Dr Thomas Ireland, the Government Medical Officer of British Guiana, who wrote;

"With a coastline such as ours, adjacent to that of the Spanish Main, it will be impossible to prevent its introduction into this colony if immigrants who go there continue to grow it".

After much consideration, the Commission stated;

"In the case of other countries, where the use of the drugs has been prohibited, the Commission do not find, in the literature available to them, many arguments for prohibition, In Turkey it rests upon the theory accepted by Orthodox Muhammadans that hashish, being a narcotic its use must of necessity be injurious, while in Egypt, the prohibition emanated from Turkey. It must be added that the Commission have no scientific information regarding the strength of the article of commerce called hashish and it may differ to some extent from the Indian products. From the description of its manufacture, it appears to resemble more the charas of Yarkand, than the ganja or bhang of India".

One of the most interesting aspects of the report, revealed the huge charas trade between India and Yarkand, a remote Himalayan region, in what was Turkestan.

Yarkand had always been an important trading centre, part of the old silk road which linked Kashgar and Bukhara, with North West Afghanistan, Kashmir and over the Karakoram Pass into Northern India. In the early 19th century, this route, known as the Black Jade Road, was used by Yarkand charas traders, who hauled hundreds of tons of it on horses and yaks, into northern India, where it was exchanged for grains, dried fruits, nuts and other goods. India's appetite for charas was such, that in the 19th and early 20th century, it imported more than anyone else in the world.

Turkestan, a wild, unruly province, first conquered by China in the Han Dynasty, was inhabited by the Uyghurs, Muslims who spoke a Turkish dialect of Arabic. The area around Yarkand was the centre of the Turkestan charas trade, although many believed that the very best came from Bukhara. Colonel Chopra's report, given nearly 40 years later, sums up beautifully, the method used to produce it;

"The female flower heads are first dried, then broken and crushed between the hands into a powder which is passed through sieves so that it attains the finest consistency of sand or sawdust. This powder, which is still green, is stored in bags made of rawhide for four to five months during the winter. At the onset of hot weather, the material is taken out and exposed to the sun for a short time, to allow the resin to melt. It is stored again in hide bags and after a few days, the agglutinated mass, is again taken out and kneaded well by means of wooden rods, so that a certain amount of oily matter appears on its surface. The process of kneading is continued till each bag yields about one to two pounds of oil. At this stage, charas is transferred into new hide bags and is ready for distribution and sale".

It is interesting to note, that it is still made much in the same way in parts of Afghanistan, Pakistan, Kashmir and China. The trade was already well established long before the Commission was formed and it was, by all accounts, a profitable one and, more importantly, an international one, as the Commission noted;

"Charas is practically a foreign article. Small amounts are imported from Nepal and Gwalior, but the bulk comes from Yarkand through the Himalayan passes, or to a much smaller degree, through the routes on the frontier of Afghanistan. It would not be a very difficult matter to stop these imports, though the co-operation of the Kashmir Darbar would be necessary in regard to Yarkand charas. It may therefore be accepted, that the supply of charas might be cut off without much difficulty, though as this article forms the principle import from Yarkand, the prohibition of charas would paralyse, if not extinguish, the trade with this country".

As one witness explained;

"With regard to the Yarkand trade, that the imposition of a duty so high as to be practicably prohibitive, would considerably injure that trade, because the Yarkand trader, in exchange for his charas, takes back the products of the Punjab or Kashmir back to his own country. The extinction or serious injury of the trade would, of course, be a very regrettable circumstance".

The Commission discovered that it was a two-way trade.

Some Muslim traders in Kashmir and Pakistan didn't wait for the Yarkand caravan to arrive, they loaded up horses with goods of all kinds and went to Yarkand or Tibet, to trade them for charas. As the report stated;

"Consumers would not take to other intoxicants, because the intoxication of charas is not like that of opium or other intoxicants. The greatest loss would be that of the traders of Hoshiarpur and Amritsar, who take merchandise to Ladakh and Yarkand and bring back charas".

It was clearly a well-defined, regulated trade, which catered for connoisseurs as well as occasional smokers. The complexities of its manufacture were beautifully described by Dr R.J Bouquet, in his report concerning different methods of production;

"The very best quality resin is collected from uncut plants. At the time when the seeds are formed, the cultivators, dressed in leather, move about the plantation. The resin sticks to their clothes, which are then scraped from time to time with a blunt curved knife. The paste, while still sticky, is kneaded by hand in copper pans. Dirt and impurities are eliminated, and the substance is divided up into little lumps, which are often given the form of sticks, sometimes flat and sometimes tapering, weighing from 30 to 40 grams".

"Others roll the resinous female tops between the palms of their hands, the charas being collected by scraping the fingers on the edge of a knife, a method which produces the very best quality, this variety is rare and is greatly valued".

Dr Bouquet also offers a valuable insight into other methods used in Chinese Turkestan;

"When the charas is collected from cut plants, it takes the form of a greenish-yellow powder, which is sifted so as to get rid of waste vegetable tissues and impurities. It is generally packed in cloth or skin bags, which are steamed above a pan of water. When cooled and compressed, the substance gradually agglutinates and forms a compact and resonant block".

Charas extracted from dried plants was graded according to the method used;

"The freshly dried tops are given three successive rubbings between fine matting. The produce of the first rubbing constitutes the superior quality known as Rup".

"The second gives Tahgalim, which is less valued; and the third is generally smoked by the cultivator, since it has very little commercial value. Traders can easily tell whether charas has been collected from uncut plants or from those which have been cut and dried; in any case, the first kind is always more expensive".

The British hated to give up any form of trade, especially a profitable, international one, and this probably influenced their decision. Non-interference with the additional benefit of revenue, was considered to be more sensible than prohibition.

In the case of bhang, the Commission was unanimous;

"The Commission are prepared to state that the suppression of the use of bhang would be totally unjustifiable. It is established that this use is very ancient, and that it has some religious connotation among a large body of Hindus; that it enters into their social customs; that it is almost without exception harmless in moderation, and perhaps in some cases, beneficial; that the abuse of it is not so harmful as the abuse of alcohol; that its suppression, involving the extirpation of the wild hemp plant, would be a matter of great difficulty; that such a measure would be extremely unpopular, and would give rise to widespread discontent; and if successfully accomplished, it would lead to the use of more hurtful stimulants".

Some witnesses were against all intoxication, Rev W.B Phillips, working with the London Missionary Society stated;

"What with liquor and opium and hemp drugs of various kinds, all licensed by Government, it does seem as if the population were terribly exposed to degrading influences".

"It is not my province to face the difficult task of dealing with these evils, but I do feel it is my duty, to set forth as strongly as possible, the assurance that very much mischief is being worked in the country by the various intoxicants so freely and largely sold. I hardly care to distinguish between them, they are all bad".

There was overwhelming opposition to the prohibition of ganja, Mr Driberg, Commissioner of Excise in Assam stated;

"It would be useless to prohibit the use of ganja in a province like Assam, surrounded as it is by independent hill people, who would cultivate it in their hills and smuggle it down with little risk of detection. Any prohibition will only lead to the increase of illicit consumption and to the secret use of the drug".

Like the charas trade, ganja smoking was considered to be a serious business, and like any business, it catered to public demand;

"There are three kinds of ganja";

a) *"Flat Ganja: The cut stalks are tied together in bundles, the large leaves are eliminated, and only the inflorescences, which are stuck together by the exuded resin, are kept. The bundles are placed on the ground and trampled underfoot to flatten them. The bundles are then untied, and the product sorted and packed under the name of Large Flat, according to the length and breadth of the stems".*

b) *"Round Ganja: Instead of being trampled underfoot, the tops are rolled in the hands, until they have become rounded and tapered in shape. This kind of ganja is always packed in bundles, generally of twenty-four pieces".*

c) *"Chur-Ganja or Rora: The tops, detached intentionally from the plants, or accidentally from the flat or round ganja, constitute what is known as Bora. This is generally delivered to the consumer in the form of a coarse powder".*

"Only the best quality flat ganja is traded throughout the country, the other two kinds are consumed in the regions where they are produced and for the most part, they are smoked".

Devi Dayal, editor of a newspaper in Lahore was clearly very familiar with the Yarkand traders, because he uses the Uyghur word for charas;

"My present belief is that there is no such thing as moderation in the use of chars, because when a charsi visits another, he offers him the chillum and they smoke in company. The smoke is thus repeated frequently".

He was clearly not in favour of its use, although I found his comments amusing. The opinion of the Commission was that although the trade and use of cannabis should be free to continue, further legislation and taxation was required.

It concluded its inquiry by stating;

"Viewing the subject generally, it may be added that the moderate use of these drugs is the rule, and that the excessive use is comparatively exceptional. The moderate use practically produces no ill effects. In all but the most exceptional cases, the injury from habitual moderate use is not appreciable. Excessive use may certainly be accepted as very injurious, though it must be admitted, that in many excessive consumers the injury is not clearly marked. The injury done by the excessive use is, however, confined almost exclusively to the consumer himself; the effect on society is rarely appreciable. It has been the most striking feature in this inquiry, to find how little the effects of hemp drugs have obtruded themselves on observation".

On the recommendations made by the Commission, Act XII of 1896 was passed, which enabled the Government to control the cultivation, importation and transportation of bhang, ganja and charas throughout the country.

This allowed Indians to continue to use it, while also providing additional revenue for the British Government. Under the new Act, cannabis was only allowed to be cultivated in certain states and all cannabis products were required to be stored in secure, bonded warehouses, from where they were issued to licenced vendors, only after the duty had been paid.

The Yarkand charas trade continued to thrive, and due to increased taxes, traders began using more circuitous, hazardous routes through the mountains, that were not patrolled by the British authorities.

Higher taxation only resulted in an increase of illegal smuggling, which was not only restricted to the Yarkand route, but also over the Khyber pass, from Afghanistan.

Although it is very difficult to estimate India's consumption of cannabis resin at the end of the 19th century, it must have been considerable and even though it was more expensive than ganja, it was considered by many to be far more desirable.

It was particularly popular in the Central Provinces of Nagpur, the orange groves of India, where many a worker sat under the shade of a tree in the late afternoon and enjoyed a chillum or two of fine Yarkand chars, or charas as he would have called it.

Regular ganja smokers would have considered it to be a treat, since it was far more mellow and dream-like than ganja, which was more of a stimulant.

In a 1957 report, compiled by Colonel Chopra, India had 2,400 hectares of ganja under licensed cultivation in 1895. However, it is important to remember, that this figure is based on what was taxed and I suspect that this probably represented only a fraction of what was actually produced.

Everything changed in 1930, when the British introduced new legislation, but more about that later.

THE OPIUM WARS

I think many readers will be surprised to learn, that the main reason why cannabis was prohibited, was due to the irreparable damage that was heaped upon the Chinese nation, by British and American opium dealers.

All the good work that had been carried out by Sir William O'Shaughnessy, Michael Donovan, Garcia da Orta and many others, was sacrificed to allow the Americans and their British cousins, to wash away the sins of the past.

I don't know who coined the phrase, "crime doesn't pay" because if history teaches us anything, it demonstrates that crime pays exceedingly well and the bigger the crime, the bigger the pay-out. With the exception of the Atlantic slave-trade, which benefitted everyone but the Africans, the so-called opium wars of the 19th century, must rank as one of the biggest crimes ever committed.

During the course of more than 70 years, British and American traders, with the support of their respective governments, illegally exported thousands of tons of opium into China every year, purely as a means of lining their own dirty pockets.

It wasn't due to public demand or pressure from missionary societies that they eventually stopped, it was mainly due to the fact that the Chinese were producing their own, which made the market a lot more competitive and as a result, less profitable. By that time, they had made so much money during the previous 70 years they didn't care because they were able to diversify their interests, launder their ill-gotten gains and look for other profitable ways to invest their vast fortunes.

The Chinese were left with a nation of more than 25 million addicts, and the former international drug smugglers and their governments, were left with a huge pile of cash and their reputations in tatters.

It has been estimated that between 1820 and 1824, ten thousand crates a year, the equivalent of 750 tons, were smuggled into the country. By 1825 the amount of opium sold in China had increased to nearly 20,000 crates and by 1835, this had risen to over 50,000 crates a year.

Each crate contained approximately seventy-five kilos of raw opium, which amounted to 3,750 tons in 1835 alone.

Russell & Co had at least 10% of this trade and they became the biggest American trading company in Canton. Samuel Russell, having made his fortune, returned to America in 1836, although the company continued to trade until it closed in 1891. He built a huge mansion in his hometown of Middletown in Connecticut and filled it with Chinese antiques and works of art which he took back with him.

He spent the rest of his days enjoying his wealth, entertaining his friends, throwing lavish parties and enjoying the accolades that were heaped upon him, before he died in 1862. The house, *Samuel Wadsworth Russell House*, which he named after his son, is now a major tourist attraction.

By 1837, opium represented nearly sixty percent of all Chinese imports and by 1839; the money spent on opium was the equivalent of twice the government's annual budget. There were now an estimated ten million opium addicts in China, with another ten million occasional, recreational users. These figures are even more astounding when you consider that this was an illegal activity.

The financial burden that the trade placed on the Chinese economy was devastating, since, during the same period, China lost 38 million Spanish silver dollars that were used to pay for the opium. This caused even more problems for the Chinese economy because without silver, the exchange rate for copper coins fell drastically from 1000 coins for a silver dollar, to over 1,700, which in effect, increased inflation by nearly 100%.

With so many people now using it on a daily basis business slowed, the standard of living dropped, and public services were crippled. One leading Chinese official was so worried that he wrote a letter to the Emperor;

"If we continue to allow this trade to flourish, in a few years we will find ourselves not only without any soldiers to resist the enemy but also without enough money to equip the army".

The Chinese Emperor realised that drastic action had to be taken and he sent Lin Zexu to Canton to put a stop to the opium imports. He ordered all the opium that was on the British and American ships to be taken off. There were more than twenty thousand crates in all, amounting to over 1,500 tons and these were placed in large pits and burned in public.

Shortly after this was done, he wrote a letter to Queen Victoria explaining the reasons for his actions. He suggested that it would be better if Britain not only prohibited the sale of it, but also banned the production of it in India, since that was the source of all the problems. He concluded by saying that profiting from the misery of others was not only immoral, it was also against the laws of Heaven.

I don't know what Queen Victoria's response was, if indeed she did respond, but I do know that production of opium in India increased and that the Chinese trade continued.

Although it was widely used in Britain, they were fully aware of how addictive it was. Thomas de Quincey's book, *The Confessions of an Opium Eater* had been published in 1822 and this graphic account of the life of an English opium addict, made very disturbing reading.

Samuel Taylor Coleridge, an English romantic poet was another well know addict, consuming nearly 100 drops of laudanum every day to feed his habit and Patrick Bronte, the brother of Emily and Charlotte, was also a regular client at the chemist shop in Haworth, where he purchased his.

The British and American traders were outraged at their loss of nearly two million pounds and both demanded compensation from their governments. Britain refused to pay, arguing that since the Chinese had destroyed their goods, it was the Chinese who should pay.

Although the British Government were not directly involved in the opium trade, they were collecting huge revenues from the tax imposed on the Imports of tea, which at the time was taxed at 5 shillings a pound. Since the opium was sold to the Chinese for silver, which was used to buy the tea, it was in the country's interest to support the traders. It was a vicious circle and the British Government, who was caught in the middle, ordered the East India Company to send an expeditionary force from India as a means of exerting pressure on the Chinese Emperor, and this marked the start of the first opium war.

After the British destroyed a number of towns along the Chinese coast and sinking a large fleet of Chinese ships, the Emperor surrendered and as a result, in 1842, the Treaty of Nanking was signed. Not only did this give Britain the status of "The Most Favoured Nation" the Emperor was also forced to pay the opium traders three million dollars in compensation, relinquish the island of Hong Kong and allow the British to have diplomatic representation in Peking.

The opium trade of course continued and flourished even more. Along with the East India Company and Russell & Co, the largest opium dealer was Jardine Matheson & Co, founded in 1832 by two Scottish traders, William Jardine and James Matheson.

Jardine knew better than most how damaging opium was, because he had studied medicine at Edinburgh University. While working as a surgeon on a ship owned by the East India Company, he soon realised that opium smuggling was far more profitable than being a surgeon and being a man of few scruples, he decided to get in on the act.

His timing was perfect, because in 1833 the House of Commons refused to renew the contract which gave the East India Company a monopoly for trading in the east. It was now a free for all and Jardine Matheson, like many other companies, made an absolute fortune. By 1841 their company owned 19 sailing clippers, the fastest boats of their day, which they used for shipping tea, silk, spices and other commodities to England and for picking up opium from India on the return journey. They also owned hundreds of smaller vessels which they used for their opium smuggling operation.

In 1844, Jardine Matheson & Co moved from Canton and set up their opium empire in Hong Kong, which was now a British Colony. They bought their first piece of land in 1841 for the sum of £565 which they used to open their first office on the island. Many years later, the company built the Excelsior Hotel on the same site which is now owned and operated by the Mandarin Oriental Hotel Group, which the company still own.

Using the money that they made from their opium business, Jardine Matheson invested heavily in Hong Kong, building offices, an ice-making factory and wharves and shipyards to maintain their fleet. They also used their wealth by offering financial services and loans to other companies who were keen to exploit the illegal trade.

With Hong Kong now a British Colony and the East India Company no longer enjoying a monopoly on trade, the opium business became even more lucrative. Many corrupt Chinese officials were only too happy to help the foreigners and it was comparatively easy to smuggle the opium into mainland China where it was sold for enormous profit.

This was a golden period for companies like Jardine Matheson, tea in England was now extremely popular with those who could afford it and the silk that they exported was sold all over Europe, along with porcelain and other goods that they were exporting.

Success however is often accompanied by problems and by 1854; Chinese imports into Britain were nine times higher than exports, which resulted in a huge trade deficit. The solution of course was to smuggle more opium into China but in order to do that, Britain needed China to open up more free ports, which the Chinese Emperor refused to do.

Britain needed another war and in 1856, a minor incident involving the seizure by Chinese officials of a small boat that was smuggling salt, provided Britain with the opportunity they had been waiting for.

Britain argued that since the boat was a registered British vessel, the Chinese were in breach of the 1843 Treaty of Bogue. This basically meant that the vessel was subject only to the legal jurisdiction of the British Consul. Britain's argument failed to impress the Chinese and things quickly escalated out of control and in no time at all, the second opium war began.

The British Navy came to the rescue and after a number of clashes and a few more Chinese towns were destroyed and the old Summer Palace reduced to rubble, the Emperor once again surrendered and in 1860, the Treaty of Tientsin was signed.

China was forced to legalise the importation of opium and under the treaty, foreign traders were allowed to import the drug without having to pay any tax on it.

Another five ports were opened up for foreign use and for the first time, foreign traders were allowed to travel inside China, thus exerting their influence over the whole country. Similar treaties were signed with the Americans and the French and many companies like Jardine Matheson opened up offices and warehouses in Shanghai and other ports.

Hampden Coit DuBose, born in 1845 in Darlington, South Carolina, was the son of a Presbyterian preacher. I don't know why he decided to go to China, I'm sure that there were lots of good causes that he could have devoted himself to in South Carolina, but like many, he felt that his religious zeal would be put to better use in foreign lands.

DuBose arrived in China in 1872 with his wife Pauline and began working with the Southern Presbyterian Church missionary group. He immediately noticed the detrimental effect that opium was having on the local population and with the support of other missionaries, he formed the Anti-Opium League.

The opium trade was in full swing at that time, but some of the big foreign traders were already diversifying into other areas due to the fact that the Chinese had begun to grow their own. He gradually gained support from other missionaries and Christian medics who were working there. Eventually some of the Chinese who were working with the missionaries began to confide in him. Over the following two years, he travelled extensively throughout the country, and this enabled him to determine the full extent of the trade which, by 1875, had grown considerably, in order to satisfy the demand which had been growing since 1820.

Local Chinese farmers had realised that opium poppies could be grown in almost any soil and so they too got in on the act. Domestic cultivation grew enormously, and Chinese traders realised that they could use it to pay for their goods. Chinese officials all over the country encouraged local farmers to grow it, since they could use the profits to pay government taxes. The opium business was no longer controlled by foreigners, but they had made so much money from it, they no longer cared.

With opposition to the trade growing in England, in the late 1870's, Jardine Matheson, the largest foreign opium dealers, diversified their interests and left the opium business in the hands of the Chinese, who were now growing enough to meet the huge demand.

By the 1880's even the Chinese who had initially attempted to suppress the drug, were now dependent on the money that it created.

In 1899, the Anti-Opium League published a book called, *Opinions of over One Hundred Physicians on the Use of Opium in China*, which outlined the extent of the opium problem in the country.

In 1901, the Qing Government launched a new campaign to suppress it, but this was opposed by Chinese farmers who claimed that they would be wiped out by the loss of their most profitable crop. Wholesalers, retailers and members of some of the most influential families in China, who were themselves opium addicts, also opposed the government. The Anti-Opium League influenced the British Government who, in 1906 issued a statement saying that the opium trade was morally indefensible.

Dubose drafted a petition for the abolition of the trade and after collecting more than a thousand signatures, he submitted it to the Chinese Emperor, who, in 1908 issued a formal edict, banning the trade, but the damage had already been done. In the same year, the British Government published a White Paper, which depicted a map of China showing the amount of opium that was produced in each province. The result was so shocking, it prompted the Lord Chief Justice to write;

"*We English, by the policy we have pursued, are morally responsible for every acre of land in China which is withdrawn from the cultivation of grain and devoted to that of the poppy: so that the fact of the growth of the drug in China aught only to increase our sense of responsibility*".

The map illustrated that the total production of opium in 19 provinces was 8,787 tons. This once great, proud nation, who had given the world silk, paper and tea and who had been the envy of the world for more than 600 years, had been reduced to a nation of junkies. Dubose wrote a letter to U.S Senator John McLaurin, urging him to call upon the American Government, to own up to its own responsibility for the part that it had played in the opium trade.

THE INTERNATIONAL OPIUM CONVENTIONS

The U.S.A called for a meeting of all interested parties, to discuss the opium problem. Representatives of 13 nations attended the International Opium Conference, held in Shanghai on February 1st, 1909 and during the course of a month, they discussed the problems at length.

It was agreed at the end of the conference, that they would meet again in the Hague for a formal convention, at which it was hoped they would all sign an international treaty, prohibiting the cultivation and use of a drug that had caused such much damage to the Chinese nation.

Italy was concerned about the flourishing, illegal hashish trade in its North African colonies, which it had acquired after a brief war with Turkey in 1911. They wanted to impose international controls on the cultivation of cannabis, which confused many of those attending, since cannabis remedies were common at the time. Many felt that any legislation concerning its use, was a matter that should be dealt with at a national, not international level.

Dr Hamilton Wright, a member of the U.S delegation who was responsible for drafting U.S domestic drug legislation, had already failed to include cannabis in the Smoking Opium Exclusion Act of 1909, and with his support, Italy was granted an addendum which was added to the conference;

"The conference considers it desirable to study the question of Indian hemp from the statistical and scientific point of view, with the object of regulating its abuses, should the necessity thereof be felt, by international legislation or by an international agreement".

In January 1912 the International Opium Convention took place in the Hague, Holland. The treaty, known as the Hague Convention, stated;

"The contracting Powers shall use their best endeavours to control, or to cause to be controlled, all persons manufacturing, importing, selling, distributing and exporting morphine, cocaine, and their respected salts, as well as the buildings in which these persons carry such an industry or trade".

It was signed on January 23rd, 1912 by China, Germany, the U.S.A, Britain, France, Italy, Japan, the Netherlands, Russia, Persia, Siam and Portugal. It was due to be effective on February 11th, 1915 but due to the First World War, it did not come into effect until June 28th, 1919 when it was incorporated into the Treaty of Versailles.

The Americans, keen to implement the Hague Convention as soon as possible, introduced the Harrison Narcotics Tax Act, otherwise known as the Opium and Coca Leaves Trade Restrictions Act, signed by President Woodrow Wilson on December 17th, 1914 which became effective on March 1st, 1915.

As a result of the International Opium Convention, Britain introduced the Dangerous Drugs Act in 1920.

This restricted the use of opium, morphine, cocaine and heroin and for the first time, under this new act, addiction, which was formerly considered to be a disease, was now regarded as a criminal act, punishable by imprisonment. Notices were published in newspapers and periodicals, which advised doctors and medical practitioners of the new law.

Following the carnage of the Great War, the League of Nations was formed. Its main purpose was to avoid further conflict through the use of arbitration, the reduction of weapons and to take action against acts of aggression by imposing economic sanctions, or military force if necessary. Another purpose of the League was to improve the lives of ordinary people by putting into place, a series of measures that were designed to provide humane working conditions, the eradication of slavery, disease and the illegal opium trade throughout the world.

A Covenant was drawn up, which would bind all members to adhere to these principles and although it was a noble idea, it was doomed to failure from the very start, because the U.S.A refused to ratify the treaty. I think the reason was quite simple, had America joined the League, it would have been obligated to end segregation, discrimination and the exploitation of African Americans, who, under the treaty, were considered equal to white Americans, a notion that many in America were uncomfortable with.

Although the U.S had refused to join the League of Nations, it still wanted to exert its influence over international regulations concerning drugs. The Americans felt that the Hague Convention of 1912 had not sufficiently addressed the opium problem and it put pressure on the League to convene a new conference, and in November 1924, members of the League met at its headquarters in Geneva, Switzerland.

The first Geneva Convention was supposed to focus on opium producing countries who, under the previous treaty, were only permitted to sell it through government-run monopolies and agencies. It had also been agreed that all producers were required to end opium production within 15 years and that a second convention would be held the following year to discuss further proposals.

Before the convention was concluded, the issue of cannabis was once again raised and members were asked to consider a report, that had been submitted by South Africa in November 1923, which it had sent to the Advisory Committee on Traffic in Opium and other Dangerous Drugs. South Africa had introduced a ban on the cultivation, sale, possession and use of cannabis in 1924. Their report stated that in their opinion, cannabis was as dangerous and addictive as opium and they were concerned that it had not been included in the international treaty.

Brazil were also keen to introduce international legislation to prohibit the use of cannabis. The plant is not indigenous to South America and was probably introduced to Brazil by African slaves from the Congo and Angola. This is supported by the fact that in the 19th century, Brazilians often called it, "fumo de Angola". In the Brazilian sugar plantations, many owners allowed their slaves to grow it, so that they had something to smoke in the evenings after finishing their work and eventually it spread to the indigenous population.

At the beginning of the 20th century, members of the Brazilian medical fraternity became concerned about the health of the nation. Rodrigues Dória, a former governor and the President of the Society of Legal Medicine, wrote a scathing report on cannabis, which he submitted to the Pan-American Scientific Congress, held in Washington in 1915. He described it's use as a "pernicious and degenerate vice" and said that it had been introduced by wild, savage blacks, who were now determined to demoralise the Brazilian nation, in revenge for the slave-trade.

The Advisory Committee requested that members submit reports based on their own views and experiences but Mohammed El Guindy, leader of the Egyptian delegation, insisted that immediate talks regarding cannabis should be implemented without further delay.

Egypt had a long history of cannabis use, which was so popular among the poorer classes that when Napoleon arrived in 1798, many of his troops began smoking it in local cafes when they were off duty. The French Emperor, worried that it would have a detrimental effect on his army, issued orders that anyone caught smoking it, would immediately be sent to prison for three-months.

Henry De Montfried, in his book *Hashish*, gives a full account of the life of a hashish smuggler, who purchased it from Greece and smuggled it into Egypt, a lucrative business right up until the 1930's. His description of the way in which it was produced in Greece, is very similar to how it is made today in Lebanon;

"The plants were stored in a barn during the winter and in the early spring, they were beaten to a pulp to produce a fine powder, which was sieved and put into cotton sacks and then pressed".

It's a great book and one of the earliest written on the subject.

Egypt first prohibited its use in 1868, when it was governed by the Sultan of Turkey and when this was unsuccessful, he instigated a campaign to eradicate it completely and by 1884 even its use was a criminal offence, punishable by a lengthy prison sentence. Corruption was rife, especially among customs officials and the trade continued. Greece had banned its use in public places, but this had very little effect and it was widely used in the cafes around the port of Piraeus, from where it was smuggled by local fishermen, into Turkey and Egypt.

The Egyptian Government, having failed so miserably to prevent the trade, probably felt that an international ban was the only possible solution to their problem.

During Guindy's hysterical and at times, theatrical speech, he claimed that hashish was an even greater threat than opium, saying that its use had led to an increase in the number of people admitted to insane asylums. He insisted that failing to ban it would have a disastrous effect on the whole world.

Howard Marks, author of *Mr Nice*, and at one time, one of the biggest cannabis smugglers in the world, gave a wonderful, comical rendition of Mohammed Guindy's speech, during his UK tour, when he was promoting his book. He staggered around the stage like a drunk at a stag party, as he informed the audience of the horrors inflicted on those who were foolish enough to smoke it and his impersonation of a lunatic cannabis addict was particularly amusing.

Guindy's claim that hashish was responsible for up to 60% of all cases, involving people who had been admitted to asylums due to insanity, was so exaggerated, one could easily be forgiven for thinking that Mr Guindy himself, was at the very least, suffering from delusions himself.

A 1921 report, prepared by the Abbasiya Asylum in Cairo, Egypt's largest mental hospital, stated that of the total 715 patients that had been admitted, only 19 were attributed to the use of hashish, while 49 were entirely due to alcohol. The report also concluded that hashish was not the cause of insanity, merely a condition associated with the disease.

Most of those attending the Convention had very little experience of cannabis and therefore their knowledge was limited at best, but Guindy's Oscar-winning performance had a profound effect on many of the delegates who were there, who were no doubt shocked by what they had heard.

Britain, France and India opposed Egypt's proposal, on the grounds that they had not submitted their request to the secretary and therefore it was not within the scope of the Convention to include hashish in the international treaty.

With support from South Africa, Turkey, Greece, Brazil, America and others, Guindy insisted that the matter should be placed in the hands of the committee. Guindy's provision stated;

"*The use of Indian hemp and the preparations derived therefrom may only be authorised for medical and scientific purposes. The raw resin, charas however, which is extracted from the female tops of the cannabis sativa, together with various preparations including hashish, of which it forms the basis, not being at present utilised for medical purposes and only being susceptible of utilisation for harmful purposes, in the same manner as other narcotics, may not be produced, sold or traded in, under any circumstances whatsoever*".

The committee later reported that they were in favour of a complete ban on cannabis, which was supported by 13 of the 16 nations represented, only Britain, India and Holland opposed the move.

In 1925, the members met again in Geneva for another International Opium Convention, often referred to as, the 1925 Geneva Convention. The Americans saw it as an opportunity to impose international controls over a wide range of issues concerning drugs, including restricting their use to scientific and medical use.

They proposed rigorous, uncompromising controls on drug production throughout the world, including the cultivation of the opium poppy, coca bush and the cannabis plant and when these were rejected, the U.S delegation refused to sign the treaty and walked out in disgust.

Unhappy that the conference was unable to arrive at an agreement in respect of opium smoking, China refused to sign, and they also withdrew and from that moment, both the U.S and China focused their legislation based on the original Hague Convention of 1912.

Britain however decided to follow the advice of the Advisory Council and in 1925, the Dangerous Drugs Act of 1920 was amended. This reversed the previous position on drug addiction, which was once again regarded as an illness, not a crime. The amended Act also restricted the importation of cannabis, which, for the first time, was listed as a dangerous drug. In 1928, the Act was amended again, to include the prohibition of the use and possession of cannabis and in 1930, the British Government in India introduced legislation aimed at putting an end to the Yarkand charas trade, which had been flourishing as a result of a peculiar clause in the 1925 Geneva Convention;

Article 11: Section 1

a) "The Contracting Parties undertake to prohibit the export of the resin obtained from Indian hemp, and the ordinary preparations of which the resin forms the base, to countries which have prohibited their use".

b) "In cases where export is permitted, a special import certificate must be issued by the government of the importing country, stating that the importation is approved for the purposes specified in the certificate, and that the resin or preparation will not be re-exported".

China had refused to sign the 1925 Convention and India had not prohibited the use of cannabis in India, so it was a perfectly legal trade that was able to continue, even after the international conventions had been signed. The trade was still flourishing in 1928, as the Indian Government report stated;

"Charas is imported from Central Asia (Yarkand), these imports are controlled as closely as the native production, a special warehouse having been established at Leh in which they are deposited and from which they are distributed".

The report stated that 53,554 kilos passed through the warehouse in 1923, which is just under 54 tons. We should not forget, that this figure only relates to what was declared by the Yarkand traders. There were many others who were not inclined to pay the tax and duties imposed by the British Government, and there was also a highly lucrative illegal trade with Afghanistan. As the report noted;

"With a view to stop the smuggling from Central Asia via Chitral, a warehouse has been established at Chitral and the preventative staff on the North West Frontier Province has been strengthened".

This was bandit country, home of the Pathans, a fierce warrior tribe who controlled routes over the Khyber pass to Afghanistan, where huge amounts of cannabis resin was produced for the Indian market.

In south west Pakistan, which was still British India at that time, it was also being smuggled from Kandahar in southern Afghanistan, to the British Province of Baluchistan from where it was distributed to the markets of central India. As a way of deterring illicit importation, the British Government lowered the duty;

"With a view to suppressing the wholesale illicit import of charas into India, duty thereon has been reduced from 60 Rupees to 20 Rupees per seer into the Punjab, Baluchistan, the North West Frontier Province and Delhi. The Excise Staff in Baluchistan was also strengthened, with a view to exercising more effective control over the smuggling of charas from across foreign territories".

Such a huge decrease in duty must have reflected the high demand and perhaps the British authorities felt that it was better to get a lower rate of tax on 60% of the trade, than a higher tax on only 20% of it. In 1931, a government report stated;

"The only preparation of the hemp plant imported from abroad is charas. It is imported from Yarkand in central Asia, under a transport-in-bond pass granted by the British Joint Commissioner at Leh, by persons licenced by the Punjab Government. Charas is also imported from Central Asia via Chitral".

According to tax records, in 1930, 1,976 units arrived at the warehouse from Yarkand, 334 from Chitral and 134 from Afghanistan, all of which amounted to around 95 tons. But again, we should remember that the vast majority of it was smuggled into India.

It was the Chinese who put an end to the Yarkand trade, when they introduced new legislation to curb the production of opium, towards the end of the second World War.

In keeping with the international conventions which recognised cannabis as a narcotic, they also banned the production of charas throughout Chinese Turkestan, including of course Yarkand.

Smugglers then looked to Afghanistan and Nepal, as principle producers but the lack of Yarkand charas also marked the beginning of commercial, domestic production in Kashmir and Himachal Pradesh. The Kashmiri's used the same technique as the Afghans, while in Himachal Pradesh, hand-rubbed charas became a cash crop for rural communities living in remote villages in the Himalayas.

It was entirely due to the illegal opium trade and the guilt of those responsible, that precipitated the prohibition of cannabis which only adds to the shame of those involved.

Opium had been used medicinally in India for several thousand years, and although there was some recreational use, there were very few addicts. The first opium factory in India, was founded by Lord Cornwallis in 1820 at Ghazipur, in Utter Pradesh. It was done because of the need to produce it on an industrial scale, in order to supply the lucrative, illegal, Chinese market.

It was totally hypocritical of the British, who, in their quest to flood China with Indian opium, had also created a huge number of Indian addicts, to then complain about the use of bhang, ganja and charas.

Those in power at the time, sought to exert their influence in ways that best suited their own purposes. It was the age of discovery, but it was also one of exploitation, imperialism and capitalism. It was also the age of arrogance, when those who knew very little, had the power to impose their ignorance on others.

The proof they say, is in the pudding, and history has proved conclusively, that the International Opium Conventions were not only a complete failure, they were responsible for creating problems that, up until then, didn't even exist.

THE PANAMA CANAL ZONE INVESTIGATIONS

The use of marihuana by American troops stationed in Panama, was first revealed during the Panama Canal Zone Military Investigations, which began in 1916 and lasted until 1918, when they were finally completed. Although its use was frowned upon, since the troops only smoked it during their free time, it wasn't considered to be a problem.

There must have been a huge increase in the number of troops using it, because on January 20th, 1923, a circular was issued by orders of the Panama Canal Department, prohibiting its use. It had little effect on the troops, who simply retreated to quiet, rural locations, during their time off but in 1925, a committee was appointed by the Governor, to investigate the use of it by military personnel.

Formal hearings were held, where the Post Commanders of Fort Clayton and Fort Davis, both gave testimonies. The committee also visited a hospital for the insane, where they observed troops smoking it, as well as a number of physicians and several members of the Canal Zone Police Department, who were also regular marihuana smokers.

Written statements were submitted, oral accounts were noted down and military records were investigated, in order to detect any possible link between marihuana use and delinquency. After an eight-month investigation, in December 1925 the Committee reached the following conclusion;

"There is no evidence that marihuana as grown here, is a "habit-forming" drug in the sense in which the term is applied to alcohol, opium, cocaine, etc, or that it has any appreciably deleterious influence on the individuals using it. We recommend that no steps be taken by the Canal Zone authorities to prevent the sale or use of marihuana, and that no special legislation be asked for".

The circular, which had forbidden the possession of marihuana was rescinded on January 29th, 1926 and in December 1928, the law prohibiting its possession and use in Panama, was repealed. Smokers could breathe a sigh of relief, but it wouldn't last long because most of the senior officers in the U.S military, disagreed with the report. They felt that its use lowered morale, made the troops lazy and more prone to belligerent behaviour.

A 12-month study was commissioned on June 23rd, 1928 by the Department Commander of the Canal Zone. This required that all medical cases of marihuana intoxication had to be submitted to the Surgeon-General. Violations, in respect of discipline that involved the use of marihuana or alcohol also had to be submitted, along with other violations that may have occurred as a result of marihuana smoking.

The committee were very clear what they wanted, stating;

"It should be understood that only concrete facts are desired, opinions or hearsay evidence are not wanted".

On June 17th, 1929 the Department Surgeon presented his evidence to the Chief of Staff, saying;

"The inquiry into the use of marihuana by soldiers of the Department had been in effect a full year. The reports of the twelve months indicate that the use of the drug is not widespread and that its effects upon military efficiency and upon discipline are not great. There appears to be no reason for reviving the penalties formerly exacted for the possession and the use of the drug".

It was a blow to the old school brigade, but they weren't finished, it was American officers who ordered the troops, not judicial inquiries. The Commander, issued an order on December 1st, 1930 which stated;

"The smoking of marihuana impairs the efficiency of the soldier and is forbidden. Soldiers smoking marihuana or using it in any way will be brought to trial for each and every offense".

In May the following year, under pressure from the military, the Governor ordered yet another inquiry in order to ascertain once and for all, the effects of marihuana use, by American troops.

The committee decided to hospitalise enlisted men who were known smokers and have them observed by a psychiatrist.

They felt this would be the most practical method to obtain reliable, first-hand information. Studies of the effects on the soldiers included a complete neuropsychiatric examination, a clinical study of the troops after smoking marihuana, and an additional study to determine signs and symptoms of any withdrawals.

In order to obtain as much information as possible, all the men's files were scrutinised to see if there was any link between crime, disobedience, delinquency and the use of marihuana. They had three main objectives; identify the extent that marihuana was being used, examine the physiological effects and whether or not it was linked to unruly, rebellious behaviour.

The report stated;

"During the period from December 1931, to October 1932, for an average of six days in each case, thirty-four soldiers, collected from four posts in the Panama Canal Department, were observed in Gorgas Hospital for the effects of smoking marihuana. These men, all known to be or suspected of being marihuana smokers, volunteered to enter the hospital, tell all they knew about the use of marihuana among soldiers in Panama and submit to any tests desired".

The length of service among the group was anything from 2 to 5 years, with an average of 18 months. All the men were aged from 19 to 33 and they smoked anything from 1 to 20 marihuana cigarettes a day. Most averaged 5 and the length of time they had been smoking varied from 2 months to 4 years, with an average of 14 months.

Their mental state was described as;

"None exhibited psychotic symptoms. 62% per cent were constitutional psychopaths and 23% were morons, a total of 05% mentally abnormal".

Users told the psychiatrist that it made them feel, "brushed up", "high" or "peppy", that it increased their appetite and helped them to sleep.

The report noted;

"These soldiers stated that marihuana was cheap and easy to procure in Panama and that they used it for "a pleasant pastime", usually during hours off duty when they had nothing else to do to amuse themselves. They stated that practically all recruits tried marihuana and those who liked it usually continued its use. Their average estimate of the number of habitual marihuana smokers in their respective organisations was approximately 10%".

The effects observed by the psychiatrist were noted as follows;

1. "No deprivation symptoms were observed even in those who admitted smoking eight to ten cigarettes the day previous to admission to hospital".

2. "With the exception of three, all after smoking showed symptoms of mild intoxication. They lost reserve, became animated, laughed without adequate cause, and talked foolishly. During this stage, which lasted for half an hour to an hour or so, neurological and mental tests were performed as well as previously".

3. "All stated they were very hungry after smoking and the quantity of food consumed at their subsequent meal conformed this statement".

4. "Pulse rate was markedly increased from a few moments after smoking the first cigarette to an hour or more. There was no appreciable variation in blood pressure before and after smoking. There were no other distinctive physiological changes observed, other than a tendency to sleep, in which some indulged for a short while an hour or two after smoking".

5. "No ill effects from smoking marihuana for several days in succession were observed, even when the soldiers were given marihuana ad libitum".

The Committee concluded;

1. *"The smoking of marihuana is quite common among soldiers in Panama".*

2. *"Morons and psychopaths are believed to constitute the large majority of habitual smokers".*

3. *"Marihuana as grown and used on the Isthmus of Panama is a mild stimulant and intoxicant. It is not a "habit forming" drug in the sense that the derivatives of opium and cocaine are such drugs, as there are no symptoms of deprivation following its withdrawal".*

4. *"Physiological effects, observed in addition to intoxication, were a marked increase in pulse rate and in appetite and the induction of sleep".*

5. *"No mental or physical deterioration effects of smoking marihuana could be demonstrated, but with this statement should be considered, the fact that the soldiers observed were all young men, who had smoked marihuana for an average of less than two years".*

6. *"From a medical standpoint the habitual use of marihuana, as of other stimulants and intoxicants, should be considered detrimental to health".*

7. *"Nothing was learned during the investigation to change our impression that the use of marihuana by civilians on the Canal Zone is so slight as to be negligible".*

8. *"The evidence obtained suggests that organisation commanders in estimating the efficiency and soldierly qualities of delinquents in their commands have unduly emphasised the effects of marihuana, disregarding the fact that a large proportion of delinquents are morons or psychopaths, which conditions of themselves would serve to account for delinquency".*

These assertions of its use by psychopaths and morons, became the hallmark of the campaign that swept across America in the 1930's. The Committee made two recommendations;

1. *"The present military regulations prohibiting the introduction, sale, possession or use of marihuana on military reservations, should continue in force, as they are believed to restrict the use of marihuana among soldiers".*

2. *"With the evidence obtained and considered by the committee, no recommendations for further legislative action to prevent the sale or use of marihuana in the Canal Zone, Panama, are deemed advisable under existing conditions".*

THE REEFER MADNESS CAMPAIGN OF THE 1930'S

Harry J Anslinger, the son of a Swiss barber and a German mother, began his Government career when he was appointed to the U.S Department's, Bureau of Prohibition as Assistant Commissioner. Shortly before prohibition ended, the U.S Government decided to form an independent department to fight the drug menace and in 1930, Anslinger was appointed as the first Commissioner of the Federal Bureau of Narcotics, established on June 14th, 1930.

When prohibition was repealed in 1933 and Americans were once again allowed to consume huge amounts of alcohol, many of those who had supported prohibition looked around for a new cause. Marihuana was the obvious choice.

Under the Pure Food and Drug Act of 1906, manufacturers were required by law to state the contents of their tinctures, remedies and patent medicines, if they contained any derivative of opium, cocaine, alcohol or cannabis.

In 1907, the Poison Act was introduced, in order to clarify what substances were deemed to be dangerous, alcohol of course was not included but cannabis was. Massachusetts went even further in 1911, when they passed legislation requiring cannabis to be issued only on prescription and in 1919, New York and Maine followed suit. California adopted a similar policy when after several amendments to the 1907 Poison Act, the possession of extracts, tinctures and other preparations containing cannabis, was classified as a misdemeanour.

Louis Armstrong was already smoking cannabis on a daily basis, when he became a regular feature at the Savoy Ballroom in Chicago. He recorded "muggles" in 1928, a great instrumental which many regard as one of his best. Muggles was a slang word for marihuana, although Jazz musicians like Louis, called it "gage". His love for smoking it began a few years earlier, when he moved to New York to play with the Fletcher Henderson Orchestra.

In 1930, due to the depression, many jazz clubs were forced to close, and a number of prominent jazz musicians stopped playing and took other jobs. Sidney Bechet started working as a tailor, before moving to Paris, where he resurrected his career and many of the great bands broke up. Frank Sebastian, a part-time actor and a jazz aficionado, invited Louis to play at his New Cotton Club in Culver City, near Los Angeles. Frank's club, the most popular night spot during the prohibition era, was the first in California to feature black orchestras and Louis was more than happy to move to a sunny, warm climate.

On November 13th, 1930, during a break between shows, Louis and fellow musician Vic Berton, went outside to the parking lot to smoke a joint where they attracted the attention of two narcotic agents, who promptly arrested them.

Thomas Brothers documented the story in his excellent book; *Louis Armstrong: Master of Modernism*. According to the author, Louis and his friend were allowed to finish their concert before they were taken to the local police station and charged. The popular magazine *Variety*, published the story under the headline;

"Drugs charges against Jazz Band Musicians".

According to Vic's brother, Ralph, Louis and his friend thought it was funny at the time and they spent what was left of the night laughing and joking, as they sat in their cell at the police station. They appeared in court in March the following year, when they were both sentenced to 30-days imprisonment and a heavy fine. The judge warned Louis about the evils of marihuana and told him to give it up. They spent 9-days in prison, before Frank and his influential friends paid the fine and persuaded the judge to set them both free. Louis sang a song as he left, as a tribute to his fellow prisoners.

On September 16th, 1934 the New York Times published an article with a headline that read;

"Use of Marihuana Spreading in the West".

The article, which claimed that even children were buying it, went on to say;

"Although as appalling as its effects on the human mind and body as narcotics, the use of marihuana appears to be proceeding unchecked in Colorado and other Western States with a large Spanish-American population. The drug is particularly popular with Latin Americans and its use is spreading to all classes".

It was a sad day for African Americans, Jazz musicians, Mexicans and medical practitioners all across America, when Harry J Anslinger was appointed. He not only declared war on them all, he also made it his personal mission, to eradicate its use in America.

When prohibition ended, Harry was keen to expand his Bureau's activities by deciding to focus his efforts against Mexicans, who he blamed for introducing marihuana smoking to the U.S. Anslinger maintained that this had been carried out by degenerate, revolutionaries who had followed Pancho Villa, claiming that the use of marihuana, caused wild, violent, psychotic tendencies.

He wasn't a Louis Armstrong fan, he claimed that Jazz was voodoo music, made by marihuana smoking negroes, which decent white folks had to be protected from. They were making the best music in the country, but if Anslinger had succeeded, the world would have been deprived of the music of Louis Armstrong, Duke Ellington, Coleman Hawkins and many others.

Jazz is perhaps, America's greatest cultural contribution to the world, although at the time it wasn't considered as such. A few, like Billy Holiday and Charlie Parker eased the pain that they suffered, as a result of racial segregation, discrimination and brutality, with heroin, but the vast majority of Jazz musicians were getting high on reefers.

Anslinger attributed the belligerence of the negro towards his white superiors to marihuana, a drug which he said, made the negro think that he was equal to his white masters.

His campaign, consisting of what we would call today, "fake news", reached hysterical proportions by the middle of the 1930's. He would do anything to get a good story and one of his classic scams concerned Victor Licata, a young, disturbed man, who had been found guilty of hacking his family to death with a machete. Anslinger re-arranged the facts, changed the evidence and planted the motive, to suit his own needs and then re-wrote the story, which was published by William Hearst, the "King of Yellow Journalism", who specialised in dark, shocking stories which gave graphic accounts, of the most distasteful events imaginable. His version of the incident, which was published in Hearst's *American Magazine*, was as follows;

"An entire family was murdered by a youthful addict in Florida. When officers arrived at the home, they found the youth staggering about in a human slaughterhouse. With an axe he had killed his father, mother, two brothers, and a sister. He seemed to be in a daze, he had no recollection of having committed the multiple crimes. The officers knew him ordinarily as a sane, rather quiet young man; now he was pitifully crazed. They sought the reason. The boy said that he had been in the habit of smoking something which youthful friends called "muggles", a childish name for marijuana".

The story was picked up by newspapers in every State of America. Nobody ever questioned Anslinger at the time, but it was revealed many years later that the young man in question had a long history of mental illness and had never smoked marijuana in his life.

He regenerated the old white myth that jazz and marijuana encouraged white women to have sexual relations with Negroes. His racist comments were considered to be normal by the majority of white Americans and that only encouraged him. By 1936 his anti-marihuana campaign was in full swing and during one of his many radio broadcasts, he described marihuana as;

"The deadly, dreadful poison that racks and tears not only the body but the very heart and soul of every human being who once becomes a slave to it in any of its cruel and devasting forms".

On other occasions, he warned the listener of some of those devasting forms, by saying;

"Marihuana is a short cut to the insane asylum, smoke marihuana cigarettes for a month and what was once your brain will be nothing but a storehouse of horrid spectres".

His love of make-believe tales of horror, was never greater than when the stories were of a violent nature. In another interview, he claimed;

"Hashish makes a murderer who kills for the love of killing, out of the mildest mannered man".

Anslinger's campaign reached a crescendo when a film called *Reefer Madness* was released to the general public in 1936. The written prologue, presented in the form of a government health warning, states the following;

"The motion picture you are about to witness may startle you. It would not have been possible otherwise, to sufficiently emphasize the frightful toll of the new drug menace which is destroying the youth of America in alarmingly increasing numbers. Marihuana is that drug, a violent narcotic, an unspeakable scourge, the real Public Enemy Number One".

"Its first effect is sudden, uncontrollable laughter, then comes dangerous hallucinations, space expands, time slows down, almost stands still. Fixed ideas come next, conjuring up monstrous extravagances, followed by emotional disturbances, the total inability to direct thoughts, the loss of power to resist physical emotions, leading finally to acts of shocking violence, ending often in incurable insanity. In picturing its soul-destroying effects, no attempt was made to equivocate. The scenes and incidents, while fictionalised for the purposes of this story, are based upon actual research into the results of marihuana addiction. If their stark reality will make you think, will make you aware that something must be done to wipe out this ghastly menace, then the picture will not have failed in its purpose. Because the dread Marihuana may be reaching forth next for your son or daughter or yours".

Looking at the film today one can only laugh, but *Reefer Madness*, one of only many similar films that appeared at the time, illustrates the power of "fake-news", which attempts to confuse, confound and convince unsuspecting people that the lies that are portrayed are the truth, the whole truth and nothing but the truth.

The film focuses on Bill and Mary, an all-American high-school couple, who are introduced to Jack, the local dope dealer. After smoking one joint, Bill becomes an addict, his life spirals out of control and he drops out of school, preferring to spend his time at Jack's house, where girls danced, giggled and played Jazz on the piano. Mary becomes worried and goes to Jack's house to confront Bill but instead, Jack persuades her to smoke a joint. Within a few minutes, she begins to giggle incessantly, while being groped on the sofa by one of Jack's friends.

There are a lot of crazy scenes in the film, which tries to portray itself as a horror film, complete with a very dramatic soundtrack. I don't want to spoil it for those who have not yet seen it, and anyone who has an interest in "Yellow Journalism" should, but needless to say, it does not have a happy ending.

It's absurd to think that Anslinger may have actually believed anything he said but there is no doubt, that even when he was presented with reports written by qualified doctors and respected experts, which contradicted his views, he chose to ignore them.

After spending years contemplating his nasty little plan, he finally drafted the Marihuana Tax Act of 1937 and even his choice of name, was intended to deceive.

Previous legislation had always referred to the wicked weed as either *Indian Hemp* or *Cannabis*. Some believe that Marihuana or Marijuana is a Mexican slang word, which combined the popular names of Maria and Juan. Anslinger perceived, quite rightly, that white Americans would consider it to be a Mexican curse if it had a Spanish name.

He immediately realised, that by making marihuana a tax issue, it would have a much greater appeal to the U.S House of Representatives, where the bill, as a tax measure, would be first presented. After all, the government was only too happy to consider any means of raising additional revenue.

Anslinger described his proposal as;

"An Act to impose an occupational excise tax upon certain dealers in Marijuana, to impose a transfer tax upon certain dealings in Marijuana, and to safeguard the revenue there from, by registry and recording".

The Act imposed a $1 an ounce tax on registered users who were supplied by doctors, pharmacists and other medical practitioners, who had registered with the government. Physicians were allowed to supply people who had not registered, providing they had applied for a permit as a "transferee" and paid a $100 an ounce tax, as a transfer fee.

Under the law, people who were not registered and who wanted to apply for a permit, had to complete a form giving their name, address, occupation and details concerning the amount they were buying from a registered practitioner. The law required that a copy of the form had to be submitted to the Internal Revenue Services, who would supply a copy to law enforcement officers on request, in return for a small administration fee.

Anslinger knew that marihuana smokers would be unable to pay the $100 an ounce tax and unwilling to furnish the authorities with their names and addresses, but his plan was not to tax marihuana, it was to persecute those who used it.

The American Medical Association opposed the bill, which they said had been prepared in secret and their legislative counsel Dr William Woodward, objected to the use of the word marihuana by stating;

"Marihuana is not the correct term, yet the burden of this bill is placed heavily on the doctors and pharmacists of this country who did not realise that they were losing cannabis".

He questioned Anslinger's claims of marihuana addiction, its propensity to incite violence and the possibility of over-doses but it was too late because it was as they say, "a done deal". The bill was passed as a direct result of the International Opium Convention, which had, by 1925, included cannabis as a drug, not a medicine. President Roosevelt signed the Marihuana Tax Act on August 2nd, 1937 but it did not take effect until October 1st.

On October 3rd, only two days after the act came into effect, Moses Baca, a 23-year-old son of Mexican parents, became the first person in the U.S to be busted under the new Act. He lived on the top floor of a boarding house in the Five Points area of Denver, an African American neighbourhood full of clubs where Duke Ellington, Ella Fitzgerald and other Jazz legends regularly entertained the local customers.

He was arrested when he returned home drunk and started beating his wife. The police arrived and after charging him for being drunk and disorderly, they searched his room and discovered a paper-bag containing a quarter of an ounce of marihuana. He was immediately charged under the Marihuana Tax Act and on October 8th, Federal Judge John Foster Symes, sentenced him to 18 months imprisonment.

Baca was well known in the local community for his passion for drinking "jungle juice". This was a drink made from the paste of "Sterno", a brand name for a type of stove that was developed in America at the end of the 19th century. An early advertisement described it as follows;

"Here's a can of paste that looks like cold cream and is just as safe. Take off the lid, touch a match to the paste and you have the clearest, hottest flame you ever saw, just what you want to boil an egg or heat baby's bottle. Quicker, hotter, easier than gas or electricity. No wires, no tubes, cannot spill".

It was promoted using the slogan;

"Sterno – Canned Heat".

It was extremely popular during the prohibition era, when hobo's and down-and-outs emptied the can, strained the paste though a sock, and then mixed it with fruit juice. Made from ethanol and methanol it was mixed with an acidic oxidising agent, to make it burn hotter and of course, it was highly toxic.

Tommy Johnson, an American bluesman, recorded a song about it in 1928 called "Canned Heat Blues", from which the blues band, "Canned Heat" took their name.

Samuel Caldwell, a 57-year-old former convicted bootlegger, was arrested on October 5th for selling three ready-rolled joints. When the police searched his room at the Lothrop Hotel, a dosshouse in Denver that was frequented by travelling salesmen, they found 4 pounds of marihuana.

Unlike Baca, Caldwell didn't smoke, but when prohibition ended, he decided to smuggle weed across the state border as a way of making money. He appeared in court on the same day as Moses Baca and became the first person in the U.S.A to be busted for marijuana trafficking. Judge Symes sentenced him to 4 years and less than two weeks later, both men were transported to the Federal Penitentiary at Fort Leavenworth, Kansas. The judge justified the sentences by claiming;

"*I consider marijuana the worst of all narcotics, far worse than the use of morphine or cocaine*".

It sounds too crazy to be true, but these are facts that cannot be denied. Anslinger took a personal interest in both cases and sat at the back of the court, beaming like the proverbial Cheshire cat, as Judge Symes announced the sentences. Shortly after the hearing, he praised the District Attorney, the Judge, the conviction and the sentence, informing the *Denver Post*;

"*These men have shown the way for other District Attorneys throughout the nation. Marijuana has become our greatest problem. Its sale and use has found its way into at least twenty-five States*".

On October 17th, the *Minneapolis Journal* informed its readers;

"*There is more human misery caused by dope than anything in the world*".

The newspaper, keen to re-assure the white citizens of Denver that the authorities were going to stamp-out this evil menace that threatened to destroy the world, went on to say;

"*Investigations early last week disclosed a ring of marijuana peddlers who recruited users of the mind-weakening and violence-breeding narcotic from the high schools and junior high schools of the city. When police raided the place, four officers fought for nearly ten minutes to subdue one slight 33-year-old man who was possessed with a "maniacal rage" police said because he was under the influence of the "killer drug"*.

The Second World War forced the U.S Government to change its approach regarding the use of industrial hemp and although the Marihuana Tax Act of 1937 remained unchanged, the U.S Government encouraged American farmers to grow it.

When the Japanese invaded the Philippines, the United States Department of Agriculture commissioned a promotional film, called, *Hemp For Victory*. It was made to inspire American farmers to grow Indian hemp, extolling its virtues as a valuable source of rope, cordage, canvas and other products. These precious materials were all vital to America's war effort and with no prospect of importing them, domestic production was the only alternative.

The film was a huge success and between 1942 and 1945, nearly half a million acres were used for the production of Indian hemp.

Fiorello La Guardia, the Mayor of New York, was an outspoken critic of the 1937 Act and in 1939, after consultations with the American Medical Association, he commissioned a study to investigate Anslinger's claims.

A sociological study was carried out by six police officers who rented a small apartment in Harlem. They spent a lot of time in poolrooms, bars, grills, dance halls and brothels, as well as parks, subways and other public places, where they observed the marihuana trade and its effects on the local population.

According to their observations and inquiries, marihuana was cheap and freely available and that its sale and distribution was not controlled by criminal gangs but by users. Clinical studies were also carried out, mostly with inmates who were serving time in New York prisons, many of whom were marihuana smokers.

The report, titled, *The Marijuana Problem in the City of New York: Sociological, Medical, Psychological and Pharmacological Studies*, was finally published in 1944.

Dealing with the physical effects, the report stated;

"The clinical studies were conducted with an experimental group of 77 persons, 72 of whom were inmates of various New York Prisons. Forty-eight of these subjects had used marijuana previously and some had been heavy users of opiate narcotics. Both orally ingested cannabis concentrate, and ordinary marijuana cigarettes were administered in various quantities. A feeling of euphoria, occasionally interrupted by unpleasant sensations, was the usual response to cannabis".

"Also noted were other common aspects of a marijuana 'high', such as laughter and relaxation. No signs of aggression occurred, although some indications of anti-social feelings were expressed. Dizziness, a light floating sensation, dryness of the throat, thirst, an increase in appetite (particularly for sweets), unsteadiness and a feeling of heaviness of the extremities, were among the common somatic symptoms noted".

When comparing users to non-users, the report stated;

"There is definite evidence in this study that the marijuana users were not inferior in intelligence to the general population and that they had suffered no mental or physical deterioration as a result of their use of the drug".

It concluded that marihuana use was relatively safe, that it did not result in insanity, users were not prone to acts of violence and that it was not addictive, stating;

"The practice of smoking marijuana did not lead to addiction in the medical sense of the word, did not lead to morphine or heroin or cocaine addiction, and no effort was made to create a market for opiate narcotics by stimulating the practice of marijuana smoking. Marijuana was not the determining factor in the commission of major crimes, nor was it the cause of juvenile delinquency. Finally, the publicity concerning the catastrophic effects of marijuana smoking in New York City is unfounded".

Anslinger condemned the report as being unscientific. It was a claim that he could not make in respect of the British 1893-1894 report but that was no longer relevant, since Britain had already prohibited the use of cannabis in 1928.

Even before the Second World War had ended, the Cold War began and to meet this new menace, Anslinger decided to change tack. In 1948, he addressed Congress, informing them that marihuana was an even greater threat than he had previously imagined. He informed them that new research demonstrated that marihuana smokers became so passive, they were incapable of fighting and that if it was not stamped out, the communists could simply walk into America and take it over without a fight.

Members of the American Congress were shocked by his revelations and fuelled by their fear of communism, without even bothering to check his latest evidence, the Boggs Act, named in honour of Hale Boggs who introduced it, was signed by President Truman on November 2nd, 1951. This was designed to deter the use of drugs, by imposing mandatory prison sentences, even for possession. When Anslinger addressed Congress, he told them;

"The danger is this: Over 50% of those young addicts started on marihuana smoking. They started there and graduated to heroin; they took the needle when the thrill of marijuana was gone".

He justified the mandatory, minimum sentences by saying;

"Short sentences do not deter, in districts where we get good sentences, the drug traffic does not flourish".

Dr Harris Isbell, an acknowledged researcher, was opposed to the inclusion of marihuana, saying;

"Marihuana smokers generally are mildly intoxicated, giggle, laugh, bother no one, and have a good time. They do not stagger or fall, and ordinarily will not attempt to harm anyone. It has not been proved that smoking marihuana leads to crimes of violence or to crimes of a sexual nature. Smoking marihuana has no unpleasant after-effects, no dependence is developed on the drug, and the practice can easily be stopped at any time. In fact, it is probably easier to stop smoking marihuana cigarettes than tobacco. In predisposed individuals, marihuana may precipitate temporary psychoses and is, therefore, not an innocuous practice with them".

Under the Boggs Act, a first offence for the possession of heroin, cocaine or marihuana, carried a minimum sentence of 2-years imprisonment, up to a maximum of 5-years, plus a fine of $2,000. On a second conviction, offenders would receive a minimum of 5-years and a third conviction carried a penalty of a minimum of 10-years and a maximum of 20.

This signalled the start of a purge by U.S law enforcement agencies all across America. On January 4th, 1952, more than 500 people were arrested, prompting newspapers to publish articles with more sensational headlines.

African Americans were once again targeted, especially in the south, where many ended up working on chain-gangs, repairing roads in rural areas, much in the same way as they were portrayed in Cool Hand Luke, a 1960's film starring Paul Newman. In reality however, the chain-gangs of the early 1950's predominantly consisted of black Americans, not whites.

The Boggs Act led to a heroin epidemic, as former marihuana smugglers realised that it was a lot easier to smuggle small amounts of heroin across the Mexican border, than it was to smuggle large, bulky bags full of weed. Although the penalties were the same, heroin was far more lucrative and, due to its size, a lot easier to conceal.

Anslinger informed the U.S Government that he needed even more powers and tougher controls, to combat the menace and in January 1956, the U.S Senate ordered a special committee to look into the problem.

The 9-page document described the illicit narcotics trade and in April, the committee submitted a 21-page report which focused on the treatment and rehabilitation of heroin addicts. According to the report, America had more addicts than any other western nation, with a large percentage being under the age of 21. Heroin addiction was cited as the cause of nearly 50% of all crimes committed in urban areas and 25% of all crimes committed in America. The committee reported that it was inevitable that this contagious disease would continue to grow, unless all addicts were removed from society for compulsory treatment and those that could not be cured should be placed in isolation.

For the first time, America realised that it had a huge smuggling problem as more and more addicts crossed the Mexican border. One female addict told the committee that she hid $1000 worth of heroin in her vagina, and smuggled it across the border at Nuevo Laredo, every week for nearly a year.

Anslinger demanded stiffer penalties, claiming that existing ones failed to deter would be smugglers, dealers and users.

The committee proposed that existing laws in respect of search and seizure should be scrapped and that Anslinger's men should be authorised to tap telephones, carry firearms and arrest without warrants. It also proposed that addicts and marihuana users should be forbidden to leave the country, and that the Federal Bureau of Narcotics should be enlarged and given more resources in order to combat the menace.

Hale Boggs was put in charge of another committee, to investigate the situation further. He was completely opposed to the treatment of heroin addicts in clinics, stating;

"To permit a Government institution to engage in the ghastly traffic in narcotics, is to give the Government the authority to render unto its citizens certain death without due process of law. The most effective weapon against the spread of addiction and the elimination of existing addiction, is severe punishment in the form of mandatory sentences which effectively deters traffickers".

As a result, the Narcotics Control Act was introduced, which was signed by President Eisenhower on July 18th, 1956. I think I am right in saying, that it was the quickest piece of legislation ever to have taken place, all done and dusted within a three-month period.

Under the new Act, a first offence for marihuana possession, carried a minimum sentence of 5-20 years imprisonment and 10-40 years for succeeding convictions. Those charged with smuggling marihuana would receive the same sentences but under a new clause, anyone convicted of selling heroin to a minor, would receive a minimum 10 years to life and, if the judge saw fit, the death penalty. The Act also stipulated that all discretion to suspend sentences or grant probation was prohibited and that anyone convicted of a drug offence would not be eligible for parole, with the exception of first offenders.

Narcotic agents and customs officers were given authority to carry guns, to serve warrants and to arrest anyone who was suspected of committing a drug offence, without a warrant.

Convicted drug offenders, addicts and users, were required to register and obtain a form before leaving the country, which they were required to submit on re-entry, failure to do so, would result in a minimum 1-3 years imprisonment and a $1000 fine.

The severity of the Narcotics Control Act of 1956 became evident a year later, when a young Mexican American by the name of Gilbert Zaragoza, was arrested for selling heroin to a 17-year old addict, who was working as an under-cover agent for the Federal Bureau of Narcotics in Los Angeles.

Zaragoza, himself an addict and unable to obtain treatment, resorted to selling heroin as a means of obtaining that which his body craved the most. He was charged and prosecuted under the new section of sales-to-minors. The judge, who clearly wanted to make a name for himself, recommended the jury to request the death penalty, which they were not prepared to do, so the judge sentenced him to the maximum sentence permissible, life imprisonment.

He told Zaragoza, who apparently had an IQ of less than 70, that society was going to use his life to;

"Set an example to others".

As he walked around the exercise yard of the Federal Prison, I can't begin to imagine what he must have felt. Even the most vicious, nasty criminals had an opportunity of parole, but he would remain there for the rest of his miserable life, although it wasn't long before others joined him.

President Eisenhower could, and should have, granted him a pardon but he was far too busy fighting the communist threat, to be worried about a mentally defected, Mexican American.

Had Zaragoza been a nice, clean cut, white American kid, the judge may have treated him differently, but he wasn't, he was a Mexican American and in the eyes of the judge, that was probably his biggest crime.

Harry Jacob Anslinger, the first Commissioner of the Federal Bureau of Narcotics, remained at his post for 32 years, under 5 U.S Presidents. On May 20th, 1962, on his 70th birthday, the mandatory retirement age for a man in his position, he submitted his resignation to President Kennedy.

It was not the end of his cannabis crusade, in recognition of his knowledge and expertise, he was appointed as the United States Representative to the United Nations Narcotics Commission, where he was able to continue his crusade on a truly, international level, something which he had been doing for more than thirty years.

GLOBAL PROHIBITION – THE SINGLE CONVENTION

America emerged from the war as the new super-power and keen to once again exert its influence over global drug policies, it decided to use the international community as a vehicle, to put into place a system to regulate, control and enforce policies that were in keeping with its own views.

It had already been established that the League of Nations was going to be disbanded. America, having refused to ratify the treaty when it was formed, had only ever been an observer but now that it was the world's most powerful nation, it was determined to play a leading role in what would become, the United Nations.

Even before the Nuremburg trials had started, the General Assembly of the League of Nations, in one of its final meetings before its demise, met in London on February 12th, 1946.

On February 18th, the following resolution was made;

"The Economic and Social Council, in order to provide machinery whereby full effect may be given to the international conventions relating to narcotic drugs, and to provide for continuous review of, and progress in, the international control of such drugs".

I think it's incredible that considering the problems that the world, and Europe in particular faced at the end of the war, that anyone would feel it was necessary to even think about drugs, but America was so concerned, they proposed the formation of a special body to deal with the issue.

The Commission on Narcotic Drugs held its first meeting on November 27th, 1946 at Lake Success in New York and its role had been clearly defined by the Economic and Social Council;

a) *"Assist the Council in exercising such powers of supervision over the application of international conventions and agreements dealing with narcotic drugs, as may be assumed by or conferred on the Council".*

b) *"Carry out such functions entrusted to the League of Nations Advisory Committee on Traffic in Opium and Other Dangerous Drugs by the international conventions on narcotic drugs as the Council may find necessary to assume".*

c) *"Advise the Council on all matters pertaining to the control of narcotic drugs and prepare such draft international conventions as may be necessary".*

d) *"Consider what changes may be required in the existing machinery for the international control of narcotic drugs and submit proposals thereon to the Council".*

e) *"Perform such other functions relating to narcotic drugs as the Council may direct".*

Although America had officially only been an "observer" in the League of Nations, its presence in the drug department had been there from day one, when Harry Anslinger was appointed as the American representative of the Advisory Committee.

Harry would have been in his element, drafting international conventions was right up his alley and he clearly had every intention of making his Marihuana Tax Act of 1937, the benchmark for global cannabis policy The Commission was made up of 15 members, representing countries that were defined as;

"Important producing or manufacturing countries, or countries in which illicit traffic in narcotic drugs constitutes a serious social problem".

These were identified as China, Egypt, Turkey, Iran, India, Mexico and Peru. Britain, America, Russia, France and Canada, who represented the allied victors were naturally given a seat, along with one for Holland, Poland and Yugoslavia.

This was a significant event for two reasons; the first is that the Advisory Committee would now be working for the Commission and the second is that under the Articles of the United Nations, they were entitled to put forward proposals not only to the U.N, but also to the General Assembly.

Although Anslinger had been a huge influence on the Advisory Council, America had not ratified the treaty, so he was only there as an invited observer and therefore, ineligible to vote.

Countries like Greece, Thailand, Uruguay and Spain, who had previously been represented on the Advisory Committee were left out, along with Belgium, Portugal and Switzerland. It's surprising that Greece, who had already been identified as a major cannabis producer and Thailand, a country that had a huge opium problem were not given a seat on the Commission.

I suspect that the inclusion of Poland and Yugoslavia was more of a political decision, than one based on merit, since it acknowledged Russia's influence in eastern Europe. Their inclusion provided a better balance between east and west, although of course, it would be the Americans who would call the shots.

Another resolution, passed by the Economic and Social Council stipulated;

"The Commission is authorised by the Council to appoint in a consultative capacity, and without the right to vote, representatives of bodies created under the terms of international conventions on narcotic drugs".

This of course allowed them to use groups like the Permanent Central Opium Board and the Drug Supervisory Body, both of whom had played important roles in the drafting of previous treaties and over the next ten years, the Commission gradually formulated its plan for a global drug policy.

The history of the Single Convention can be traced back to July 28th, 1958 when the Economic and Social Counsel of the United Nations, decided to convene a plenipotentiary conference, for the adoption of a Single Convention on Narcotic Drugs, to replace the existing, multilateral treaties that were already in place. In a nutshell, its aim was to become the single mechanism, through which it could influence, establish and enforce, drug legislation and policies throughout the world.

On January 24th, 1961, the United Nations Conference, for the adoption of a Single Convention, began in New York at the United Nations offices in Manhattan, and it was attended by representatives of 73 countries. Also present were non-governmental organisations like the International Criminal Police Organisation, the International Conference of Catholic Charities and the International Federation of Women Lawyers. Two international bodies were also present in the form of the Permanent Central Opium Board and the Drug Supervisory Body. General Safwat, Director of the Permanent Anti-Narcotics Bureau of the League of Arab States was also invited.

The world was a very different place, to what it was in 1925, when America had refused to sign the 1925 Geneva Convention. Having already passed the Marihuana Tax Act in 1937, it was determined to impose its views on everyone present. As the biggest, single contributor to the United Nations budget, it was determined to get its money's worth.

Carl Schurmann of the Netherlands was elected as President and 18 Vice-Presidents were appointed from countries which included, Switzerland, USSR, U.S.A and the U.K, along with others like India, Turkey, Thailand, Pakistan and Peru. Mr G.E Yates was appointed as the Executive Secretary and his Deputy was Mr Adolph Lande. A general committee was formed with an additional 13 committees that were given specific roles, designed to focus on various aspects of the treaty.

Five Resolutions were passed that laid out their objectives;

Resolution I -Technical Assistance on Narcotic Drugs

This expressed the hope that adequate resources would be made available to fight against the illicit traffic, in the form of expert advisors and training for national officials.

Resolution II – Treatment of Drug Addicts

This declared that the most effective methods of treatment of addiction was hospitals, that had a drug-free atmosphere.

Resolution III – Illicit Traffickers

This recommended that the criminal records of convicted foreign drug traffickers, that were kept by the International Criminal Police Organisation, would be made available to all members.

Resolution IV – Membership of Commission on Narcotic Drugs

This invited the Social and Economic Counsel to increase the membership of the Commission on Narcotic Drugs.

Resolution V – International Control Machinery

This invited the Social and Economic Counsel to implement measures which would ensure the simplification of the international control machinery, as soon as possible.

A preliminary statement attached to the treaty, explained its purpose;

"Recognising that the use of narcotic drugs continues to be indispensable for the relief of pain and suffering and that adequate provision must be made to ensure the availability of narcotic drugs for such purposes. Recognising that the addiction of narcotic drugs constitutes a serious evil for the individual and is fraught with social and economic danger to mankind".

"Conscious of their duty to prevent and combat this evil, effective measures require co-ordinated and universal action. Acknowledging the competence of the United Nations in the field of narcotics control and, desirous that the international organs concerned should be within the framework of the Organisation. Desiring to conclude a generally acceptable international convention to replace existing treaties on narcotic drugs, limiting such drugs to scientific and medical use, and providing for continuous international co-operation and control for the achievement of such aims and objectives".

It many ways it all sounded very reasonable, a noble effort to ensure that the horrors of the opium trade could never be repeated, but a closer study of the Articles contained within the Convention, reveal some very disturbing elements. These need to be pointed out, simply because they form the heart of the problem that we are faced with today.

Article 4 – General Obligations

"The parties shall take such legislative and administrative measures as may be necessary";

    a) *"To give effect to and carry out the provisions of this Convention within their own territories";*

    b) *"To co-operate with other States in the execution of the provisions of this Convention; and";*

c) *"Subject to the conditions of this Convention, to limit exclusively to medical and scientific purposes the production, manufacture, export, import, distribution of, trade in, use and possession of drugs"*.

This basically meant that everyone who signed the treaty, the UK included, gave up their sovereign right to introduce laws and regulations of their own making. In choosing to sign the treaty they agreed to adhere to those laid out in the Single Convention.

Article 5 – The International Control Organs

"The Parties, recognising the competence of the United Nations, with respect to the International Control of Drugs, agree to entrust to the Commission on Narcotic Drugs of the Economic and Social Council and to the International Narcotics Control Board, the functions respectively assigned to them under this Convention".

Under this article, the United Nations, having set the parameters of the Single Convention, were then in a position to enforce them.

Article 9 – Compositions and Functions of the Board

The Board, as defined in Article I, is the International Narcotics Control Board, the United Nations equivalent of the Federal Bureau of Narcotics.

Article 9 states that the Board will consist of 13 members, 3 with medical, pharmacological or pharmaceutical experience, chosen from a list of 5 persons nominated by the World Health Organisation. The remaining 10 were chosen from a list of persons nominated by Members of the United Nations, and by Parties that were not even members of the U.N. It further stated that the members should be persons who, by their "competence, impartiality and disinterestedness, will command general confidence".

The use of the word "disinterestedness" is for me, a paradox, because logic dictates that only those with an interest should have been appointed. Certified medical practitioners and scientific researchers would have commanded a far higher degree of confidence and credibility, than those with experience in drug enforcement.

All previous international treaties had focused on opium and cocaine, or derivatives of them.

At the second Geneva Convention in 1925, cannabis had already been included, but due to the number of oppositions, it had never been fully ratified. However, due to the legislation that was already in place in the U.S, America once again insisted, that cannabis should be prohibited.

A number of countries were opposed to the American view. The Indian delegation in particular, objected to the religious and social intolerance towards their social and religious customs. In an act of appeasement, cannabis leaves and seeds were removed from the list of controlled substances, which allowed the cultivation, sale and use of *bhang* to continue.

Article 1 – Definitions

d) *"cannabis means the flowering or fruiting tops of the cannabis plant (excluding the seeds and the leaves when not accompanied by the tops) from which the resin has not been extracted, by whatever name they may be designated".*

e) *"cannabis plant means any plant of the genus cannabis".*

f) *"cannabis resin means the separated resin, whether crude or purified, obtained from the cannabis plant".*

However, they insisted that India and others like Nepal, banned ganja and charas, but allowed a transitional period of 25 years, before they were required to comply.

Article 49 – Transitional Reservations

f) *"The use of cannabis for other than scientific or medical purposes must be discontinued as soon as possible but, in any case, within twenty-five years of the coming into force of this Convention as provided in paragraph 1 of Article 41".*

The Single Convention listed all substances in different categories and the U.S.A insisted that cannabis was placed in the most dangerous category. Cannabis was listed as both a Schedule 1 substance and Schedule 4 substance, officially described as one that was; highly addictive, had no medical applications and was unsafe, even under stringent medical supervision. This confirmed its status as a narcotic which was first suggested by Linnaeus, the Swedish botanist in 1762, and was therefore treated in the same way as heroin.

Barbiturates, tranquilisers and amphetamines were not prohibited under the Single Convention, the Commission had already decided that these drugs should be regulated at a national level, not an international one.

The Office of Legal Affairs of the United Nations claimed that there was an understanding at all stages during the course of the drafting of the treaty, that the Convention was not applicable to these types of substances.

I suspect that the main reason was to keep the major pharmaceutical companies happy, who make a fortune producing drugs that contain these substances, even though most people accept the fact that they are highly addictive.

It is another example, of the blatant hypocrisy of a system that generates huge revenues from the sale of alcohol and tobacco but imprisons those who choose to smoke marihuana.

The Single Convention was signed on March 30th, 1961 in New York and it was later amended in 1972 and again in 1988, making it the most comprehensive, international treaty ever conceived.

It was Reefer Madness all over again, although like Mickey Mouse and MacDonald's, it was shipped all over the world, as a warning to all would be cannabis smokers. In a 1962 issue of the *Bulletin of Narcotics*, published by the United Nations Commission on Narcotic Drugs, they proudly announced;

"After a definite transitional period, all non-medical use of narcotic drugs, such as opium smoking, opium eating, consumption of cannabis and chewing of coca leaves, will be outlawed everywhere. This is a goal which workers in international narcotics control all over the world have striven to achieve for half a century".

THE CHOPRA REPORT

Colonel R.N. Chopra was a highly educated Indian, of a type much admired by the British. He graduated from Cambridge, getting his BA in natural sciences in 1905 and in 1909, an MA. After leaving Cambridge, he worked for a while at St Bartholomew's Hospital in London, under the guidance of Walter E Dixon, in the pharmacology department, a relatively new form of scientific studies.

Chopra became Professor of Pharmacology at the Calcutta School of Tropical Medicine in 1922 and is regarded by many, as a visionary in the field of pharmaceutical science, and the founding father of Indian pharmacology. He was made a Companion of the Order of the Indian Empire in 1934 and in 1941, he was awarded with a Knighthood.

In 1957, he was a member of the Expert Advisory Panel on Addiction-producing Drugs, a committee that was formed by the World Health Organisation, to investigate the effects of the use of dangerous drugs. As a leading world expert, his report on cannabis use in India, published in 1957, formed the basis of the plenipotentiary conference which first proposed the Single Convention. At the time of writing his report, only 6 states were legally allowed to issue licences for the cultivation of cannabis.

The introduction of the Dangerous Drugs Act in 1930, had attempted to end the illegal charas trade with Yarkand, but that was still flourishing, due to the ingenuity of the traders, who discovered new, safe routes through the mountains. According to Chopra's report, in 1953 more than 16 tons of illicit ganja was seized by Indian officials, who estimated that it represented only 2% of the trade.

That being the case, India was consuming 800 tons of cannabis a year, although again, the figure is probably much higher, due to the fact that it grew wild in many parts of the country and therefore many had no need to buy it.

In the same year, 468 kilos of charas were seized, again, considered to be only 2% of the illicit trade, estimated at nearly 250 tons. Commercial quantities of domestic hand-rubbed charas, was also being produced in Himachal Pradesh and Kashmir, so consumption was probably a lot higher than Chopra estimated. His report to the Advisory Committee was interesting for a number of reasons, as a chemist and pharmacologist, he immediately recognised its potential;

"Cannabis undoubtedly has remarkable therapeutic properties, unfortunately its chemistry is still not quite clear. It is possible that studies, particularly on the synthetic variations which might be produced from it, may bring about advantages to be derived from its use as a therapeutic agent. In contrast with opium and its derivatives, the drug has no constipating action, it does not depress the respiratory centre; and there is little or no liability to addiction formation".

It is a great pity that Sir Nath Chopra is not here today, because I am certain that if he was, he would be leading the way in the field of cannabis pharmaceuticals. Unfortunately, the world was very different in 1957 and Chopra more or less, dismissed its use in modern medicine, pointing out that it had already been deleted from the British Pharmacopoeia, saying;

"During the last decade or so, cannabis preparations have not figured at all in the practise of western medicine in India. We have recently made inquiries from some of the large hospitals, attached to the medical colleges and other institutes and our belief has been confirmed, that cannabis is hardly used in the practice of modern medicine at the present time. Most of the eminent physicians, to whom inquiries were addressed said that they have neither used, nor are willing to use cannabis preparations in their practice".

He described some interesting veterinary applications, including a ganja poultice made for cattle suffering from "foot sore diseases" as well as the use of bhang for calming the cows before milking, which he dismissed by adding;

"Such use is largely based on hearsay and tradition".

Some of his comments regarding local customs, were amusing;

"The belief regarding the stimulant effects of cannabis on the sexual organs has existed for a long time among a section of the population. In moderate doses cannabis is believed to promote sexual desire, and it is not an uncommon practice among the younger, newly married folk, to drink beverages and eat sweets containing bhang".

"Among profligate women and prostitutes, bhang sherbet used to be a popular drink in the course of the evening when their paramours visited them. This practice has, however, been replaced by the use of alcohol".

He could not ignore the religious aspects of cannabis in India, although it is clear, that as an educated Hindu, his views were very different to that of the common man;

"Even today, a religious mendicant smoking ganja is not only tolerated, but is looked upon with some veneration by ignorant people and is even considered to possess supernatural powers of healing disease and infirmities. The enormous influence that cannabis and its associations had on the mind of the credulous and ignorant classes in India, and the tradition that was built up around it can thus be easily imagined".

I have no doubt that Chopra meant well, his report was extremely thorough, but due to his English education, he was looking at it from a British point of view, not an Indian one. His description of bhang drinking by the religious classes was particularly scathing;

"The deliberate abuse of bhang is met with almost entirely among certain classes of religious mendicants in this country, their main purpose being to get into a state of frenzy which, according to their traditional ideas, induces mental concentration and communion with God. Such a frenzied state is used as a cloak for impressing the credulous illiterate masses and creating in them a sort of religious fervour".

Chopra divided Indian cannabis users into 4 groups.

1: These consisted of labourers, domestic servants, whose use was described as;

"These people are the principle consumers of ganja and charas. They take these as food accessories in order to relieve fatigue after their work and for mild euphoric effects to relieve the monotony of their daily vocations and existence. They necessarily stick to small doses and as a rule, they are able to carry on with their ordinary work. They suffer little or no injury to their general health from the habitual use of the drug".

2: This group included those who used it purely for recreational purposes;

"The members of this group are idlers and persons mentally below average who take to the habitual use of cannabis in order to induce a state of oblivion. or to overcome feelings of inferiority and the sense of inhibition. Ganja and charas are mostly used by this group and the damage to their health is more perceptible".

3: This group was a little more up-market;

"This practice exists mostly amongst the idle and the rich who wish to seek pleasure and new sensations, often of a sexual nature. Such use, prolonged and carried to excess, is apt to cause injury to the gastro-intestinal tract, resulting in dyspepsia and impairment of vitality and general health, and later in damage to their nervous system".

4: This included sadhus, Shaivites and other religious sects;

"Cannabis drugs are used in all forms by them in order to overcome the feeling of hunger and to help them concentrate on religious and meditational objectives".

Chopra's views of the effects of cannabis, were very different to those expressed by the Indian Hemp Commission in 1894, according to him;

"Excessive indulgence in cannabis is apt to produce in healthy individuals and more so in susceptible individuals, mental confusion which may lead to delusions with restlessness and disordered movements. Intellectual impairment as well as disorientation may show itself in various ways, such as weakening of moral sense, habit of telling lies, prostitution and theft. The addict may become egotistic and unreliable, and may have recourse to theft, pilfering, sex perversion and other disgraceful practices. Sometimes indulgence may release subconscious impulses and lead to violent crime".

He was a firm believer in the Single Convention;

"When imports of charas were stopped, consumption of ganja and bhang increased a good deal. If the increase was not officially recorded, it was because illicit consumption prevailed. In all countries, smugglers, lured by the extravagant rewards that their nefarious trade offers, try to foil the efforts of the governments to protect the health, physical and mental, of the population. The narcotic problem is therefore an international one. Gangs of international traffickers exist and shift their operations from country to country wherever the government control is ineffective".

Sir Chopra's report was very well received by his fellow members of the World Health Organisation's Advisory Panel and I have no doubt that it played a key role in the drafting of the Single Convention.

In 1985, with the 25-year transitional period nearly at an end, Rajiv Gandhi, the Indian Prime Minister, faced with economic sanctions, complied with the Single Convention, by introducing the Narcotic Drugs and Psychotropic Substances Act.

Bhang of course was exempt, since the Single Convention did not prohibit leaves and seeds of the cannabis plant. Under the new Act, ganja and charas simply joined the list of other prohibited substances like opium, morphine, heroin and cocaine.

The penalties imposed were unnecessarily harsh; the minimum sentence for violating the act was 10 years imprisonment and as a result, those who had previously been involved in the ganja trade, switched to heroin, which provided much bigger profits, for the same risk.

Heroin was easier to hide which made transportation and concealment much easier, especially for the hawkers who roamed the markets, streets and villages, plying their trade. It was only a job for them, from which they earned just enough, to support their families. As is always the case, only a few were getting rich out of it, for everyone else it was either a poorly paid job or an addiction.

Almost overnight the entire trade shifted from peddling ganja and charas to heroin or morphine. This slowly created a huge drug problem in India, especially in large urban centers like Delhi, Bombay and Calcutta. Poor people, who had earlier smoked chillums packed with ganja, could no longer get the weed, so many began "chasing the dragon" instead.

It had a disastrous effect on the country, creating tens of thousands of heroin addicts all across the country. India had never had a drug problem before, but as a result of being forced to comply with the Single Convention, it inherited a heroin epidemic of massive proportions.

THE WOOTEN REPORT OF 1968

In response to the rise of cannabis use during the 1960's, the British Government commissioned the Advisory Committee on Drug Dependence, to compile a report on the use and effects of cannabis in the UK. Barbara Wooten, Baroness of Abinger, a British economist and social scientist, was appointed Chairman of a subcommittee, which consisted of 11 people, including several of the most respected experts in the field of drug use and dependency.

The report showed that convictions for cannabis offences had doubled in 1966, from 626 in the previous year, to 1,119 and that they had doubled again in 1967 to 2,393.

During the early 1950's, the vast majority of drug seizures by British customs concerned marihuana, mostly on ships from Indian and African ports, which was thought to have been mainly used by immigrant workers and jazz musicians. Investigations carried out by the committee, showed that by the mid 1960's, the vast majority of those convicted, were predominantly white, middle-class users.

These were supplied by a loose network of amateur smugglers, who were not seeking to exploit their customers and as a result, it was not considered to be a criminal activity carried out for financial gain, in-spite of the penalties imposed on those who were caught.

Witnesses confirmed the fact that cannabis smoking in the UK was a social, rather than a solitary activity and most felt that its use enhanced creativity and "self-expression", as well as producing a sense of "well-being".

On July 24th, 1967 the Times published a full-page advertisement which had been paid for, and signed by 50 prominent people which included, Dr Francis Crick, Fellow of the Royal Society, author Graham Greene, the political activist Tariq Ali, artist Graham Hockney and The Beatles;

> *"The law against marijuana is immoral in principle and unworkable in practice".*

"The prohibition of cannabis has brought the law into disrepute and has demoralized police officers faced with the necessity of enforcing an unjust law".

"Uncounted thousands of frightened persons have been arbitrarily classified as criminals and threatened with arrest, victimisation and loss of livelihood. Many of them have been exposed to public contempt in the courts, insulted by uninformed magistrates and sent to suffer in prison".

"The use of cannabis is increasing, and the rate of increase is accelerating. Cannabis smoking is widespread in the universities, and the custom has been taken up by writers, teachers, doctors, businessmen, musicians, scientists, and priests. Such persons do not fit the stereotype of the unemployed criminal dope fiend. Smoking the herb also forms a traditional part of the social and religious life of hundreds of thousands of immigrants to Britain".

"It is almost certainly correct to state that the risk to cannabis smokers of becoming heroin addicts is far less than the risk to drinkers of becoming alcoholics".

The advertisement also contained statements from established respected, medical practitioners, including a very dismissive quote, published in the Times three months earlier. Dr David Stafford-Clark, Director of Psychological Medicine at Guy's Hospital in London, stated;

"Certain specific myths require objective confrontation since otherwise they recurrently confuse the issue, and incidentally divert the energy and attention of police and customs and immigration authorities in directions which have very little to do with the facts and much more to do with prejudiced beliefs. The relative innocence of marijuana by comparison with alcohol is one such fact, its social denial, a comparable myth".

A lyrical laid-back statement from Dr Anthony Storr, was also included, which had previously been published in the Sunday Times earlier in the year, and one that I feel best describes the mood of the day;

"Marijuana is not a drug of addiction and is, medically speaking, far less harmful than alcohol or tobacco. It is generally smoked in the company of others and its chief effect seems to be an enhanced appreciation of music and colour and together with a feeling of relaxation and peace. A mystical experience of being at one with the universe is common, which is why the drug has been highly valued in Eastern religions".

A quote that was previously published in the Guy's Hospital Gazette in 1965, summoned up the situation in a sentence.

"The available evidence shows that marijuana is not a drug of addiction and has no harmful effects, the problem of marijuana has been created by an ill-informed society, rather than the drug itself."

It was a very powerful, social statement at the time, which concluded with a 5-point-plan.

1: *"The Government should encourage research into medical applications".*

2: *"Smoking cannabis on private premises should be legal".*

3: *"Cannabis should be removed from the dangerous drugs list".*

4: *"Possession should either be legally permitted, or considered as a misdemeanour, punishable by a fine of not more than £10 and not more than £25 for subsequent offences".*

5: *"All persons now imprisoned for possession of cannabis should have their sentences commuted".*

It was the year of Sgt Pepper, a time when things were changing so fast, it was hard to keep up with them and some of us believed that anything was possible.

The Wooten report was very critical of British legislation and of the sentences imposed on convicted offenders;

"We believe that the association of cannabis in legislation with heroin and the other opiates is entirely inappropriate and that new and quite separate legislation to deal specially and separately with cannabis and its synthetic derivatives should be introduced as soon as possible. We are also convinced that the present penalties for possession and supply are altogether too high".

This view demonstrates that the Single Convention, which failed to differentiate between cannabis, coca leaves and the opium poppy, was clearly an error of judgement on the part of those responsible for drawing up the treaty, those who agreed to its format and most of all, on the part of everyone who signed it. That decision was more than inappropriate, it was criminal, as the report noted;

"The maximum penalties for any offence relating to cannabis are, on summary conviction, a fine not exceeding £250 or imprisonment for not more than 12 months or both. And, on conviction on indictment, a fine not exceeding £1,000 or imprisonment for not more than 10 years or both. These penalties are common to all drugs prohibited or controlled under the Dangerous Drugs Act 1965, including heroin".

The Single Convention had turned normally law-abiding British citizens into criminals, with all the ramifications that go with it, a fact that was highlighted by the committee;

"Over two-thirds of all cannabis offenders (and nearly all found guilty of possessing more than I Kg) did not have a record of non-drug offences. Nine out of ten of all cannabis offences were for possessing less than 30 grams. About a quarter of all cannabis offenders were sent to prison (or borstal, detention centre, or approved school); only about 13% were made subject to a probation order; and about 17% of first offenders were sent to prison. In considering the scale of penalties our main aim, having regard to our view of the known effects of cannabis, is to remove for practical purposes, the prospect of imprisonment for possession of a small amount and to demonstrate that taking the drug in moderation is a relatively minor offence. We would hope that juvenile experiments in taking cannabis would be recognised for what they are, and not treated as antisocial acts or evidence of unsatisfactory moral character".

The report described the illicit market as;

"Annual volume of seizures by the customs has been fairly steady over the past decade or so. Individual cases have shown that large supplies have been brought in by highly organised smuggling. According to witnesses, there is also a substantial traffic in small amounts carried by persons returning from holidays abroad or, sent mainly to immigrants by post from their home countries".

"Several witnesses felt that amateur smuggling was now becoming more organised. Lebanon, Pakistan and Cyprus were mentioned as major sources and it has been suggested that hashish now forms some 80% of the traffic".

In its evaluation of the cannabis smoker, the report stated;

"The professional group are fundamentally law-abiding; discriminating in the use of cannabis for introspective and elation as well as for social relaxation. Involved in life, often to the point of social protest; not much interested in experiments with LSD; generally disinclined to take amphetamines or alcohol, tending to stop the use of cannabis on marriage, or when the risk of prosecution was felt to be inimical to career prospects. The unskilled group is similarly industrious and law-abiding and see nothing wrong or harmful in its use".

The report was very critical of the way the law failed to differentiate between users and suppliers and the reason given appeared to be one of assumption, rather than detection;

"The Dangerous Drugs Act 1965 imposes the same penalties for unlawful possession as for unlawful supply. A high maximum penalty for possession has been justified in the past by the argument that it must allow for due punishment of the trafficker, who is more likely to be found in possession than in the act of supply".

On the aspect of criminality, the report stated;

"From our study of the statistics and other evidence about the supply of cannabis in the United Kingdom we have come to the conclusions that the traditional view of the supplier as a large-scale criminal is an over-simplification, and that having a heavy maximum penalty for possession to allow for punishment of the large-scale trafficker exaggerates the criminality of drug-taking itself. It seems clear that in cannabis "society" there is a regular give and take of the drug and that many users are in a position to supply it, and do supply it, in very small quantities without real criminal intent. Having reviewed all the material available to us we find ourselves in agreement with the conclusion reached by the Indian Hemp Drugs Commission appointed by the Government of India (1891-1894) and the New York Mayor's Committee on Marihuana (1944), that the long-term consumption of cannabis in moderate doses has no harmful effects".

With regards to the addictive nature of cannabis, the report stated;

"Unlike the "hard" drugs. such as heroin, cannabis does not produce tolerance. Consuming the same, sometimes even a smaller amount of cannabis, continues to produce the original effect. Unlike heroin, cannabis does not cause physical dependence and withdrawal effects do not occur when its use is discontinued. The majority of users regard cannabis as pleasurable and so continue its use, but if they decide to give it up, they do not usually experience difficulty".

Baroness Wooten and her colleagues fulfilled their obligations and provided the British government with enough information to reassess their position in respect of cannabis. Like all the other reports that had gone before, it was ignored, simply because the politics of the day would not allow it. The attitude of the establishment at the time was summed up by the UNODC (United Nations Office of Drugs and Crime), who published a report in January 1969, under the title; *Approbation of Drug Usage in Rock and Roll Music.*

The paper, written by S. Taqi, is a savage condemnation of the 1960's counter-culture, its fashion, ideas and above all, its music;

"Perhaps no other artistic outlet has as striking an influence on the lives of British and American youth as rock and roll music. Television and feature films, certainly, must also be considered influential over the young, but their potential power is somewhat diluted by the fact that they must cater simultaneously to both adult and teen-age tastes in order to survive financially".

"The rock and roll music industry in contrast, depends almost exclusively on the youth market for its profits, thus, the rock and roll product is 100% aimed at the ears of teenagers and young adults. (A teenager or young adult in music business terms, can be anyone from about the age of 9 up to 24 or 25)".

My parent's generation completely underestimated the early 1960's music scene, which they viewed as merely a trend that would soon pass, but by 1967 it was obvious to everyone that it was here to stay. As the UNODC report noted;

"One survey by an American music-trade paper, Billboard, has shown that 64% of American youngsters living at college have their own phonographs, with average collections of 40 LP's and 79 45's. Frank Zappa, a noted rock and roll artist and Jazz magazine's musician of the year for 1968, has said that pop music is the real religion of young people today. In recent years the rock and roll industry has produced a consistent flow of records focusing on illicit drug usage and often approving of it as a form of recreation and relaxation".

The author of the paper completely disregards songs like My Generation and Won't get Fooled Again by the Who, which reflected the views of British youth, who were no longer prepared to accept the values of previous generations, who had plunged the world into two world wars.

His report is very critical of The Beatles; he most certainly would have read the Wooten Report, as well as seeing the Times Advertisement which they had all signed, and as a result he laid much of the blame on them. It is however an entertaining document and one which I feel is worthy of further examination.

The author's comments about *Mellow Yellow*, a big hit for Donavon in 1966, are very amusing;

"This song perhaps best exemplifies how far a suggestion can go, intended or unintended, as it became the anthem of a short-lived American joke-fad, known as banana-smoking. It had been discovered that one could get "high" by smoking the baked, scraped-off insides of a banana peel: the joke was that perhaps the banana, like marihuana, should be outlawed, and the United Fruit Company prosecuted for pushing drugs".

I remember a story about people getting stoned from smoking banana skins, but I always associated *Mellow Yellow* with sex, not smoking bananas, but then, I am not an American.

He wasn't a Beatles fan;

"*Sgt. Pepper is one of the largest selling records of all time; it was the number one LP of 1967 and, amazingly, was the number seven record of the following year. The Beatles, who were easily the most powerful and influential force in popular music, had evolved from clean-cut boyish figures into shaggy mystical underground heroes. At about the same time that Sgt. Pepper hit the sales racks, some of the Beatles admitted they had used LSD, and the album itself caused something of an uproar because of its alleged references to drugs*".

The author pointed out the obvious connection with Lucy in the Sky with Diamonds and LSD, and then went on to say;

"*A Day in the life is the one that perhaps stirred the most controversy. Some immediately said the song was about a drug experience, although one of the Beatles was quoted as saying it was only about a dream. Still, the song does have a line in which the narrator says he made his way up some stairs and then had a smoke, and shortly afterwards he began to dream. The Song ends with Beatle John Lennon remarking that he would love to turn on the listener*".

It was a great album, a musical innovation at the time, using recording techniques that had never been used before, but the author is of the opinion that the world would have been a better place without it;

"*The Beatles maintain a god-like status in the eyes of many of the young people who produce so much of the record industry's material. They are earnestly considered extraordinary talents and even musical geniuses. If they had chosen to ignore the drug trend or to remain discreet about it, the course of the trend might have been somewhat different*".

"*The Sgt Pepper album, however, was a green light of sorts to their vast following and indicated that the drug experience was indeed "in" as songwriter's material*".

It's surprising that he didn't blame them for the hippy invasion of India, but the overland trail to Kathmandu was already in full swing by the time the album came out, although the author does note;

"*The Beatles, soon after the album's release, announced that they were through with their drug phase, and were now off to India to study meditation*".

He was clearly a man who was out of touch with the times, but I think he had a soft spot for Elvis Presley;

"*The true importance of the music perhaps, is that through the controversy it aroused, it bred among the young a great, easy-going familiarity with pot and LSD*".

"If ten years ago Elvis Presley had been arrested for a narcotics offence, there doubtless would have been a profoundly shocked reaction and his career would certainly have been jeopardised. Today, when Beatle John Lennon is arrested for a drug offence, none of this shock is in evidence, and his career rolls cheerfully along. Being arrested for a drug violation is almost fashionable, and certainly nothing unusual".

If Elvis had been busted for marihuana, I don't think it would have done his career any harm, he was far too big at the time. It didn't ruin Louis Armstrong's career, who smoked it every day of his life and many would argue that it inspired him to create some of the best music the world had ever heard. Having been busted for it in 1930, he had his own views; As he wrote in a letter to his manager;

"All that grief over a mere small pittance such as gage, something that grows out in the backyard among the chickens. I just won't carry on with such fear over nothing and I don't intend to ever stop smoking it, not as long as it grows. There is no one on this earth that can ever stop it all from growing. No one but Jesus, and he wouldn't dare, because he feels the same way that I do about it".

Unlike Louis, who blew his horn as well as his joints, Elvis was a victim of drug abuse, but his was of the pharmaceutical variety, legally prescribed by his doctor, although of course, the author was unaware of that at the time.

The establishment had a very fixed way of looking at things, they were against any form of change and I think that they had great difficulty with young people expressing themselves;

"Whereas some public figures are careful not to be seen smoking ordinary cigarettes for fear of influencing young people, the Beatles and other like-minded pop musicians have seen fit to be reported as having experimented with LSD and having smoked "pot" for fun. They have musically reinforced their attitudes in the public mind by releasing a profusion of drug-slanted pop songs".

The report concluded by stating;

"The end result of it all perhaps, is that when, sooner or later, an urban child, who lives in the ordinary world, not in the pop world where a drug conviction can be shrugged off, is offered a marijuana cigarette or a dose of LSD, he will remember them not as something his health and hygiene teacher spoke warningly about, but as something Mick Jagger, or John Lennon or Paul McCartney has used and enjoyed".

To his detriment, the author failed to acknowledge that there were as many anti-war songs as there were pro-drug ones. Donovan's *Universal Soldier* and Hendrix's *Machine Gun* are only two examples but there are hundreds of others.

Lyrics not only expressed views on drugs, but on a wide range of social issues not least of all racism, the war in Vietnam and the impending threat of a nuclear war.

The paper also fails to recognise the influence of blues music on bands like the Beatles, the Rolling Stones and many other British groups, who were very much against the racist attitude that was so prominent in America at that time. During the 1930's, music was one of the few vehicles available for artists like Billie Holiday to express their views. Songs like *Strange Fruit*, a graphic description of negro lynching's, was a poignant reminder of what was going on in America at the time.

British bands were doing the same thing, even though the issues were different. The Beatles song, *Taxman* highlighted the fact that at that time in Britain, they were paying 19 shillings tax on every 20 they earned, others focused on the clash of social values and ideals, creating the notion of "us" and "them".

They were probably Britain's biggest export at the time, and it was their taxes and those of the Rolling Stones, Led Zeppelin, Pink Floyd and others, that enabled the British Government to continue to pay its war debt to America.

Racial equality and the democratic rights of African Americans was not something that the American influenced, UNODC, felt comfortable writing about, preferring instead to focus its efforts on anti-drug propaganda, although it did at least acknowledge its inconsistency in respect of alcohol;

"The belief is often expressed that there is something seriously wrong with a society than bans marijuana and at the same time allows alcoholic beverages to flow freely. Though the competent international bodies have voiced opinions on this score, no one, the United Nations included, has yet answered this question to the pop world's satisfaction: and that is what counts".

The British Government introduced the Misuse of Drugs Act in 1971. Cannabis was separated from Heroin, by categorising it as a Class B, as opposed to a Class A substance, prison sentences for possession were increased and the persecution of cannabis smokers intensified.

This was graphically illustrated at the Windsor Free Festival in 1973, when police, armed with truncheons and accompanied by police dogs, invaded the field in the early hours of the morning, when the peaceful hippies were sleeping. The police ripped up tents, beat people senseless and cleared the site, it was the last time that a free festival was held on Crown land.

Drug squads were formed by every police force in Britain and raids became a common occurrence, as Britain's police force enforced the new regulations.

It was the death of Sgt Pepper and the birth of a police state.

TIMOTHY LEARY V UNITED STATES

Timothy Leary, High Priest of the psychedelic generation, was a colourful character and one of the most influential people of flower power generation of the 1960's.

He is best known for his studies and experiments with psychedelic drugs, such as LSD and psilocybin, which he believed had enormous therapeutic potential. However, it was his appeal against a marihuana conviction, that finally caused the downfall of the Marihuana Tax Act of 1937, that had the biggest ramifications for the youth of America.

When Richard Nixon was appointed President of the United States in 1968, he described Leary as;

"The most dangerous man in America".

Leary's legal battle began when he was busted at the U.S border with Mexico, in Laredo Texas, in December 1965.

He left New York on December 20th, with his son Jack, his daughter Susan and his girlfriend, Rosemary Woodruff. From there they drove to Mexico for an extended holiday, during which time Leary planned to carry out research for a book that he intended to write about the use of *Psilocybe Mexicana,* psychedelic mushrooms that were used by the Mazatec tribe as part of their religious rites.

The party arrived at the Mexican border in the afternoon of December 23rd but were told that they would have to wait until the following day to apply for an extended visa. Rather than spend the night there, they decided to go back to Texas and resume their journey the following day.

A U.S custom's officer noticed marihuana seeds on the floor of the car and after a closer inspection, he found a very small quantity of marihuana in the glove box and as a result, decided to search everyone.

Leary's daughter had hidden a small amount of marijuana and three partially smoked marihuana cigarettes in her underwear. Her father, who naturally wanted to avoid any implication in his daughter's guilt, accepted full responsibility.

After admitting that the marihuana belonged to him and him alone, he was charged under the Marihuana Tax Act of 1937 and U.S Code 28, (176a) which relates to smuggling. Leary was charged on three counts;

1: That he had knowingly smuggled marihuana into the U.S.

2: That he had knowingly transported and facilitated the transportation and concealment of marihuana with the knowledge that it had been illegally imported.

3: That he was a transferee of marihuana and had knowingly transported, concealed, and facilitated the transportation and concealment of marihuana, without having paid the transfer tax imposed by the Marihuana Tax Act of 1937.

Leary admitted purchasing the marihuana in New York prior to his departure for Mexico but said, in his defence, that he had no idea of its origins.

On March 11th, 1966 Leary was tried before a jury in the Federal District Court, for the Southern District of Texas. After both sides had presented their evidence, the District Court dismissed the first count of smuggling, which was the only possible outcome. An examination of Leary's passport would have revealed that he had not entered Mexico and it was highly improbable that he had bought the marihuana from Mexican customs officials.

After deliberating the evidence, on the direction of the judge, the jury found Leary guilty on the other two counts. He was sentenced to 20 years and fined $20,000 for illegal transportation and 10 years and a fine of $20,000 for failing to pay the transfer tax. The Judge ordered the sentences to run consecutively, which meant that Leary would have to serve 30 years in prison and pay a fine of $40,000.

The severity of the sentence, and Leary's high profile, ensured that it made headlines all over the world. I remember the case very well, although at the time, I was completely unaware of the absurdity of the Marihuana Tax Act. There is no doubt that it was his reputation as a "guru" of the psychedelic age which prompted the judge to award Leary the maximum sentence allowed by law. He clearly disagreed with the views expressed in a report published in 1967, under the title;

The Challenge of Crime in a Free Society, which stated;

"On July 23rd, 1965, recognising the urgency of the Nation's crime problem and the depth of ignorance about it, President Johnson established this Commission on Law Enforcement and Administration of Justice, through Executive Order; 11236".

There is a whole section devoted to marihuana and I have no doubt that Leary was inspired by the following;

"The Federal Law controlling marihuana is a tax statute, enacted in 1937 and enforced by the Bureau of Narcotics. On its face the statute authorises marihuana transactions between persons, such as importers, wholesalers, physicians and others, who have paid certain occupational and transfer taxes. But in fact, since there is no accepted medical use of marihuana, only a handful of people are registered under the law and for all practical purposes the drug is illegal. Unauthorised possession, which in this context means possession under almost any circumstance, is a criminal act under Federal tax law".

After the Commission examined sentencing procedures, which included the mandatory minimum sentences, it concluded;

"There is a broad consensus among judges and correctional authorities that discretion should be restored. Application of the mandatory minimums has had some measurable results. At the close of fiscal 1965 there were 3,998 drug law violators in all Federal institutions. This number represented 17.9% of all persons confined. The average sentence being served by the drug-law violators was 87.6 months and 75.5% of them were ineligible for parole. These figures compare with the 2,017 drug-law violators confined at the close of fiscal 1950, comprising of 11.2% of all persons confined at that time".

The Commission accepted the recommendations made by the President's 1963 Advisory Commission, which first examined the penalties imposed on drug offenders;

1: "The smuggling or sale of large quantities of narcotics or the possession of large quantities for sale, would subject the offender to mandatory minimum sentences. Probation, suspension of sentence and parole would be denied".

2: "The smuggling or sale of small quantities of narcotics, or the possession of small quantities for sale, would subject the offender to some measure of imprisonment, but not to any mandatory minimum terms. Suspension of sentence would not be available, but parole would".

3: "The possession of narcotics without intent to sell. The sentencing judge would have full discretion as to these offences".

4: "All marihuana offences. The sentencing judge will have full discretion".

It is interesting to note that the Commission separated marihuana from narcotics, but these words of wisdom from the Presidential report had very little impact on Leary's judge. I can't begin to imagine how he felt, it must have all seemed like a bad trip at the time, but he appealed against the conviction and was given bail, pending his appeal.

Over a two-day period, in December 1968, the U.S Supreme Court considered the facts that were placed before them by both the prosecution and Leary's defence team. The case, like the Indian Hemp Drugs Commission of 1893-1894 is a fascinating document. It was the first time that the U.S Supreme Court had an opportunity to investigate the mechanisms and machinations of the Marihuana Tax Act of 1937 and to investigate the true purpose behind it.

I have no doubt, that Harry J Anslinger, Public Enemy Number One, followed the proceedings with great interest, after all, he was the person responsible for drafting it.

Although he had retired from service in 1962, his reputation, and that of the Federal Narcotics Bureau was now a matter of public scrutiny.

Leary's main defence rested on the fact, that under the Marihuana Tax Act of 1937, he was required by law to register himself as a marihuana user. In order to comply with the transfer provisions of the act, he would have been forced to provide the authorities with information that would have incriminated him, which he said, was a blatant violation of his rights under the 5ᵗʰ Amendment.

Another peculiarity of the case was the origin of the marijuana that Leary had been busted with.

Under the U.S Code 28, it was a crime to import or facilitate, the transportation of illegally imported marihuana, with knowledge of its illegal importation. Furthermore, under section 17 (a) of that code, possession of marihuana was considered to be sufficient evidence in itself, that the defendant knew that it had been illegally imported. This was a dangerous supposition on the part of the U.S Government, because it presumes that all marihuana sold in the U.S was imported, although this was not the case.

During the course of the appeal, which was heard over a two-day period in December 1968, the court decided to focus first on Leary's claim, that full compliance of the act was in breach of his civil rights under the 5ᵗʰ Amendment.

The 1937 Act consisted of two parts; the first imposes a tax on all transfers of marihuana and the second is an occupational tax imposed on all marihuana dealers, and it was the second part which the court considered first. Section 4751 provides that all persons who "deal" in marihuana shall be subject to an annual occupation tax. Subsections required that specified categories of persons, such as importers, producers, physicians, researchers and millers, pay varying annual rates. Persons who "deal" in marihuana who do not fall into any of the specified categories are required to pay $3 a year.

Section 4753 provides that at the time of paying the tax, the taxpayer must "register his name or style and his place or places of business" at the nearest district office of the Internal Revenue Service.

The court then considered the first part of the Act, concerning the tax imposed on all transfers of marihuana.

Section 4741 imposes a tax "upon all transfers of marihuana which are required by Section 4742 to be carried out in pursuance of written order forms". This section further provides that on transfers to persons registered under Section 4753, the tax is $1 an ounce, while transfers to persons not registered, the tax is $100 an ounce.

The tax was required to be paid by the transferee "at the time of securing each order form".

Section 4742 makes it unlawful for any person, "whether or not required to pay a special tax and register under Sections 4751-4753", to transfer marihuana except pursuant to a written order form to be obtained by the transferee. It also required the Internal Revenue Service to "preserve" in its records, a duplicate copy of every order form it issued.

Section 4773 assures that the information contained in the order form will be available to law enforcement officials. It also provides that the duplicate order forms required to be kept by the Internal Revenue Service, shall be open to inspection by Treasury personnel and state and local officials charged with enforcement of marihuana laws, and that upon payment of a fee, such officials shall be provided with copies of the forms.

Section 4744 makes it unlawful for a transferee to pay the transfer tax either to acquire marihuana without having paid the tax, or to transport, conceal, or facilitate the transportation or concealment of, any marihuana so acquired.

Leary was convicted under Section 4744 of the Marihuana Tax Act of 1937, after admitting that he had not obtained an order form or paid the transfer tax.

When Leary failed to comply with the Act in late 1965, possession of any quantity was a crime in every one of the 50 states, including New York, where the transfer took place and Texas where he was arrested and later convicted. However, almost all states, including New York and Texas, had exemptions making lawful, under specified conditions, possession of marihuana by;

a) State-licenced manufacturers and wholesalers.

b) Apothecaries.

c) Researchers.

d) Physicians, dentists, veterinarians, and other medical personnel.

e) Agents or employees of the foregoing persons or common carriers.

f) Persons for whom marihuana had been prescribed or to whom it had been given by an authorised medical person.

g) Certain public officials

Individuals in the first four exemptions, are among those compelled to pay the occupational tax; Sections 4751-4753.

It is extremely unlikely they would remain unregistered, failure to register renders them liable not only to an additional $99 per ounce transfer tax, but also to severe criminal penalties. Persons covered in the remaining three exemptions appear to be wholly exempt from the order form and transfer tax requirements.

When Mr Leary failed to comply with the Act, those persons who might legally possess marihuana under state law were virtually certain either to be registered under Section 4753 or to be exempt from the order form requirement. It is reasonable to assume that possessors who were both unregistered and obliged to obtain an order form constituted a "selective group inherently suspect of criminal activities". Full compliance with the transfer tax provisions, would have required Mr Leary, to identify himself as a member of this "select" and "suspect" group.

As the Supreme Court noted;

"We can only decide that when read according to their terms, these provisions created a "real and appreciable" hazard of incrimination".

The court then addressed Leary's conviction of transporting illegally imported marihuana. It concluded that there were only 5 ways that those in possession of marihuana, could have known for certain that it had been imported;

1: The user might have been aware of the proportion of marihuana consumed in the U.S and deduced that theirs was illegally imported.

2: The user might have smuggled the marihuana themselves.

3: The user might have learned by indirect means, that the marihuana that was furnished by their supplier had been illegally imported.

4: The user may have specified their preference for foreign marihuana when making their purchase, or their supplier may have informed them of its origins.

5: The user might have been able to determine the source of the marihuana, by its appearance, packaging or taste.

With regards to the first possibility, the court concluded that although the majority of users were aware that marihuana was imported from Mexico, it was extremely likely that they either had no knowledge of the proportion that was imported, or they believed that the proportion was considerably lower than may have actually been the case. In respect of the second possibility, the court accepted that some users may have imported it themselves, but they concluded quite rightly, that the vast majority of users, obtained it from American suppliers.

The third possibility was rejected outright, since the court was of the opinion that imported marihuana passed through a number of hands before reaching the consumer and at each stage, a different story was probably used to protect suppliers.

Distribution of any illegal product is, by its very nature, a clandestine operation and a closely guarded secret. Suppliers operate on a "need to know" basis, in order to protect their source and their own anonymity, so it's reasonable to assume relatively few customers could have been aware of its origins.

With regards to the fourth possibility, the court accepted that some users may have had a preference for Mexican marihuana and that some suppliers, occasionally furnished information in respect of its origins. However, if this information was not volunteered, the court concluded that most buyers would be reluctant to ask, for fear of being thought of as a government informant.

Dealing with the last possibility, the court was of the opinion that since all marihuana belonged to the same species, *Cannabis Sativa*, it was extremely difficult to distinguish the difference between marihuana that had been imported and that which had been domestically cultivated.

The court accepted that Mexican marihuana was often packed into bricks and wrapped in Mexican newspaper. These bricks usually weighed a kilo, but the vast majority of consumers purchased it either by the "bag", about one-fifth of an ounce, by the "can", about one ounce, or in rare cases, by the pound. It follows then, that by the time it reached the consumer, it had probably been re-packaged several times and therefore only a small percentage of users could have known of its origins from its packaging.

In respect of taste, while the court accepted that consumers were able to differentiate between good and bad marihuana, they concluded that most were unable to identify its origins simply by its taste or smell.

John S. Martin Jnr represented the U.S Government and his team included, Solicitor General Griswold, Assistant Attorney General Vinson and Beatrice Rosenberg. In Leary's corner were Robert J. Haft, his lawyer, a team from the American Civil Liberties Union and Joseph S. Oteri of the National Students Association.

The Government claimed that the regulations of the Act did not allow a person to register, unless their activities were permissible under his laws of jurisdiction and that no one would be permitted to obtain an order form and pay the transfer tax, unless they had registered.

They also claimed that the Act was designed to prohibit non-registered people, like Mr Leary, from dealing in marihuana.

The Government denied the existence of a substantial hazard of incrimination at the time Mr Leary acquired his marihuana, because he would have known that he could not obtain an order form and therefore, would not have applied for one, and because there was no risk that an unsuccessful claim would have been brought to the attention of law enforcement officials.

When questioned however, the Government had to admit that there had never been an attempt by a non-registered person to pay the tax. The legislative history of the 1937 Act was of particular interest to the Supreme Court. Since the Act had been disguised as a Tax Bill, it originated in the House of Representatives. At the start of the first hearing before the House Ways and Means Committee, the Treasury's Department's Assistant General Counsel, Clinton M. Hester, told the House;

"The purpose of this bill is not only to raise revenue from the marihuana traffic, but also to discourage the current and widespread undesirable use of marihuana by smokers and drug addicts".

He further stated;

"The bill would permit the transfer of marihuana to anyone but would impose a $100 per ounce tax upon a transfer to a person who might use it for purposes which are dangerous and harmful to the public".

At that point in the proceedings, Leary and his team must have realised that they had the Government on the run, but the best was yet to come. When Clinton M. Hester appeared before a subcommittee of the Senate Finance Committee, he clarified the situation even further, which left the Supreme Court in no doubt, as to why the bill was passed in 1937. Hester told the committee;

"The $100 transfer tax is to prevent the drug from coming into the hands of those who will put it to illicit use".

The House of Representative and the Senate's report, describe the purpose of the transfer provisions in much the same way as Hester had;

"Congress has the power to enact a tax that is so heavy as to discourage the transactions or activities taxed. These cases sustain the $100 tax imposed, upon transfers to unregistered persons".

The Supreme Court concluded;

"Upon this evidence, we have no hesitation in concluding that the interpretation that the Government would give to the transfer provisions is, contrary to the manifest congressional intent, that transfers to non-registered people be taxed, not forbidden".

The court agreed with Leary, that full compliance of the transfer provisions would have created a real and serious threat of self-incrimination, in violation of his right under the 5th Amendment.

They further added;

"The foregoing shows that at the time Mr Leary acquired the marihuana, he was confronted with a statute which on its face permitted him to acquire the drug legally, provided he paid the $100 per ounce transfer tax and gave incriminating information, and simultaneously with a system of regulations so out of keeping with the statute as to be ultra vires".

I had to get the dictionary out for that one, it's not a phrase that is commonly used, except of course by lawyers who seem to have an entirely different language to the rest of us. According to Collins, *ultra vires* means;

"Beyond the legal power of a person, agent, corporation etc".

Clearly, Harry J. Anslinger had operated beyond the power given to him.

The Supreme Court considered the question of "presumption", in respect of Leary's conviction of transporting marihuana with the knowledge that it had been illegally imported and they concluded quite rightly that a criminal statutory presumption must be regarded as "irrational" or "arbitrary" and as such, unconstitutional. I would have loved to have seen the look on Harry J Anslinger's face, when the Supreme Court of the United States delivered its verdict on May 19th, 1969. In a unanimous decision, penned by Justice John Marshall Harlan II, the court declared the Marihuana Tax Act of 1937 to be unconstitutional and Timothy Leary's conviction was overturned.

Mr Justice Brook, concurring in the result said;

"I concur in the Court's outright reversal of the petitioner's conviction on Count 3 of the indictment. I also concur in reversal of the petitioner's conviction on Count 2 of the indictment, based on 21 U.S.C. 176(a). Congress has no more constitutional power to tell a jury it can convict upon any such forced and baseless inference than it has power to tell juries they can convict a defendant of a crime without any evidence at all from which an inference of guilt could be drawn"

After leaving the court a free man, Leary announced his intention of running for the Governorship of California, under the slogan of;

"Come together, join the party".

On June 1st, he joined John Lennon and Yoko Ono in Montreal, where they performed their famous "love-in", informing the world's press that they were campaigning for world peace.

Timothy Leary had an interesting life.

On January 21st, 1970 he was sentenced to 10 years imprisonment for his conviction of the two cannabis cigarette butts that he had been arrested with in 1968, and another 10 years for a previous conviction in 1965, prior to his arrest at the U.S border. He escaped from prison, went on the run, had numerous adventures in Algeria, Switzerland, Austria, Lebanon and Afghanistan, before ending up back in prison in the U.S in 1973.

In 1976, he was released and settled down in Laurel Canyon where he continued to write and give lectures until he died in May 1996. Some of his ashes were placed in a Pegasus Rocket, along with those belonging to Gene Roddenberry, the creator of Star Trek.

The rocket was launched on April 21st, 1997 and after orbiting the earth for 6-years, it finally exploded, scattering its remains into the cosmos.

THE LE DAIN REPORT OF 1970 – A CANADIAN PERSPECTIVE

Within weeks of Timothy Leary's victory in the U.S Supreme Court, the Canadian Government appointed a Commission of Inquiry into the Non-Medical use of Drugs. Dean Gerald Le Dain Q.C, was appointed Chairman and the Commission published its interim report in April 1970.

During the course of its investigation, which was carried out along the same lines as the Indian Hemp Commission of 1893, it held 21-days of formal hearings in a wide variety of venues which included colleges, schools and universities in 12 major Canadian cities. They also held informal meetings in coffee shops, youth clubs and bars where people were free to speak about their use, views and experiences with drugs.

Its purpose was to listen to those who were directly or indirectly involved in the Canadian drug scene, particularly, young marihuana users. In order to gain their trust and to encourage everyone to speak freely, witnesses were guaranteed that their statements and testimonies would not be used by law-enforcement agencies and that their identities would remain anonymous.

As a result, nearly 12,000 people took part in the study, providing the commission with a wealth of information which was then considered by a wide variety of doctors, psychologists, chemists and social scientists. Their interim report began on a very positive note;

"Opinions and feelings have poured forth in the hearings with great spontaneity, particularly in the more informal settings. The Commission has been deeply impressed, and on several occasions moved by the testimony which it has heard".

"As a result of the initial phase of its inquiry, the Commission is more than ever convinced that the proper response to the non-medical use of psychotropic drugs is a question which must be worked out by the people of Canada, examining it and talking it over together. It goes to the roots of our society and touches the values underlying our whole approach to life. It is not a matter which can be confined to the discrete consultation of experts, although experts obviously have their role, and a very important one, to play".

It is important to remember that when this study was carried out, the hippie movement, which promoted peace and love as opposed to war and hate, was in full swing and many of the views that were expressed reflected an attitude of hope for a better future. The Vietnam war was at its height, African Americans were fighting for civil liberties, and the prevailing view among young people all over the world was that it was time for a change, as the report noted;

"In our conversation with students and young people, they have frequently contrasted marijuana and alcohol effects to describe the former as a drug of peace, a drug that reduces tendencies to aggression while suggesting that the latter drug produces hostile, aggressive behaviour. Marijuana is seen as particularly appropriate to a generation that emphasizes peace and is, in many ways, anti-competitive".

Many of those that took part in the study, freely admitted that they smoked marihuana simply to get high, which the commission accepted was justification in itself;

"The use of marijuana for pleasure, must not be interpreted as meaning that the motivation is trivial. On the contrary, it is one among many indications that the younger generation has profoundly re-evaluated the proper role of pleasure in human life".

Others expressed more idealistic views, similar to those that were highlighted in the Wooten Report, two years earlier in Britain, as the Canadian report noted;

"While pleasure, curiosity, the desire to experiment, and even the sense of adventure are dominant motivations in drug use, there is no doubt that a search for self-knowledge and self-integration and for spiritual meanings are strong motivations with many".

It was the search for spiritual meaning that contributed to the rise of interest in Eastern philosophies, which caused many to take the overland trail to India, in search of something more meaningful, than that which western societies offered;

"The positive values that young people claim to find in the drug experience bear a striking similarity to traditional religious values, including the concern with the soul, or inner self".

"The spirit of renunciation, the emphasis on openness and the closely-knit community are part of it, but there is definitely the sense of identification with something larger, something to which one belongs as part of the human race".

Much of the cynicism that young people felt at the time, was due to two World Wars, the war in Korea, the ongoing war in Vietnam and the threat of a future nuclear war. All of these were perceived as a total failure on the part of previous generations, which had failed to combat the real issues concerning atomic weapons, human rights and poverty. As a result, young people were not prepared to believe the propaganda perpetrated by the media, especially with regards to the use and effects of marihuana, which was often distorted, as the report noted;

"Many of the young people who have appeared before us have been critical of the drug education to which they have been exposed. The conclusion we draw from the testimony we have heard is that it is a grave error to indulge in deliberate distortion or exaggeration concerning the alleged dangers of a particular drug, or to base a program of drug education upon a strategy of fear. It is no use playing "chicken" with young people; in nine cases out of ten, they will accept the challenge".

Those living in large cities, particularly Montreal and Toronto, began to adopt a more British approach, in terms of what they smoked, as the Commission stated;

"The Royal Canadian Mounted Police, representatives of the Department of Justice, and a number of witnesses have reported that marihuana, long the staple of the drug-using subculture, is now being replaced by hashish in some parts of the country. This shift in popularity can probably be attributed to a growing difficulty in obtaining marihuana, since American and Mexican authorities have been intensifying their efforts to control its cultivation and prevent smuggling activities".

As the Canadian authorities focussed their efforts to prevent the importation of marihuana from the U.S, enterprising members of the Canadian hippie community, many of whom had learned their trade on the overland trail to India, began to import hash and charas. As the report reveals, it was a fairly lucrative business;

"Hashish can be purchased at its source for around $50 a kilo and resold in Canada at $1,400 a kilo, while marihuana costs from $20 a kilo in Mexico to $100 a kilo in southern California, and can be resold in Canada for about $300 a kilo; an ounce of hashish sells for between $75 and $100 in contrast to about $20 for an ounce of marihuana".

Estimations are speculative by nature, but it is always interesting to look at the amounts seized by the authorities.

"The R.C.M.P have provided the Commission with information about the amounts of cannabis products they have confiscated".

"In 1968, they confiscated 857 pounds of marihuana and 83 pounds of hashish. In 1969, 481 pounds of marihuana and 404 pounds of hashish".

Looking at it from a financial perspective, we can see that the wholesale value of marihuana seizures fell from $257,100 in 1968, to only $144,300 the following year. Hashish was clearly a far more profitable trade since the wholesale value of seizures rose from $116,200 in 1968, to $257,100 in 1969.

The Le Dain Commission arrived at many of the conclusions that previous reports had, with regards to the addictive nature of cannabis, the commission stated;

"It would appear that there are normally no adverse physiological effects or withdrawal symptoms occurring with abstinence from the drug, even in regular users. Psychological dependence may be said to exist with respect to anything which is part of one's preferred way of life. In our society, this kind of dependency occurs regularly with respect to such things as television, music, books, religion, sex, money, favourite foods, certain drugs, hobbies, sports or games and, often, other persons. Some degree of psychological dependence is, in this sense, a general and normal psychological condition".

These days, the same argument is often used in connection with excessive use of video games, which appear to have replaced many other forms of entertainment, particularly among the young unemployed. Prescription drugs, like amphetamines and barbiturates were also included in their report, which revealed some startling information;

"These reports would indicate that the available supplies of drugs such as the amphetamines and barbiturates far exceed the most liberal estimates of our proper medical needs. However, the amount manufactured and imported is so great as to suggest questionable prescribing judgement by some physicians".

It is important to remember that the Single Convention only required regulation, not prohibition in respect of these drugs;

"Some 55,600,000 standard doses of amphetamines, and some 556 million standard doses of barbiturates were produced or imported for consumption in Canada. A study by the Addiction Research Foundation in 1963 found evidence indicating that on an average day 7% of the Toronto population over 15 years of age would be using, on prescription, a mood-modifying drug. This study estimates that 24% of all prescriptions written in Toronto were for drugs of this type; 44% of these were for sedative and hypnotic drugs; 40% were anti-depressants and major and minor tranquilizers".

Pharmaceutical companies have made a fortune out of barbiturates and I have no doubt, that their influence on western governments is responsible for the fact that illegal possession of them carries penalties that are far less severe, than those imposed for the possession of cannabis, even though they are far more dangerous;

"In British Columbia, 109 persons died from overdoses of barbiturates in 1967; and 158 in 1968. Metropolitan Toronto Police records show that in 1968, 57 apparent suicides and 322 attempted suicides were attributed to barbiturates. Metro Toronto Police also estimate that 30 per cent of the 2,052 drunken female prisoners encountered in 1968 used barbiturates in conjunction with alcohol".

A large number of people who participated in the survey were very concerned by the use of tranquilisers, and many felt that they were far more harmful than marihuana. The commission revealed some interesting facts in respect of these drugs;

"The minor tranquillizers are among the most widely used mood modifiers. In potency, most of these drugs rank between alcohol and the barbiturates as daytime sedatives, and Canadians and Americans spend well over $500 million annually for them. Since regulations do not require either the manufacturer or the retail pharmacist to keep records of the volume of minor tranquillizers handled, it is not possible to report on the volume of Canadian production or importation".

The Canadian government can't be blamed for inadequate supervision, they were merely adhering to the regulations laid out in the Single Convention, however, that did not prevent the Le Dain Commission from drawing its own conclusions;

"It is known that the non-medical market for these minor tranquillizers is supplied, indirectly, by drug companies which manufacture or import far more barbiturates and minor tranquillizers than are required for medical purposes. How these excess amounts are then diverted to, and distributed within, the illicit market has not been adequately researched, but it appears certain that the pharmaceutical industry is well aware of their overproduction".

My generation was well aware of the danger of amphetamines, "speed kills" was a popular badge to wear and it use was also noted by the Le Dain Commission;

"Their nonmedical use has risen sharply in recent years, and witnesses appearing before the Commission expressed particular concern about the increased use of amphetamines in high dosages by the young".

The UK and the U.S.A both suffered from an amphetamine epidemic in the 1960's, and Swedish authorities were so concerned, they prohibited their use even for medical purposes.

"In Canada, the oral ingestion of amphetamines has been rising since the mid-forties. By 1964, approximately 60 million standard doses were produced for the Canadian market. This increased to more than 100 million doses in 1966, but statistics tell us little about the degree of non-medical use of amphetamines and nothing about the volume produced and distributed illicitly in Canada. It has been put to the Commission, however, that the volume of legally manufactured and imported amphetamines greatly exceeds medical needs. The relative frequency of illegal sales and thefts along the route between the manufacturer and the consumer is uncertain, and illegitimate distribution has been widely reported at all social levels of our society".

The use of this cheap, nasty drug that was freely available probably affected more levels of society than anything else, with the obvious exception of tobacco and alcohol;

"Low-dose oral amphetamine use, and dependence are not un-common in every age group. High school students swallow them for kicks, as a cheap, readily available and easily taken drug. Housewives can become habituated to the mood-elevating and energizing effect of amphetamine-type diet pills; tired professionals and executives use them; and even members of men's clubs meet to take these stimulants and strong coffee while their friends enjoy the more traditional pleasures of the afternoon cocktail".

The Rolling Stones described them as "mother's little helper".

I thought it was a brave decision on the part of the Le Dain Commission to include alcohol in the report, but since so many people who participated in the survey compared its use with marihuana, they were compelled to investigate the subject, This again revealed some worrying statistics;

"The annual average increase in the number of alcoholics since 1951 has been about five per cent. Similarly, convictions for offences associated with alcohol use rose significantly over the same period. In 1951 in Canada, there were 117,685 convictions for offences involving alcohol; by 1966, this had risen to 302,278, an increase of more than 150%. These convictions accounted for a total of between 6.3% and 8.5% of convictions for all crimes in Canada during those years".

Those who claim that cannabis is responsible for a large number of road accidents should take note of the following;

"Of particular significance is the increase in convictions for impaired and/or drunken driving. The rate of these convictions per 100,000 vehicles increased from 234 in 1951 to 448 in 1966, an increase of 92 per cent".

It is therefore not surprising that the report concluded by stating;

"One indication of our society's acceptance of the abuse of alcohol is the fact that while alcoholism has increased by almost 60 per cent since 1951, the rate of convictions for drunkenness has remained virtually stable in the population 15 years of age and older in that period (1,149 in 1951; 1,155 in 1966)".

The Commission was not in favour of immediate legalisation, not because of the dangers of cannabis, but because it felt that more work was needed in respect of education and research on the effects that legalisation would cause, but it was very critical of the penalties imposed on users;

"Its enforcement would appear to cost far too much, in individual and social terms, for any utility which it may be shown to have. The present cost of its enforcement, and the individual and social harm caused by it, are in our opinion, one of the major problems involved in the nonmedical use of drugs".

The report stated;

"The Commission is of the opinion that no one should be liable for imprisonment for simple possession of a psychotropic drug for non-medical purposes. As an interim measure, pending its final report, that the Narcotic Control Act and the Food and Drugs Act be amended, to make the offense of simple possession punishable upon summary conviction by a fine not exceeding a reasonable amount, the Commission suggests a maximum fine of $100".

The only member of the committee who did not agree with its recommendations was Professor Bertrand;

"I find myself in disagreement with my colleagues on the Commission in respect of the offence of simple possession of cannabis. In my opinion the prohibition against such possession should be removed altogether".

"I believe that this course is dictated at the present time by the following considerations: the extent of use and the age groups involved; the relative impossibility of enforcing the law; the social consequences of its enforcement; and the uncertainty as to the relative potential for harm of cannabis".

It is fair to say that the Commission was extremely concerned about the growing number of young Canadians who found themselves in court;

"The harm caused by a conviction for simple possession appears to be out of all proportion to any good it is likely to achieve in relation to the phenomenon of nonmedical drug use".

"Because of the nature of the phenomenon involved, it is bound to impinge more heavily on the young than on other segments of the population. Moreover, it is bound to blight the life of some of the most promising of the country's youth".

"Once again there is the accumulating social cost of a profound sense of injustice, not only at being the unlucky one whom the authorities have decided to prosecute, but at having to pay such an enormous price for conduct which does not seem to concern anyone but oneself. This sense of injustice is aggravated by the disparity in sentences made possible by the large discretion presently left to the courts".

I'm certain that Dean Gerald Le Dain Q.C and the members of his Commission were extremely disappointed. As usual, political ambitions on the part of those in power, coupled with pressure from the international community, prevented any possibility of taking a more enlightened approach.

Drug enforcement became a priority, and although longer prison sentences were imposed on offenders, it completely failed to prevent the drug-culture explosion, that Canada began to experience in the 1970's.

NIXON AND THE SHAFER COMMISSION

Richard Milhous Nixon was born in California in 1913, to a Quaker mother and a Methodist father, who later converted to the Quaker faith. He had a strict upbringing, Quakers did not approve of drinking, dancing and having a good time but this was considered normal in Wittier where he grew up, because it was a predominantly Quaker community. His family was not wealthy, and he often described his childhood as;

"We were poor, but the glory of it was, we didn't know it".

He was, in many ways, the all-American boy, since he could trace his family's history back to Thomas Cornell, an early American settler who was a descendant of Ezra Cornell, who founded Cornell University.

After leaving Duke University School of Law, he applied to join the FBI, but after receiving no response to his application he joined a local law firm in Wittier and was admitted to the bar in 1937. His work mainly consisted of commercial litigation for petroleum companies and other corporations and eventually opened up his own branch of Wingert and Bewley, in La Habra, California and then later became a full partner in the firm.

He applied for a commission in the navy in 1942 and was appointed lieutenant junior grade, in the U.S Naval Reserve on June 15th, 1942. In October of the same year, he was appointed as aide to the commander of the Naval Air Station Ottumwa, Iowa but, seeking a more active role in the war, he was reassigned as the naval passenger control officer for the South Pacific Combat Air Transport Command. Nixon was put in charge of logistics preparing manifests, supervising loading and dealing with mountains of paperwork that accompanied such matters, but he was very good at his job and was awarded a navy Letter of Commendation for his;

"Meritorious and efficient performance of duty as Officer in Charge of the South Pacific Combat Air Transport Command".

In January 1945, he was transferred to the Bureau of Aeronautics office in Philadelphia, assisting in the negotiations to terminate war contracts and received his second Letter of Commendation for;

"Meritorious service, tireless effort and devotion to duty".

A staunch Republican and anti-communist, he was chosen to run as Dwight Eisenhower's running mate, in the 1952 Presidential election. His youth and his political base in California, one of the biggest in America, made him a popular choice.

It was a good start, Eisenhower was elected in 1953 and Nixon served as Vice-President, during which time he made a number of foreign trips, to South East Asia.

At this point, I feel I should include a story that I found extremely amusing, concerning Vice-President Nixon and Louis Armstrong. Louis and his band were also performing goodwill tours, and the two met up at an airport in Japan, in late 1953. Louis was there to perform a series of concerts, while Nixon was there in a political capacity.

The story is related in the book, *What a Wonderful World*, by Ricky Riccardi. For some reason, Japanese customs officials directed Louis to join a queue for customs inspection. Louis was apparently very concerned, since he had 3 pounds of marihuana in his suitcase. As he stood there, sweating profusely while waiting in line, Vice-President Nixon arrived on the scene, with an entourage of photographers and reporters. He immediately noticed Louis standing in line, and is reported as saying to the Jazz legend;

"Hi Pops, can I do anything for you?"

Louis complained about the long flight and told him that he was really tired and just wanted to get to his hotel as quickly as possible. Nixon was more than happy to accommodate his fellow American, and as he picked up Louis's case, he said;

"Ambassadors don't go through customs".

Louis was obviously very relieved and he no doubt gave passers by one of his warmest smiles, as he walked outside with the Vice-President of America, carrying his stash.

His band must have had a good laugh when Louis related the story and there is no doubt, that it soon acquired an almost legendary status among fellow Jazz musicians. Louis himself always laughed about it whenever it was mentioned, and there is no doubt that Nixon was furious when he heard the story.

It's not a coincidence that less than 3 months later, Louis's wife, Lucille, was arrested by U.S customs officers in Hawaii, who discovered 14 grams of marihuana in her hotel room in Waikiki Beach. Louis attended the court case and the judge, taking into account all the good work that Louis had done for America, imposed a fine, warning her not to repeat the offense.

It was probably Nixon's way of getting his own back on Louis, who never stopped laughing about the fact that Vice-President Nixon had carried his stash through customs for him. It's a great story and I must admit, it put a huge smile on my face when I first heard it.

Eisenhower and Nixon were comfortably re-elected in 1956, but in 1958, during a goodwill tour of South America, Nixon and his wife Pat were subjected to violent demonstrations by students, angry at U.S foreign policy, which had used the CIA to oust President Arbenz of Guatemala, a socialist who opposed American domination of Guatemala's fruit industry.

It was a poor decision on the part of Eisenhower to send Nixon to South America at a time when America was conducting covert operations, to gain control over the copper mines in Chile. When Nixon was in Venezuela in 1958, his car was attacked by angry demonstrators and on his return to the U.S, he claimed that there was;

"Absolute proof that the protestors were directed and controlled by a central communist conspiracy".

The Americans have always had a problem differentiating between socialism and communism, because as far as they are concerned, they are the same thing. The fact is, the Americans were fighting the cold war and any socialist government, anywhere in the world was considered to be a threat to U.S national security.

In July 1959, Vice-President Richard Nixon visited the Soviet Union to attend an American trade fair, held in Sokolniki Park in Moscow. As the Russian Premier Nikita Khrushchev and the American Vice-President toured the exhibition, they stopped at the Pepsi-Cola stand, where Nixon offered Khrushchev a drink. It was a moment captured on camera and images of the Soviet Premier drinking the sweet, decadent, capitalist beverage were published all over the world.

Donald Kendall, who was in charge of Pepsi's international operations, was also photographed with Nixon and Khrushchev and it was this event that eventually saved Nixon's political career. In 1962, after failing to beat Kennedy in the Presidential election, Nixon decided to run for the governorship of California and when that failed, his political career appeared to be over.

He then moved to New York where he joined the legal firm of Mudge, Rose, Stern, Baldwin and Todd and on June 1st, 1963 he became a partner and the firm was re-named, Nixon, Mudge and Rose. Donald Kendall, who was now Chairman of Pepsi-Cola, engaged the former Vice-President's law firm to represent his company, and from that moment, Nixon became Pepsi-Cola's main man.

Nixon was encouraged to return to politics and after easily winning the Republican nomination, he chose Spiro Agnew, the Governor of Maryland as his running mate. He believed Agnew would help unify the Republican Party by appealing to the moderates, who had become increasingly disillusioned with the Democrats.

His campaign slogan, "Nixon's the one", appealed to conservative middle-class Americans, who felt threatened by the emerging hippie culture and Nixon portrayed himself as a figure of stability. He promised to lower the crime rate promising "peace with honour" in the Vietnam War and that under his leadership, peace would be restored in the Pacific.

President Lyndon Johnson did not run for re-election, his decision to send more U.S troops to Vietnam, the number of U.S soldiers arriving back in body bags and the inability of the U.S military to win the war, made him an unpopular choice, so it was left to Vice-President Humphries to carry the Democratic hopes.

Nixon believed it was to be a close election, but in the end, he won by a comfortable margin. He became the 37th U.S President on January 20th, 1969 and during the ceremony, his wife Pat held the family bible, purportedly opened at Isaiah 2:4;

"They shall beat their swords into plowshares, and their spears into pruning hooks".

After Leary's victory in the Supreme Court, the House of Representatives formed a subcommittee in September 1969, to evaluate the effects of alcoholism and narcotics. Judge Charles W. Halleck, of the District of Columbia Court, explained his reasons why he no longer imposed prison sentences on young marihuana smokers;

"If I send a long-haired marijuana offender to the jail even for 30 days, he is going to be the victim of the most brutal type of homosexual, unnatural, perverted assaults and attacks that you can imagine, and anybody who tells you it doesn't happen in that jail, day in and day out, is simply not telling you the truth. How in God's name, can I send anybody to that jail knowing that?"

"How can I send some poor young kid who gets caught by some zealous policeman who wants to make his record on a narcotics arrest? How can I send that kid to that jail? I can't do it. So, I put him on probation, or I suspend the sentence, and everybody says the judge doesn't care, but you just simply can't treat these kinds of people like that".

Many U.S servicemen returning from Vietnam were addicted to heroin, a habit they picked up while on leave in Bangkok. Officially, the number of heroin addicts was estimated at 63,000, in reality, the number was considerably higher.

In July, Nixon gave his first speech about drugs, designed to reassure the silent majority that his administration was aware of the problem;

"It is doubtful that an American parent can send a son or daughter to college today without exposing the young man or woman to drug abuse. Parents must also be concerned about the availability and use of such drugs in our high schools and junior high schools".

He informed the American public that Mitchell, his new Attorney General, was in the process of preparing new comprehensive measures, necessary to win the war on drugs;

"I am confident that Congress shares with me the grave concern over this critical problem, and that Congress will do all that is necessary to mount and continue a new and effective Federal program aimed at eradicating this rising sickness in our land".

The new Attorney General wasted no time informing the American public, that it order to defeat the problem, every citizen would have to play their part;

"We cannot succeed with this war on drug abuse until we enlist the active assistance of every citizen. Young people themselves can and must play a key role in this war. It is time for synthesis between the generations, a time to harness the dynamism and energy of youth and the experience of their elders for the tasks that lie ahead".

He outlined the extent of the problem by saying;

"Persons who live in ghetto areas, which have substantial numbers of narcotics addicts, literally bar the doors of their apartments at night. They are attacked in broad daylight on the streets. They are terrorised by the knowledge that the heroin addict who needs a fix will commit the most vicious crime in order to obtain a TV set for resale or a few dollars, even school children are beginning to use hard narcotics".

On October 27th, 1970 President Richard Nixon signed the Controlled Substance Act, which became effective on May 1st, 1971. Recognising that he needed to address the problem of heroin addiction, the Act contained provisions for more effective treatment of addicts, as well as rehabilitation, especially for military personnel. However, it was also clear that Nixon's war was also going to be one which targeted marihuana as well.

Nixon followed the example set by the Single Convention, which placed drugs in different categories according to their perceived threat. Cannabis had been categorised as a Schedule 4 substance, which included the most dangerous drugs such as heroin. Under the Controlled Substances Act, Cannabis was classified as a Schedule 1 substance, reserved for drugs like heroin, that had a high potential for abuse, had no accepted medical use and were considered to be unsafe, even under strict supervision.

This meant that cannabis could no longer be prescribed by medical practitioners, which explains why opium and cocaine had to be included in Schedule 2, in order to allow their use for medical purposes. Realising that the mandatory sentences that had been introduced in the 1950's had been a complete failure, he scrapped the mandatory laws, and introduced new penalties.

Under the new Act, a first offence for simple possession could result in probation or a maximum 12 months imprisonment with a $5000 fine. A second offence could result in two years imprisonment and a fine of $10,000.

The "Continuing Criminal Enterprise" clause, aimed at criminal organisations, stipulated a minimum sentence of ten-years with a maximum of life and a $100,000 fine. Subsequent offences carried a minimum of twenty-years and a fine of $200,000. In addition, the Act also incorporated other clauses which eliminated any possibility of parole, and which would enable the government to confiscate property, cash, jewellery and any other assets that were deemed to have been acquired as a result of their illegal activities. Nixon considered enforcement was the key to success and as a result, this was clearly laid out in the new Act.

Part E – Administrative and Enforcement Provisions

Sect: 508: "Any officer or employee of the Bureau of Narcotics, designated by the Attorney General may";

1) *"Carry firearms".*

2) *"Execute and serve search warrants, arrest warrants, administrative inspection warrants, subpoenas and summonses issued by the United States".*

3) *"Make arrests without warrants (A) for any offence against the United States committed in his presence, or (B) for any felony cognisable under the laws of the United States, if he has probable cause to believe that the person being arrested has committed or is committing a felony".*

4) *"Make seizures of property pursuant to the provisions of this title".*

5) *"Perform such other law enforcement duties, as the Attorney General may designate".*

Independent distributors and marihuana dealers faced a maximum of 15-years and a $25,000 fine and for a second conviction, up to 30-years and a $50,000 fine.

In his 1971 address to the American people, Nixon stated;

"America's public enemy number one in the United States is drug abuse. In order to fight and defeat this enemy, it is necessary to wage a new, all-out offensive".

Nixon was not a fan of the swinging sixties and white, middle-class students were perceived to be the biggest threat to his Presidency. Portraying them as un-patriotic hippies, who spent their time smoking marihuana and experimenting with LSD, enabled him to segregate them from main-stream society.

The Controlled Substance Act gave authorities the power to disrupt their meetings, imprison their leaders and wage a propaganda war against them in the American media.

There were many members of Congress who felt that marihuana had potential medical benefits and as a result, they were unhappy that it had been classified as a Schedule 1 substance. Some of them were in favour of an official inquiry, which they felt would ultimately lead to the re-classification of marihuana. In order to keep them happy, in 1971 the National Commission on Marihuana and Drug Abuse was established, to carry out a thorough study. Nixon appointed Raymond P. Shafer, Governor of Pennsylvania and a former prosecutor who had a reputation for being tough on crime, to head the investigation.

Nixon was worried from day one, and telephone conversations that were declassified in 2002 which were later released to the public, illustrate his concerns. Speaking to his aide, H.R Haldeman, Nixon said;

"I want a goddamn strong statement about marihuana. Can I get that out of this son-of-a-bitching, domestic council? I mean one on marihuana that just tears the ass out of them".

Articles began to appear in the American press, written by prominent psychiatrists which led some to believe that marihuana may be legalised. Nixon was furious about many of the articles, some of which had been written by medical experts, telling his aide;

"Every one of those bastards that are out for legalising marihuana is Jewish. What the Christ is the matter with the Jews Bob, what is the matter with them? I suppose it's because most of them are psychiatrists, you know, there's so many, all the greatest psychiatrists are Jewish. By God, we are going to hit the marihuana thing, and I want to hit it right square in the puss. I want to find a way of putting more on that. I want a goddam strong statement about marihuana, I mean one that just tears the arse out of them".

If those conversations had been leaked to the public, the outcome would have been very different. Politicians, like crooked businessmen and criminals are not in favour of transparency, which explains why whistle-blowers like Julian Assange are frowned upon by governments, even when they reveal information that the public has a right to know. On September 9th, 1971 Nixon met Shafer and once again the tape machine was rolling, when he told him;

"I think there's a need to come out with a report that is totally oblivious to some obvious differences between marihuana and other drugs, other dangerous drugs. Don't go into the matter of penalties and that sort of thing, as to whether there should be uniformity in penalties, whether in courts, I'd much rather have uniformity than diversity. You're enough of a pro to know that for you to come out with something that would run counter to what the Congress feels and what the country feels and what we're planning to do, would make your commission just look bad as hell. Keep your commission in line".

THE SHAFER COMMISSION

President Nixon did his very best to stack the deck in his favour. He personally selected eight members of the 13-man Commission and a Congressional Committee appointed the remaining four, but he severely under-estimated the integrity of Chairman Shafer.

The Commission held formal and informal meetings, which considered the opinions of public officials, community leaders, medical practitioners and experts, as well as students and other members of the public. They conducted surveys among judges, probation officers, health officials and members of law enforcement agencies as well as commissioning studies on the effects of marihuana and the enforcement of marihuana laws. The result of this comprehensive study, *Marihuana: A Single Understanding*, was presented to the U.S Congress in 1972 by Raymond Shafer. Its initial introduction stated;

"In order to maximize public awareness, we are apt to characterize situations as being far worse than they really are. Because any activity is commonly regarded as a move toward a solution, rhetoric and stopgap legislation sometimes substitute for rational reflection. The appointment of this Commission, and the publication of this Report, reflect the escalation of marihuana use into the realm of a social problem. Since the beginning of our official life, we have grappled with the threshold question: Why has the use of marihuana reached problem status in the public mind?"

As a way of answering this question, the report stated;

"The belief that marihuana is causally linked to crime and other antisocial conduct first assumed prominence during the 1930's as the result of a concerted effort by governmental agencies and the press to alert the American populace to the dangers of marihuana use".

"Newspapers all over the country began to publish lurid accounts of "marihuana atrocities" In the absence of adequate understanding of the effects of the drug, these largely unsubstantiated stories profoundly influenced public opinion and gave birth to the stereotype of the marihuana user as physically aggressive, lacking in self-control, irresponsible, mentally ill and, perhaps most alarming, criminally inclined and dangerous".

Investigations carried out by the Commission however, revealed a very different picture of the activities of young marihuana smokers at that time;

"In a Commission-sponsored study, of 1,776 16 to 21-year-olds, arrested in five New York counties for marihuana law violations between 1965 and 1969, only a small percentage had either previously or subsequently come to the attention of authorities for such offenses as assault or robbery".

"In fact, less than 1% of the offenders in this sample had been arrested for these offenses prior to their first marihuana arrest, and less than 3% were known to the Federal Bureau of Investigation for these offenses, subsequent to their marihuana violation".

Additional studies carried out in West Philadelphia, involving 559 residents, confirmed these statistics;

"In corroboration of the earlier findings, the researchers found no significant differences in the proportions of users and non-users, who stated that they had committed any of the aggressive or violent crimes enumerated".

Investigations led the Commission to believe that marihuana use may have an ability to reduce violent incidents;

"The data show that marihuana users were much less likely to commit aggressive or violent acts than were those who preferred amphetamines or alcohol. They also show that most marihuana users were able to condition themselves to avoid aggressive behaviour even in the face of provocation. In fact, marihuana was found to play a significant role in youth's transition from a "rowdy" to a "cool," non-violent style".

One of the major concerns that the American public had, was their belief that marihuana, like heroin, was addictive, however, the conclusion that the commission arrived at was entirely different;

"Unfortunately, fact and fancy have become irrationally mixed regarding marihuana's physiological and psychological properties. Marihuana clearly is not in the same chemical category as heroin insofar as its physiologic and psychological effects are concerned. In a word, cannabis does not lead to physical dependence. No torturous withdrawal syndrome follows the sudden cessation of chronic, heavy use of marihuana".

Many people at the time believed that the use of marihuana led to heroin use, another myth that the Commission was keen to dispel;

"Citizens concerned with health issues must consider the possibility of marihuana use leading to use of heroin, other opiates, cocaine or hallucinogens. This so-called stepping-stone theory first received widespread acceptance in 1951 as a result of testimony at Congressional hearings. The implication of these descriptions was that a causal relationship existed between marihuana and subsequent heroin use. When the voluminous testimony given at these hearings is seriously examined, no verification is found of a causal relationship between marihuana use and subsequent heroin use".

The Commission acknowledged the mistakes that had been made in the past by stating;

"The Commission believes that the contemporary American drug problem has emerged in part from our institutional response to drug use. We have failed to weave policy into the fabric of social institutions. Unless present policy is redirected, we will perpetuate the same problems, tolerate the same social costs, and find ourselves as we do now, no further along the road to a more rational legal and social approach than we were in 1914".

In conclusion, the Shafer Commission's report, concluded by stating the following;

"The Commission feels that the criminalization of possession of marihuana for personal use is socially self-defeating as a means of achieving this objective. We have attempted to balance individual freedom on one hand and the obligation of the state to consider the wider social good on the other. We believe our recommended scheme will permit society to exercise its control and influence in ways most useful and efficient, meanwhile reserving to the individual American his sense of privacy, his sense of individuality, and, within the context of an interacting and interdependent society, his options to select his own lifestyle, values, goals and opportunities".

President Nixon rejected the Commission's findings, and the war against marihuana and other drugs began. In order to enforce the new law effectively, Nixon and his cronies established a powerful, new, para-military force and in July 1973 the Drug Enforcement Agency was created. This combined the Bureau of Narcotics and Dangerous Drugs with U.S Customs Agents.

Under the provisions of the new Act, the DEA was given sole responsibility for making any changes or alterations, in respect of the classification of the drugs that were contained in the 5 Schedules.

It must be noted that in 1965, less than 25,000 Americans were arrested for marihuana offences but by 1975, this figure had increased to over 400,000.

The Act also stipulated that the Director of the DEA could only be appointed by the President, which enabled Nixon to ensure that the right man was given the job.

One of the first overseas offices of the DEA was in Kabul. They went there to monitor opium production, since under the Single Convention, Afghanistan was a licenced producer of opium, used by American pharmaceutical companies for the manufacture of barbiturates. There was also a thriving black-market, for cannabis resin and "hash oil", much of which was smuggled into America. The DEA quickly discovered the need for diplomacy, when in 1973, they uncovered a plot to ship 40 kilos of "hash oil" to the Afghan Embassy in Washington. They believed that the Afghan King's personal valet was behind the scheme, as a cable from their office in Kabul, published by Wikileaks, which stated;

"Involvement of Mohammed Rahim Panjshiri and unidentified accomplices in Afghan Embassy, Washington, in plan to smuggle 40 kilos Hashish Oil to U.S in late May 1973. Rahim Panjshiri is long-time family retainer in Palace who has extremely close relationship to H.M King Zahir, to whom he serves as personal valet. Panjshiri long notorious here as smuggler of many items, such as lapis and gold, and widely believed by Afghans to handle such transactions for account of members of Royal Family, as well as for his own pecuniary interests".

After sending their initial cable, the DEA soon realised that it had underestimated the bond between the King and his trusted valet and several days later they sent another cable to Washington;

"All elements of U.S Government should understand delicacy of case. Panjshiri is bound to King by tight Afghan-style bond of honour and gratitude for services he performed for Royal Family during period when throne itself was threatened. He is closer to King than any of King's sons and is undoubtedly privy to many Royal secrets. Any direct effort by foreign officials to move against him in Afghanistan would, we believe, be viewed by King as intolerable affront to dignity of throne. There is no possibility, in our judgement, that he would ever be prosecuted here for any drug offence".

The DEA office in Kabul informed Washington of the need for good relations, as their cable stated;

"Future of all our efforts here to develop anti-narcotics programme under U.N leadership is at a crucial stage. King's continued support absolutely essential for continued progress. Enforcement action in this case must, therefore, be handled in a way which does not force King to choose openly between Panjshiri and foreign policy advisory presence. Royal Afghan pride could make that an unpleasant choice for U.S interests in overall narcotics effort here".

The Afghani hashish trade continued to grow, and after following the money trail, the DEA office in Kabul, sent another cable to Washington;

"A recent DEA investigation of the seizure of a significant quantity of hashish in the United States, revealed that numerous unusual financial transactions, are apparently being conducted which involve Kabul money-merchants, U.S banks and financial interests in India and Switzerland".

Kathmandu was the international centre of the hippie generation when Nixon took control. Its colourful foreign residents and visitors, many of whom had recently completed their studies at Yale, Harvard, Oxford, Cambridge and other universities. Woodstock was cool, but being in Kathmandu was way, way cooler. Its laid-back ambience represented everything Nixon was against and he was determined to put an end to it.

He got his opportunity when the old King died and his son, Birendra, inherited the crown in 1972. The DEA opened an office in Kathmandu in 1973 and in return for U.S aid, amounting to around $50 million dollars, the new King prohibited the use of cannabis, closed the hashish shops and escorted many of its foreign hippie visitors to the Indian border. It was in many ways, a personal victory for Nixon.

A cable sent from the DEA office in Kathmandu the following year, summarised the situation in Nepal at that time;

"Nepal is not an opium producer although very small quantities of opium poppies may grow wild in the hill areas of western Nepal. The very real narcotics problem in Nepal has stemmed from the substantial growth of cannabis, which is the source of hashish and a highly concentrated hashish oil. It has been banned since July 1973, following a government decision not to renew licences. However, some Nepali hashish is consumed in Nepal both by Nepalese for use in religious festivals and by the foreign hippie community, many of whom have been attracted to Nepal because of the availability of drugs. The size of this foreign community has, however diminished considerably over the last year, reflecting the government's decision to tighten up on drug control".

It was the end of the Kathmandu generation and the birth of the Goa brigade, where the international hippie brigade, set up their new headquarters in a warm, tropical coastal region of what was formerly, Portuguese India but was now the Indian State of Goa.

The DEA soon discovered that the hippies were not the only ones involved in the Kathmandu drug scene, as a later secret cable shows;

"Yet another problem faced by the draft narcotics control legislation, is the alleged involvement in drug trafficking of high-level Nepalese government officials, some close to the Royal Family. There are even rumours that the Royal Family itself is, or at least has been, involved. (Preceding two sentences should be regarded as highly sensitive and given appropriate protection)".

The DEA in Kathmandu once again urged caution, in another top-secret cable to Washington it stated;

"It is important to recognise that foreign representatives should move with caution, finesse, and an understanding of Nepal's perception of the international narcotics problem. Any action which the Government of Nepal might view as undue pressure, would swing considerable sentiment to the side of those opposed to legislation, In this respect there have already been charges that Nepal is being forced to act on narcotics because of the interest of foreign governments, including the United States, who it is said do not understand Nepal's problems".

"Our policy in Nepal has been to mute this criticism by keeping a low profile and allowing the U.N to be the main focus for narcotics control activities in Nepal. We believe it is in our best interests to continue this policy".

It made perfect sense to Nixon, it was far better to leave the paperwork to the United Nations, the DEA was far more effective working in the wings.

REAGAN - THREE STRIKES AND OUT

When Ronald Reagan was appointed President in 1981, his wife, Nancy, instigated a national campaign, using the slogan;

"Just Say No".

Reagan's policy of zero tolerance, was illustrated by his view that it was easier to prevent people from using illegal drugs, by putting them in prison, than to effectively stop the flow of illegal Mexican marihuana. He also faced a new challenge in the form of crack-cocaine, a highly addictive, refined paste, later turned into rocks, which could only be smoked.

Reagan didn't approve of what Nixon had done, he viewed America's problems as a result of what he described as the liberalism of the 1970's. He believed that Nixon's war on drugs had failed because it had been too lenient and in 1986, he signed the Anti-Drug Abuse Act. This re-introduced mandatory sentencing, first used in the 1950's, which Nixon had scrapped. Reagan saw them as a deterrent. The Senate Minority Leader, Robert Byrd, justified the re-introduction of mandatory sentences, by stating;

"A major drug offender must know that there will be no escape hatch, through which he can avoid a term of years in the penitentiary. He must know in advance, exactly how lengthy that prison term is going to be. He must know that no matter how good a lawyer he gets, how experienced, how expensive, how well-known and how clever and sharp, that lawyer will not be able to keep him out of jail, once he has been found guilty in a court of law".

Reagan's new Act retained Nixon's scheduling system, and marihuana remained a Schedule 1 narcotic. Anyone caught distributing more than a kilo of heroin or 5 kilos of cocaine, a ton of marijuana or more than 50 grams of crack-cocaine, received a mandatory minimum sentence of 10-years, with a maximum of life. Subsequent offenders received a minimum of 20-years to life.

Offenders who were lower down the chain were treated a little more leniently. Anyone caught with more than 100 grams of heroin, 500 grams of cocaine, 5 grams of crack-cocaine, or more than 100 kilos of marihuana, received mandatory, minimum sentences of 5-years, with a maximum of 40 years.

Subsequent offences carried a mandatory minimum term of 10-years with a maximum of life.

These new sentences reflected the fact that crack-cocaine was now viewed as the new menace. It seems illogical that a person convicted of possessing 5-grams of it, was subjected to the same penalties as someone convicted of possessing half a kilo of normal cocaine but in reality, it was due to the fact that crack-cocaine was now the predominant drug in areas inhabited by African Americans and Hispanics.

Offences involving less than 50 kilos of marihuana, were not subject to a mandatory sentence and the judge was free to give anything from 1-20 years and on a subsequent conviction, anything up to 30 years.

To ensure that Reagan's prisoners served their full sentence, the Act included the following;

"The new act provides that a court may not place on probation or suspend the sentence of any person sentenced under any provisions providing for imposition of mandatory terms of imprisonment, It also provides that such persons may not be released on parole, during the term of imprisonment imposed. Thus, a person sentenced to a term of imprisonment, in excess of the applicable mandatory minimum, must serve the entire term of imprisonment imposed, not merely the applicable mandatory minimum".

There were no mandatory sentences for first time offenders, convicted of simple possession. They could receive fines of up to $5,000 or if they were unlucky or their face didn't fit, up to a year in prison. On a second conviction, the fine and the maximum sentence were doubled.

Probation was also re-introduced, for first time offenders, convicted of possession, which enabled wealthier white families, with the aid of a good lawyer, to keep their kids out of prison, provided they demonstrated a willingness to kick the habit.

The Act also introduced various drug-free initiatives, leading to compulsory drug tests in factories, offices and other workplaces.

The prison population rose dramatically, as more and more African Americans and Hispanics were convicted of offences involving crack-cocaine and things were made even worse when a later amendment introduced the Three-Strikes Law, which created a mandatory minimum of 25-years imprisonment for repeat offenders.

NORML (National Organisation for the Reform of Marihuana Laws) petitioned the DEA to remove marihuana from the list of Schedule 1 substances, to allow medical practitioners to prescribe it to their patients.

It took them more than 10 years to obtain a hearing and in September 1988 DEA Chief Administrative Law Judge, Francis L. Young ruled in favour of re-classifying marihuana as a Schedule Two substance, declaring;

"Marihuana, in its natural form, is one of the safest therapeutically active substances known to man".

In his conclusion, Judge Young stated;

"The evidence in this record clearly shows that marihuana has been accepted as capable of relieving the distress of great numbers of very ill people and doing so with safety under medical supervision. It would be unreasonable, arbitrary and capricious for the DEA to continue to stand between those sufferers and the benefits of this substance in light of the evidence in this record".

Judge Young's ruling was a non-binding recommendation and it was rejected by the DEA Administrator John Lawn, in December 1989. It wasn't surprising, the Administrator of the DEA is appointed by the President, so Lawn was no doubt influenced by Reagan's policy of zero tolerance. His loyalty to the Republican party, was a far greater priority, than his duty to do what was right.

When George W. Bush was elected, he allocated even more money to combat drug use, although it had very little effect.

The DEA is now a global organisation with offices in more than 70 countries. It has an annual budget of more than $2 billion, it employs nearly 11,000 people of which 5,000 are special agents and a further 800 Intelligence Analysists. The starting salary for a special agent is between 50 and 55 thousand dollars a year and after 4 years of service, they can expect an annual salary of nearly $100,000. Its Aviation Division, based in Fort Worth Texas, consists of 106 aircraft and 124 pilots.

In 2005 the DEA seized $1.4 billion worth of drug-trade related assets and $477 million worth of drugs but according to the Office of Drug Control Policy, the total value of illegal drugs sold in the U.S is $64 billion. This gives the DEA an efficiency rating of less than 1% and according to figures given for 2014, the average cost of an arrest was nearly $100,000.

The Americans know better than anyone that prohibition does not work. In the 1920's, the prohibition of alcohol gave rise to the birth of American gangsters like Al Capone, so it is not surprising that drugs are now the major source of income for organised crime.

Drug trafficking is now the third biggest industry in the world, after oil and arms and in spite of the huge amounts of money that is spent trying to combat this illicit trade, the situation is worse than ever.

In 2011 there were 1.6 million people in U.S prisons, of which, more than 325,000 had been convicted for drug offences.

The use of prison labour is now a multi-billion-dollar industry, but the vast majority of convicts work for little or no pay, performing menial tasks that are unlikely to boost their job prospects when released.

Federal Prison Industries, also known as UNICOR, was created in 1934. It is owned by the Federal Bureau of Prisons and inmates are paid anything from $1 to $4 a day.

Under the present law, all inmates are required to work, unless they are either sick or physically disabled. In 2016, UNICOR had nearly 70 factories, operating in more than 50 Federal prisons, producing a wide range of goods including clothing, textiles, electronics, office furniture and industrial products, which earn the U.S Government more than $500 million a year.

This large corporation is responsible for overseeing prison labour, it is responsible for regulating wages and establishing safe working conditions and while it claims to provide inmates with "vocational training", the reality is very different.

At a UNICOR facility in a prison in California, the inmates, re-cycle old cathode computer monitors. Standard industrial safety regulations require the use of a mechanical crusher to minimise the risk of flying glass as well as an isolated system to prevent lead and other toxic substances from being released into the atmosphere, but at the UNICOR facility, inmates were required to smash the monitors with hammers.

With such a huge, labour force available, it is not surprising that Corporate America is now exploiting prisoners as a way of reducing production costs. Capitalism has always sought to exploit workers and American prisoners now offer an even cheaper alternative to the use of third-world labour. It's known as "insourcing" and for shareholders and CEO's of large corporations, it is regarded as a profitable alternative.

Under the Work Opportunity Tax Credit, a relic of Bush's Welfare to Work legislation, businesses are given a $2,400 tax credit for every work-release inmate they employ, with additional benefits if they employ inmates who are considered to be a risk. Companies are not required to provide them with health insurance, sickness benefits or holidays and there are no unions to worry about.

Female inmates in South Carolina are kept busy by producing garments for Victoria's Secret, as well as women's underwear for J.C Penny. In the late 1990's, two female inmates were put in solitary confinement, simply for divulging sensitive information to a journalist. They claimed that they were employed to switch "Made in Honduras" clothing tags, with "Made in America" ones.

It was only when prisoners were employed as an alternative to unemployed, hard-working, honest Americans, that the media became interested. When British Petroleum's, Deepwater well-head exploded, spewing out billions of gallons of oil into the Gulf of Mexico, which later began washing up on the beaches of Louisiana, local businesses were devasted. The local community suffered from post-traumatic stress, as the local economy, based on shrimp fishing, oyster catching and other aquatic industries, ground to a halt as a result of the pollution caused by the oil spill.

Many were out of work, and residents were horrified when large groups of mainly African Americans, wearing bright orange uniforms, supplied by the Louisiana Department of Corrections, suddenly appeared on the beaches.

Public meetings were held, where residents complained about B.P's policy of hiring cheap prison labour, in an area with huge unemployment, caused as a result of B.P's negligence. Prisoners swapped their prison uniforms for B.P ones, but in some areas, with a predominantly white population, Louisiana beach-cleaning prison gangs, stuck out like a sore thumb.

It was good business for the British based oil company, not only did they get an unlimited supply of cheap labour, the tax benefits they received helped to settle some of the 80,000 claims for lost revenue, that they received from local businesses, as a result of the disaster.

Louisiana has earned the title of "The Inmate State", because they have the highest incarceration rate in America, with more than 40,000 prisoners, of which 70% are African Americans, the majority of whom have been convicted of drug offences. The Louisiana Department of Corrections only has 20,000 beds, so the other 20,000 live in parish jails, privately run contract facilities or work-release centres. They are hired out to B.P or sent to work on state owned farms and factories, where they earn 10-40 cents an hour.

Cleaning oil drenched beaches is dirty work and the sweltering heat doesn't help. Conditions are so bad, inmates work in 20-minute shifts, with 40 minutes breaks in between, when they guzzle huge amounts of water to prevent dehydration. They work 12 hours a day, 6 days a week, shovelling sand soaked in oil, into large plastic bags, that are then thrown into a dumpster. The lucky ones live in work-release centres and the unlucky one's sleep in crowded, converted shipping containers, conveniently situated near the beaches.

McDonald's buy huge amounts of plastic cutlery, food containers and uniforms all of which are manufactured in prisons, but they are only one of the corporations, that are now turning to prison labour as a means of improving profit margins. Others that either use, or have used prison labour, include Microsoft, Motorola, Starbucks, Nike, Nintendo and many others.

All things considered, it is not surprising that American prisons are overflowing and there seems very little incentive to reduce the prison population. While many people would argue that prisoners get what they deserve, in a civilised world, every attempt should be made to re-habilitate offenders, but under the capitalist system, which places a higher value on money than it does on the welfare of individuals, it makes more sense to exploit them.

The U.S currently spends more than $47 billion on the war against drugs. In 2017 over one and a half million Americans were arrested on drug violations, of which more than 85% were for possession. More than 650,000 of those, were for marihuana violations, of which 90% were for possession.

America has more prisoners than anyone else in the world. In 2016, there were nearly two and a quarter million Americans in prison, of which nearly half a million were in there for drug offences.

Things are slowly changing, 22 U.S states have now either decriminalised or removed the threat of imprisonment for the possession of marihuana, but the fact remains that every 75 seconds, someone in America gets arrested for the possession of it.

In 2017, Morgan Fox, Director of Communications for the Marijuana Policy Project said;

"Arresting and citing nearly half a million people a year for a substance that is objectively safer than alcohol is a travesty. Despite a steady shift in public opinion away from marijuana prohibition, and the growing number of states that are regulating marijuana like alcohol, marijuana consumers continue to be treated like criminals throughout the country. This is a shameful waste of resources and can create lifelong consequences for the people arrested".

He concluded by saying;

"Regulating marijuana for adults creates jobs, generates tax revenue, protects consumers and takes money away from criminals. It is time for the Federal Government and the rest of the states to stop ruining people's lives and enact sensible marijuana policies".

CHILDREN BATTLE FOR LIFE

The UK Government has finally legalised cannabis-based products for medical use, a decision that was forced on them by three small children, whose suffering they could not ignore.

Newspapers in Britain have traditionally portrayed cannabis as a social evil, particularly the tabloids. In the 1970's its use was considered to be an act of rebellion, against everything that Britain stood for but the story of two children, with horrible, debilitating diseases, changed everything and perhaps, for the first time, this was a story that everyone could get behind.

Little Alfie Dingley was a six-year-old boy who suffered from a rare form of epilepsy, a central nervous system disorder, characterised by nervous twitching or violent seizures.

Alfie had his first seizure when he was only eight months old and despite treatment with conventional, anti-epileptic drugs, his seizures continued, and his health deteriorated. The doctors who treated him told his mother that in all probability, he would die prematurely.

His mother, Hannah, was devasted but refused to give up and having tried every conventional medicine available, none of which had any effect, she decided to try cannabis. Hannah and her partner Drew took Alfie to Holland where a doctor prescribed cannabis oil, which was so effective, that within a very short time Alfie's seizures were much shorter, less frequent and a lot less violent.

Cannabis oil was illegal in Britain, so they decided to stay in Holland, so Alfie could continue his treatment and as his health improved, Hannah's confidence in the power of cannabis grew. She launched a campaign, to petition the Government to allow her to have access to cannabis oil via the health service saying;

"I'm his mum, I'm not a politician, not an activist, I'm just a mum tired of seeing him suffer and I've found something that helps him, it's his human right to be well".

Her high-profile campaign collected 370,000 signatures and the British actor, Sir Patrick Stewart, accompanied her family to Downing Street where she delivered her petition. The British press lapped it up, in a world full of stories of corruption, atrocities, global catastrophes and scandals, here was a story about a cute little lad, a determined mother and a film star. After meeting Home Office Policing Minister, Nick Hurd MP, a Government spokesperson said;

"The Government has a huge amount of sympathy for the rare and difficult situation that Alfie and his family are faced with. The Policing Minister wants to explore every option and has met with Alfie's family to discuss treatments that may be accessible for him".

"No decisions have been made and any proposal would need to be led by senior clinicians using sufficient and rigorous evidence".

Alfie's mother described the plan as;

"A sincere offer because they want to help us".

The APPG, (All-Party Parliamentary Group) on drug policy reform, called on the Government to support Alfie's mother in her fight to get access to the medicine that her little boy desperately needed. Conservative MP Crispin Blunt, who is the co-chairman of the group said;

"It would be heartless and cruel not to allow Alfie to access the medication".

I would have gone further and said that it would have been a criminal act on the part of the British Government to deny him access, but politicians are not in the habit of incriminating themselves.

The Government issued Alfie a licence in June 2018, allowing Alfie's mother to legally import the cannabis oil from Holland and as his treatment continued, his health improved dramatically. Hannah told the BBC that her son had not suffered from any seizures since the treatment was reapplied, after the licence was granted, saying;

"He's going to school every day, he's riding a horse, he's riding a bike, he has a pretty much normal life".

It's not difficult to imagine the joy she must have felt, after being told that in all probability, Alfie would die prematurely.

She said;

"It's overwhelming but when I walk him to school, I know how lucky I am".

Having issued Alfie's mother with a special licence to import cannabis oil from Holland, the UK Government were forced to consider the situation on a much broader scale.

Conservative MP Dan Poulter believed there was overwhelming evidence that cannabis was also an effective treatment for multiple sclerosis and for reducing nausea in patients undergoing chemotherapy. He stated his views by telling reporters;

"When there is growing evidence of the benefits of prescribing medicinal cannabis, it seems extraordinary that we can't do so. The legitimate medical needs of patients are seen through the prism of drugs legislation from 1971. That can't be right, sensible or humane".

Following a report published at the end of June 2018, by the Chief Medical Advisor to the UK Government, on July 3rd, the Home Secretary commissioned the ACMD (Advisory Council on the Misuse of Drugs) to carry out an evaluation of cannabis-derived medicinal products. Their response was surprisingly swift; on July 19th they presented their initial recommendations and in September they submitted a full report.

The case of Billy Caldwell, a 12-year-old boy who also suffered from epilepsy, made headlines, when his mother, Charlotte, was arrested at Heathrow Airport with a supply of cannabis oil that she had purchased from a medical pharmacy in Canada. Customs officers confiscated Billy's medicine but instead of charging her for importing an illegal substance, she was invited to the Home Office where she met Nick Hurd who informed her that the medicine would not be returned.

Billy was hospitalised, because without his medication, he suffers from regular seizures on a daily basis. The family live in Northern Ireland, where a doctor had prescribed cannabis oil for Billy the previous year, but the Home Office ordered him to stop, which forced his mother to import the medication illegally. Her local MP said;

"Charlotte told me this morning that Billy had a seizure on Monday night which is heart-breaking, I do not support breaking the law, but I can appreciate the difficult actions that Charlotte has had to take as a mother".

Although Charlotte had broken the law, by preventing Billy's doctor from prescribing his medication, the Home Office was guilty of a far greater crime. Billy's mother was furious, when interviewed by the *Guardian* she said;

"Billy had a seizure this morning, it's proven to me, that on the first day since his anti-epileptic medication was confiscated, it's having a detrimental effect on him. The consequences inevitably for Billy will not be good. He's heading towards a crisis situation; without that anti-epileptic medication my little boy will die. That is the situation we are in. Nick Hurd, who planned the confiscation of my son's life-saving medicine, has signed Billy's death warrant".

A Home Office spokesperson said;

"The Home Office is sympathetic to the difficult and rare situation that Billy and his family are faced with. Whilst we recognise that people with debilitating illnesses are looking to alleviate their symptoms, Border Force has a duty to stop banned substances from entering the UK".

That last statement reflects better than anything, the United Nations Single Convention's attitude, that preventing the importation of illicit substances, is more important than saving lives.

It was bloody disgrace in my opinion, and everyone involved should have immediately tendered their resignations, because they were unwilling to do the job they were elected to do, and that is, safeguard the interests of every citizen in the UK.

As more and more newspaper reports appeared in the press, all condemning the Government's attitude, they finally realised that they could no longer sit on their arses, doing nothing. The Home Secretary finally announced that cannabis products would be available from November 1st, 2018. At a time when the government was in complete turmoil over "Brexit", it managed to introduce legislation in a matter of months.

Alfie's mum was over the moon saying;

"Today is a momentous day for every patient and family with a suffering child who wish to access medicinal cannabis".

Professor Mike Barnes, who helped Alfie's mum get her license said;

"This announcement has transformed the position of the UK in this exciting and developing field. Many of my medical colleagues are understandably unsure about the benefits. After all, medical cannabis has been illegal in the UK for generations, but I urge them all to embrace these developments. Compared to many pharmaceutical drugs, whole plant medical cannabis products are remarkable safe and, as recent high-profile cases have shown, can produce dramatic improvements for patients".

Clark French, founder and director of the United Patients Alliance, who are campaigning for the medical use of cannabis, said that they would probably only be available to those suffering from epilepsy, multiple sclerosis and cancer, stating;

"They are the three most likely to benefit, because there's a lot of research on them and a lot of media attention on those patients at the moment".

He said he was very pleased with the change in the law, but that he was cautious, saying;

"They haven't defined what is a cannabis medicine at all. We don't really know what is going on. It is definitely a step in the right direction, and it should mean that more patients will get medicine through their doctor. But we don't know whether it's going to be widespread or whether it's going to be for the high-profile cases, to get them out of the media".

"We are quite concerned that it could be like Sativex: limited to a few patients that can get it and often patients are left to fund it for themselves".

The MS (Multiple Sclerosis) Society published a report in July 2017, the Executive Summary stated;

"MS is the only condition which has a medically licenced, cannabis-derived treatment for spasticity, Sativex. However, Sativex is not available on the NHS (with the exception of Wales), because the pharmaceutical company and the relevant approval bodies have not been able to negotiate a pricing agreement, which is a major concern because many people simply cannot afford to pay for it privately".

It is not surprising that many MS sufferers have resorted to buying cannabis, without the funds to pay for expensive private consultation in order to obtain Sativex, they were left with no other option,

I think it's disgraceful that GW Pharmaceuticals, a British company who manufacture the drug, should hold the British taxpayer to ransom, by demanding the highest possible price for their product, but that's capitalism for you, which seeks to make a profit from everything, including health.

Alfie's mother assumed that under the new law, everything would be alright, and she was shocked when she discovered that cannabis oil was not included. She immediately launched another campaign, which collected 360,000 signatures in less than a week.

The Royal College of Physicians and the British Paediatric Neurology Association, who were responsible for issuing the new guidelines, said that cannabis oil had not been included because there was insufficient evidence to prove that it could be used safely or effectively, for pain relief. They also stated that doctors who prescribed medicinal cannabis for any treatment, had to be specialists in their field.

In spite of this, the National Health Service said it would continue to supply Alfie with his cannabis oil, providing the prescriptions were issued by Professor Barnes.

Alfie's mother said;

"I feel incredibly guilty, that it's only through our campaign that we have been able to secure this for Alfie, when there are so many others who will find they are unable to get the treatment because of these guidelines".

A spokesman for the Royal College of Physicians said that formal guidelines would be published by the National Institute of Health and Care Excellence in October 2019. The *Independent* put further pressure on them, when thy published a story in early April 2019 under the headline;

"Mother left in tears after medical cannabis for epileptic daughter confiscated at airport".

Emma Appleby had been prescribed cannabis oil by a Paediatric Neurologist working at the Erasmus Hospital in Rotterdam.

Her daughter, Teagan, suffers from a rare chromosomal disorder called Iso-dicentric 15 as well as Lennox-Gastaut syndrome. Emma had spent £4,500 on a 3-month supply of her daughter's medication, which was confiscated when she and her family arrived at Southend Airport .

Emma told reporters;

"I'm really gutted, they just took everything. They knew apparently, they had been notified from social media. They asked me at the border control how long we were away for. I thought they're asking questions as someone's notified them. Then they asked if I had anything to declare, and there were loads of them waiting, so I knew if I said no, I was going to get myself in deeper, so, I just said yes".

She said that customs had been told not to destroy the medicine but to seize it and said that she plans to apply for an import license and hopes that the cannabis oil will be returned to her. Alfie's mum, the first person in the UK who was allowed to legally import it from Holland in 2018, was at the airport to comfort her. It made great press, because here was another story that everyone could get behind and feel good about themselves and they did, in spades. Conservative MP Sir Mike Penning, co-chairman of the All-Party Parliamentary Group on Medical Cannabis Under Prescription said;

"This is a shattering blow for Emma and Teagan. It's a damning indictment of the way this policy has been implemented. We need compassion not entrenched positions. I will be urging all my parliamentary colleagues to get this medicine returned to Emma soonest and demanding that the Department for Health, the NHS and everyone involved gets together urgently so families don't have to go through the stress and trauma of travelling abroad to get medicine that is now legally here".

Peter Carroll, director of the campaign group, End Our Pain said;

"The law was changed for a reason. It was changed on scientific advice as well. To put these families, who have already got this stress and worry for caring for very sick children, through all the trauma. Emma has been passed from pillar to post; she's tried to do the right thing at every stage of this process".

"I call on everybody from Matt Hancock, the leaders of the NHS, the leaders of all the medical professions, I know you must all be caring people but the system that you have put in place is resulting in this kind of trauma for families like Emma's".

Peter Carroll said a request to the Home Office had been submitted, requesting an import licence on compassionate grounds but it was refused.

A spokesman for the Government said;

"The decision to prescribe cannabis-based products for medicinal use, is a clinical decision for specialist hospital doctors, made with patients and their families, taking into account clinical guidance. It is unlawful to import unlicensed cannabis-based products for medicinal use to the UK without the prescription of a specialist doctor and a Home Office importation license. Border Force has a duty to enforce the law and stop the unlawful import of controlled substances".

The fact that so many "conventional" physicians in the UK shudder at the mere mention of using cannabis-based products is not surprising, after all, the plant has been demonised in the West for a hundred years. This attitude was unacceptable in the 1970's but is even more so today, since the discovery in the late 1990's of the cannabinoid receptor antagonist and its relation to the endocannabinoids and their signalling system within the brain.

A Home Office spokesman recently said;

"There is a substantial body of scientific and medical evidence to show that cannabis is a harmful drug which can damage people's mental and physical health. It is important that medicines are thoroughly trialled to ensure they meet rigorous standards. There is a regime in place, administered by the Medicines and Health Regulatory Agency to enable medicines, including those containing controlled drugs, to be developed".

A former colleague once reminded me;

"Every great discovery begins life as a heresy".

One only has to look at the effect that cannabis oil has had on Alfie Dingley, Billy Caldwell and Teagan Appleby, to realise that it works. As a good friend of mine was fond of saying;

"If it looks like a duck, walks like a duck and quacks like a duck, you can bet your life that it's not a dog".

PHARMACEUTICAL CANNABIS

At present, there are only 4 cannabis-based products that have been approved by the European Medicines Agency. They are all pharmaceutical products, not herbal preparations, but given the choice between a synthesised, pharmaceutical vitamin, or one that has been extracted from a plant, fruit or vegetable, most people would choose the natural option.

Producing a product that meets international standards requires clinical trials, sworn testimonies from acknowledged leading experts, substantial data relating to its specific use and dosage and an accredited form of production and packaging, all of which can run into several million pounds. Companies who do this, want a reasonable rate of return, making their product very expensive, until they have recuperated their investment.

GW Pharmaceuticals, founded in 1998, is a British company and is now one of the largest producers of medical, cannabis-based pharmaceuticals in the world. Dr Geoffrey Guy, co-founder of GW, is credited for the creation of Sativex, a mouth spray containing two chemical extracts from the cannabis plant, THC (tetrahydro-cannabidiol) and CBD (cannabidiol), which has been licenced for the treatment of multiple sclerosis.

He has also been credited with the creation of Epidiolex, a pharmaceutically standardised CBD (cannabidiol), which in June 2018, was approved by the U.S FDA (Food and Drug Administration) for the treatment of LGS (Lennox-Gastaut syndrome) and Dravet syndrome, both rare forms of epilepsy.

It was launched in November 2018 and is now available on prescription in the U.S.

The Epilepsy Foundation has estimated that 4% of people in America will develop epilepsy in their lifetime, it is therefore, a potentially huge market. It stands to reason then, that Epidiolex has a very bright and profitable future and obviously, GW Pharmaceuticals are keen to protect their investment.

Under the Single Convention on Narcotic Drugs of 1961, as amended by the 1972 Protocol, GW had to work closely with both the British Home Office and the UK's Medicines Regulatory Authority, in order to comply with the Articles contained within the Convention. During the course of researching this book, I came across three items that I found particularly amusing.

1: In May 2018 Victoria Atkins, the Minister for Drugs, who should naturally be leading this debate, announced that she had voluntarily refused herself from speaking about cannabis because her husband runs a company that grows acres of it, which it supplies to GW Pharmaceuticals, obviously for either Sativex or Epidiolex.

2: The largest investor in GW Pharmaceuticals is Capitol Group Companies Inc, an American based financial services company founded in 1931, with assets of $1.87 trillion.

3: Philip May, an investment relationship manager and husband of Theresa May, the British Prime Minister, is employed by the Capitol Group.

When his wife emerged as the leading contender for the head of the Conservative Party, his employer issued the following statement;

"*He is not involved with, and doesn't manage, money, and is not a portfolio manager. His job is to ensure the clients are happy with the service and that we understand their goals*".

That sounds like a disclaimer to me, although I don't know why they felt it necessary to make any comment.

In order to understand the regulations concerning the cultivation of non-industrial cannabis, and the production of pharmaceutical cannabis products, it is necessary to look at Article 28 of the Single Convention.

Article 28 – Control of Cannabis

1: "If a Party permits the cultivation of the cannabis plant for the production of cannabis or cannabis resin, it shall apply thereto the system of controls as provided in Article 23 respecting the control of the opium poppy".

It seems absurd that under the Single Convention, cannabis cultivation and the production of cannabis-based medicines must comply with the regulations for the production of opium.

This clearly demonstrates that the two are inextricably linked, at least as far as the Single Convention is concerned because although we are informed that Article 23 also relates to cannabis, the word itself does not appear in the text.

Article 23 – National Opium Agencies

1: "A Party that permits the cultivation of the opium poppy for the production of opium shall establish, if it has not already done so, and maintain, one or more government agencies (hereinafter in this article referred to as the Agency) to carry out the functions required under this article".

2: "Each such Party shall apply the following provisions to the cultivation of the opium poppy for the production of opium";

   a) *"The agency shall designate the areas in which, and the plots of land on which, cultivation of the opium poppy for the purposes of producing opium shall be permitted".*

   b) *"Only cultivators licenced by the Agency shall be authorised to engage in such cultivation".*

   c) *"Each licence shall specify the extent of the land on which the cultivation is permitted".*

   d) *"All cultivators of the opium poppy shall be required to deliver their total crops to the agency. The agency shall purchase and take physical possession of such crops as soon as possible but not later than four months after the end of the harvest".*

   e) *"The agency shall, in respect of opium have the exclusive right of importing, exporting, wholesale trading and maintaining stocks other than those held by manufacturers of opium alkaloids, medicinal opium or opium preparations. Parties need not extend this exclusive right to medicinal opium or opium preparations".*

3: "The government's functions referred to in paragraph 2 shall be discharged by a single government agency if the constitution of the Party permits it".

Looking at the regulations, one can only assume that GW Pharmaceuticals, must be the agency that has been appointed by the British Government, although, they may not be the only one. This perhaps explains why the Capitol Group, who are the biggest investor in GW Pharmaceuticals, employed the services of the Prime Minister's husband. Men of influence are always useful to have on the payroll.

Furthermore, the Drugs Minister's husband, who by her own admission runs a company that grows acres of cannabis for GW Pharmaceuticals, must have obtained his licence from GW, since under Article 23 of the Single Convention, only the agency is authorised to issue licences in respect of cannabis cultivation. I thought it was rather amusing, that both the Prime Minister and the Minister of Drugs are both married to men who have a professional interest in the British cannabis industry.

GW Pharmaceuticals has a monopoly on the only FDA approved cannabis-based pharmaceutical, that is used for the treatment epilepsy. Epidiolex has been approved for the treatment of Lennox-Gastaut syndrome, an illness that Teagan Appleby suffers from.

It has been available since November 2018 and yet, the Paediatric Neurologist, working at the Erasmus Hospital in Rotterdam, prescribed Teagan with cannabis oil, a natural preparation, as opposed to Epidiolex, which is a pharmaceutical product.

If Epidiolex is so effective, why did he not prescribe Teagan with that? Was it because in his opinion cannabis oil was more effective? Or was it because cannabis oil was cheaper? Why are pharmaceutical cannabis-based products acceptable, when natural cannabis-based ones are not? We are all encouraged to eat fresh fruit and vegetables because they are better for us, so why does that not apply to cannabis-based medicines?

It should be remembered, that it was not American medical experts who first identified the medicinal properties of marihuana. It was in fact, sufferers of diseases like glaucoma, and multiple sclerosis who first realised that it helped to relieve their symptoms.

The most expensive, innovative marketing campaign is no substitute for "word of mouth" and as people discovered its benefits, they told their friends, who in turn told others and as a result, the medicinal marihuana industry was founded. Pharmaceutical companies like G.W Pharmaceuticals, owe a tremendous debt to the cannabis smoking community, although of course, they would oppose any plans which would allow people to grow it and treat themselves.

A report by the International Narcotics Control Board, published in 2018, stated;

"The Board has repeatedly stated that personal cultivation of cannabis for medical purposes is inconsistent with the 1961 Single Convention".

Its reasons were as follows;

"Personal cultivation of cannabis for medical purposes does not allow Governments to exercise the supervision required by the 1961 Convention over the production, manufacture, export, import and distribution of, trade in and use and possession of cannabis, the establishment of estimates of medical usage, the furnishings of related statistical returns or the implementation of the provisions of Article 28 of that Convention".

"In addition to the risks of diversion, allowing private individuals to cultivate cannabis for personal medical consumption may present additional health risks, in that the dosages and levels of THC consumed may be different from those medically prescribed".

Even though millions of Americans are now smoking marihuana to relieve a wide variety of symptoms, it is not a practice that the INCB approve of, as their 2018 report states;

"Smoking cannabis is not a medically accepted way to obtain standardised doses of cannabinoids for two reasons. First, cannabis plants vary in their composition, which makes it difficult to prescribe specific doses. Second, there are health risks to patients from inhaling the carcinogens and toxins in cannabis smoke".

In a world where cigarettes are sold and packaged to include a health warning, surely marihuana and cannabis resin could be treated the same way.

While policy makers debate the issues, scientists, researchers and medical practitioners are busy at work.

MEDICAL RESEARCH IN THE 21ST CENTURY

Although cannabis had been used for medical purposes for thousands of years, nobody had any idea of how or why it was so effective. An enormous amount of work is now being carried out all over the world, to discover new medical applications of cannabis pharmaceuticals and cannabis-based preparations, for the treatment of a wide-number of illnesses.

It is without doubt, one of the most exciting new fields in 21st century medicine, because this remarkable plant has provided science with a completely new insight into a previously unknown, chemical controlled system within the human body, which controls and regulates various bodily functions.

Victorian doctors and chemists had attempted to isolate individual components of the cannabis plant. In 1840, Schlesinger began to experiment with an active ingredient which he had extracted from the leaves and flowers of the plant and in 1848 another pioneer described a dark resin that he had extracted with ethanol, which he named cannabin.

Robert Cahn, a British chemist identified an active ingredient in 1940 that was previously unknown, which he named cannabinol (CBN), since it was thought to be unique to the cannabis plant. Several years later, Roger Adams, an American chemist, discovered another previously unknown component, which he called cannabidiol (CBD).

In 1964, Dr Raphael Mechoulam, isolated and identified one of the primary psycho-active ingredients. His discovery, named as tetrahydrocannabinol (THC) marked the beginning of intensive research, as experts scrambled to try and discover how it interacted with the human brain.

These compounds, collectively known as cannabinoids were at first thought to be unique to the cannabis plant but scientists quickly discovered identical chemicals in the human body and in the 1980's, a completely new system, using these chemicals was identified.

The discovery of the respiratory system, the central nervous system and the immune system, all led to a greater understanding of how the body functions and this new system, called the endo-cannabinoid-system (ECS), has opened up exciting new avenues of medical research.

Researchers quickly discovered that not only did the body produce its own cannabinoids, they also acted as receptors, providing the brain with crucial information. Allyn Howlett and William Devane discovered the first cannabinoid receptor in 1988, in the brain of a rat and they soon discovered that cannabinoid receptors were found throughout the body, particularly in the central nervous system, the immune system and in the gastrointestinal tract.

They help to regulate sleep, appetite, the immune system, pain and memory. These chemical messengers help to maintain the body's balance and when we cannot produce enough of them, we are more susceptible to illness and disease.

Although most people are only familiar with THC and CBD, there are many more cannabinoids that are found within the cannabis plant and all of them interact in some way with the endo-cannabinoid system within our own bodies.

These include Cannabinol (CBN), Cannabigerol (CBG), Tetrahydrocannabivarin (THCV), Cannabidivarin (CBDV), and Cannabichromene (CBC). Not surprisingly, research is now being carried out on all of these.

All of this has contributed to a huge rise in scientific research and even though it is a relatively new branch of medicine, a huge number of medical applications have already been identified.

Alzheimer's Disease

This is a neurological disorder, characterised by memory loss. Patients may also suffer from depression and a loss of appetite.

There are no conventional treatments available to control either the progression of the disease or to treat its symptoms. In 2007 the *British Journal of Pharmacology* published the findings of a study carried out by researchers at Trinity College in Ireland. The work carried out by Campbell and Gowan revealed;

"Cannabinoids offer a multi-faceted approach for the treatment of Alzheimer's disease by providing neuroprotection and reducing neuroinflammation, whilst simultaneously supporting the brain's intrinsic repair mechanisms, by augmenting neurotrophic expression and enhancing neurogenesis".

"Manipulation of the cannabinoid pathway offers a pharmacological approach for the treatment of Alzheimer's disease, that may be more efficacious than current treatment regimens".

In 2016, researchers in Israel carried out a four-week trial, assessing the safety of THC-infused oil. Following treatment, it was revealed that patients suffered with less incidences of delusion, apathy and agitation and the investigators stated;

"Adding medical cannabis oil to Alzheimer's patient's pharmacotherapy is safe, and a promising treatment option".

Other studies at the Scripps Research Institute have shown that THC slows down the formation of amyloid plaques, which are known to kill brain cells, which can often result in Alzheimer's.

Rheumatoid Arthritis

This is an inflammatory disease, often characterised by pain, stiffness and the swelling of joints, particularly in women.

Many people have reported that the use of medicinal cannabis alleviates suffering and although only limited studies have as yet been carried out, results have been extremely promising, which has encouraged further studies.

Researchers Croxford and Yamammura, working at the National Institute for Neuroscience in Japan, concluded;

"Cannabinoid therapy of Rheumatoid arthritis could provide symptomatic relief of joint pain and swelling, as well as suppressing joint destruction and disease progression".

Cancer

The most accepted use of medicinal cannabis by cancer patients is for the reduction of pain, nausea and loss of appetite, as a result of chemotherapy.

There is now a huge amount of research presently being carried out and there is no doubt, that cannabinoids may represent a new breakthrough in anticancer drugs, that retard growth and the spread of cancerous cells. It is perhaps one of the most exciting fields of research today, and although the disease offers scientists a huge challenge, the results so far are very encouraging.

A pilot study, involving patients suffering with glioblastoma multiforme, was published in the British Journal of Cancer in 2006, Guzman reported;

"The fair safety profile of THC, together with its possible antiproliferative action on tumour cells reported here and in other studies, may set the basis for future trials aimed at evaluating the potential antitumoral activity of cannabinoids".

Other researchers working in the U.S, Italy and Spain have also reported encouraging results from numerous trials, which suggests that CBD may well be an effective antineoplastic agent.

Diabetes Mellitus

There are two types of diabetes. Patients suffering from type 1 are incapable of producing pancreatic insulin and therefore rely on medication in order to survive. Those suffering from type 2 produce insufficient quantities, although this can often be controlled by dietary measures.

This disease can lead to blindness, nerve damage, kidney failure and the hardening of arteries. It is the third major cause of premature death in the U.S, after heart disease and cancer. This is a particularly interesting field of research, since it has been shown that marihuana users are less likely to suffer from diabetes, as non-users.

The University of California conducted a survey to investigate the connection between diabetes and marihuana smokers. More than 10,000 adults between the ages of 20 and 59 took part in the study which showed that past and present marihuana consumers, had a lower rate of prevalence of type 2, despite the fact that all groups possessed a similar family history of diabetes.

A 2015 study, published in *The Journal of Pain* reported that the inhalation of vaporised marihuana, reduced diabetic neuropathy in patients who were resistant to conventional analgesics. Researchers who conducted the trials stated;

"This small, short-term, placebo-controlled trial, of inhaled cannabis, demonstrated a dose-dependent reduction in diabetic peripheral neuropathy pain, in patients with treatment-refractory pain. Overall, our finding of an analgesic effect of cannabis is consistent with other trials of cannabis in diverse neuropathic pain syndromes".

Similar trials carried out in Israel and Canada in recent years support this view and there is a large number of studies presently being carried out.

Epilepsy

This is a central nervous system disorder, characterised by seizures and uncontrollable spasmodic twitching of the arms and legs. Conventional treatment includes medications or surgery, although for many sufferers it has proved to be ineffective.

Recent high-profile cases involving young British children, have demonstrated that the use of cannabis-oil, can be an effective treatment for those who have not benefitted from conventional measures.

Epidiolex, a pharmaceutical CBD preparation, is the first FDA approved treatment of Lennox-Gastaut Syndrome, a rare form of epilepsy, which conventional medicine has, as yet, had little or no effect.

Gastrointestinal Disorders

These include irritable bowel syndrome and inflammatory bowel disorders, including Crohn's disease. Symptoms include cramps, abdominal pains and inflammation of the lining in both the large and small intestine.

Many patients have reported that the use of cannabis has helped to reduce the effects and according to a survey published in 2011 in the European Journal of Gastroenterology & Hepatology;

"Cannabis use is common amongst patients with Irritable Bowel Syndrome, for symptom relief, particularly amongst those with a history of abdominal surgery, chronic abdominal pain and a low quality of life index".

Some of the most exciting research is being carried out in Israel at the Meir Medical Centre. A recent study of 30 patients, which involved whole-plant cannabis therapy, produced some interesting data;

"Fifteen of the patients had 19 surgeries during an average period of nine years before cannabis use, but only two required surgery during an average period of three years of cannabis use".

"The results indicate that cannabis may have a positive effect on disease activity, and in the need for other drugs and surgery".

Later studies, involving placebo-controlled trials, inhaled cannabis was found to decrease Crohn's disease symptoms in patients with a treatment-resistant form of the disease and nearly half the patients who took part in the trial, achieved disease remission. However, it is curious to note that the same trials, using an oral CBD preparation, failed to show similar results.

Glaucoma

This is a disease which increases the pressure on eyeballs, injuring the optic nerve which results in loss of vision or blindness. Marihuana has been found to be an effective treatment, as the National Eye Institute stated;

"Studies in the early 1970's showed that marihuana, when smoked, lowered intraocular pressure in people with normal pressure and those with glaucoma".

Human Immunodeficiency Virus

HIV invades cells in the immune system, making it susceptible to infectious diseases. According to the World Health Organisation, half a million Americans have already died from HIV and over a million more are infected, causing enormous suffering on a daily basis.

Research at the University of California, published in the journal *Neuropsychopharmacology* in 2012 stated;

"Our findings suggest that cannabinoid therapy may be an effective option for pain relief in patients with medically intractable pain, due to HIV".

In an earlier study in 2007, which involved patients smoking marihuana, the researchers concluded by saying;

"Smoked cannabis was well tolerated and effectively relieved chronic neuropathic pain from HIV-associated neuropathy, similar to oral drugs used for chronic neuropathic pain".

This has led to some experts believing that cannabis may provide an alternative treatment in health management, for those suffering with this dreadful disease.

Migraine

This is a condition that produces reoccurring headaches, which can last for three days if left untreated. It is a fairly common phenomenon, which mainly affects women and is characterised by pulsating headaches, nausea, dizziness and confusion.

A recent assessment of 121 adults, which was published in 2016 in *Pharmacotherapy* reported;

"Migraine headache frequency decreased from 10.4 to 4.6 headaches per month with the use of cannabis".

At the 2017 conference of the European Academy of Neurology, it was reported that daily administration of cannabinoid extracts, resulted in a 40% reduction in migraine frequency, in a group of 79 chronic sufferers. Research is still in its early stages, but there is sufficient anecdotal and trial evidence, to suggest that cannabis will be an effective treatment for migraine in the future.

Multiple Sclerosis

(MS) or multiple sclerosis, is a degenerative disease that attacks the central nervous system, causing muscular inflammation and a loss of coordination. Many sufferers become permanently disabled and for some, it is fatal. According to the National Multiple Sclerosis Society, more than 200 people are stricken with this condition every week.

Due to the amount of research that has been carried out, there is a wealth of information to show that cannabis has the ability to reduce pain, spasticity and fatigue. Results published in the journal of the Canadian Medical Association, demonstrated that studies carried out at the University of California in 2010, showed that marihuana smoking patients suffered from less pain and less spasticity than their placebo-controlled counterparts.

In 2012, further studies were carried out which supported previous evidence;

"Cannabis was superior to placebo in reducing spasticity and pain, it provided benefit beyond currently prescribed treatment, for patients with treatment-resistant spasticity".

It's not surprising that health regulators in numerous countries including Germany, Spain, Denmark and New Zealand, have approved the prescription use of extracts of the cannabis plant for those who suffer from this dreadful disease.

The Neurologic Institute in New York carried out trials in April 2019, involving 77 patients, which showed that;

"In addition, 34% of patients were able to decrease or discontinue other medications, including opioids, stimulants, and benzodiazepines, indicative of symptom improvement".

These findings are all consistent with those carried out by G.W Pharmaceuticals, who created Sativex, which has been approved for the treatment of MS-related spasticity in both the UK and Canada.

Parkinson's Disease

This is a progressive disorder of the central nervous system, which results in restricted movement and muscle rigidity. As yet, there is no known cure, but conventional medicines which help to alleviate the symptoms, are available. Numerous surveys have shown that the use of cannabis, is an effective treatment for alleviating some of the problems associated with this condition, especially non-motor symptoms. Trial data, published in 2017, in *Clinical Neuropharmacology* led researchers to conclude;

"The results of our study demonstrate that most users had found medicinal cannabis to improve their condition, and that the treatment was safe, without any side effects".

Researchers in the Department of Neurology at Tel Aviv University reached similar conclusions. After studies were carried out on patients who were given marihuana to inhale, their conclusion was;

"Significant improvement after treatment in tremor, rigidity and bradykinesia (slowness of movement). Other, placebo-controlled trials have found that cannabis improved sleeping patterns, reduced symptoms and provided a sense of well-being".

Further research is currently being carried out but there is no doubt that cannabis will play a key role in the future for those suffering from this debilitating illness.

Post-traumatic Stress Disorder

This is a psychiatric response to a traumatic event. Symptoms include, severe anxiety, nightmares and often, distorted memories of the event. These symptoms often persist, long after the event that triggered them and they may not respond to conventional treatments. It has been estimated that 10% of Americans suffer from this condition.

Although many sufferers have testified, that cannabis has helped greatly to reduce their stress levels, clinical trials have so far proved to be inconclusive. Some researchers have suggested that cannabis may reduce the impact of traumatic memories, through synergistic mechanisms, allowing the patient to sleep better and feel less anxious, and accumulating evidence suggests that cannabinoids may play an anti-depressive role, reducing fear and general anxiety.

Further research on its use for post-traumatic stress is continuing in the U.S and Canada.

I think it is incredible that the people in charge, sitting in comfortable offices of the Economic and Social Council of the United Nations, appear to be oblivious to the extensive work now being carried out by scientists and researchers.

In a world swamped with pharmaceutical concoctions, that is trying to adopt a greener approach to environmental problems, governments and international bodies should encourage the use and availability of plant-based medicines.

Although present research is being directed at the use of THC and CBD, there are many other cannabinoids in the plant that have as yet, not been identified. My own view, is that what has been discovered so far represents merely the tip of a giant medical iceberg, just waiting to be revealed.

As I write, more than a hundred naturally occurring cannabinoids have now been identified and there is no doubt that there are many others waiting in the wings.

It is interesting to note that researchers have recently identified other plants that also contain cannabinoids. These include the tea plant, which perhaps explains why the Chinese and Japanese, recognised its medicinal properties, although of course, at the time, they had no idea why.

I can only repeat what my good friend and former colleague said;

"Every great scientific discovery begins life as a heresy".

The sad part of the story is that of the heretics, who paid the price for this medical revelation.

There have been millions, from all walks of life, from every occupation imaginable, of all ages and of both sexes. They were harassed, arrested and imprisoned simply because of their association with this remarkable plant, and we should never forget that.

LEGALISATION AND THE UNITED NATIONS

As we approach the second decade of the 21st century, a more enlightened approach to cannabis is now being adopted, although the United Nations refuses to change its views.

A 2012 report, published by the INCB (International Narcotics Control Board), whose role is to enforce the United Nations Single Convention, stated;

"Cannabis is included under Schedules I and IV of the Single Convention on Narcotic Drugs of 1961 as amended by the 1972 Protocol because it produces dependence and has adverse public health consequences. Those consequences include injuries in motor vehicle crashes, mental illnesses such as psychoses, impaired cognitive and educational performance, disrupted adolescent development and adverse effects on foetal development. Cannabis use that begins during adolescence can damage the developing brain at a time of increased vulnerability".

I find statements like this very annoying and extremely misleading. Alcohol is the major cause of road traffic accidents, and as to the comments concerning addiction, all I can say is that whoever was responsible for writing that nonsense, clearly has a case of Reefer Madness.

Although under U.S Federal Law, marihuana is still classified as a Schedule 1 substance, medical use of marihuana has now been legalised in more than 33 U.S States. Recreational use of marihuana has been legalised in Alaska, California, Colorado, Washington, Massachusetts, Michigan, Nevada, Oregon, Vermont and Maine.

The U.S Justice Department issued the Cole Memorandum in August 2013, in an attempt to clarify how Federal Law would be enforced. This was rescinded in January 2018 by Jeff Sessions, the Attorney General, so at present, it is still unclear what the U.S Government's response will be, in respect of State Laws. From another report, issued by International Narcotics Control Board in 2012, we can see their reaction to recent legislative changes in the U.S States of Colorado and Washington, which provides us with a clue of how they will proceed;

"In the United States of America in November 2012, voters in the States of Colorado and Washington approved ballot initiatives which would allow the recreational use of cannabis. INCB has reiterated that the 1961 Convention limits use of narcotic drugs, including cannabis, to medical and scientific purposes. INCB has taken note of a statement made by the Office of the Attorney General of the United States in December 2012, subsequent to the finalisation of our report, that regardless of any changes in state law, growing, selling or possessing any amount of marijuana remains illegal under Federal Law".

"However, INCB has to underline, it is our mandate, the central role of the 1961 Convention which needs to be implemented worldwide on the national level, but also on the sub-national level".

On December 20th, 2013 President José Mujica signed Law number, 19.172, which legalised the use of cannabis for medical, spiritual and recreational purposes, making Uruguay the first country in the world, to regulate its use. The Government of Uruguay established the Institute for the Regulation and Control of Cannabis and in a presentation to the ICNB, the Vice-Minister of Foreign Affairs laid out his country's vision of the future;

"This initiative is aimed at regulating the cannabis market and to guarantee public safety".

He went on to explain that the decision was taken, to take the cannabis trade out of the hands of criminal organisations, to regulate the supply of it and to separate cannabis use from other, more dangerous drugs.

Uruguay suffered from a huge problem with pasta or paste, an unrefined form of cocaine that was highly addictive, which could only be smoked, not sniffed. Prior to the new law, Uruguay had never criminalised personal possession for any psychoactive drug but when the pasta problem escalated, they realised that they would have to introduce new legislation.

It was not a decision they took lightly, and discussions lasted for several years before they arrived at a decision that everyone was happy with. One of the first things they all agreed on was the simple fact that total prohibition, as used virtually all over the world, had proved to be a complete failure.

Regulation of cannabis was seen as a way of combatting the pasta trade, by allowing young people with a legal alternative, while at the same time, imposing heavy penalties for the possession, distribution and importation of dangerous drugs. With a regulated cannabis market, law enforcement agencies would then be free to focus their efforts on combatting the pasta trade.

The Uruguayan Government recognised that total prohibition had been a complete failure and I am certain that they agreed with the European Parliament Committee, who, in 2003 submitted a proposal recommending the scraping of the Single Convention;

"Despite massive deployment of police and other resources to implement the U.N Conventions, production and consumption of, and trafficking in, prohibited substances have increased exponentially over the past 30 years, representing what can only be described as a failure, which the police and judicial authorities also recognise as such".

"The policy of prohibiting drugs, based on the U.N Conventions of 1961, 1971 and 1988, is the true cause of the increasing damage that the production of, trafficking in, and sale and use of illegal substances are inflicting on whole sectors of society, on the economy and on public institutions, eroding the health, freedom and life of individuals".

Faced with the choice of repeating the mistakes that everyone else had made, which ultimately would have had little or no effect in combatting the pasta trade, they decided to try something different. As President José Mujica later said;

"Somebody had to be the first, so it was up to us".

It must be stressed that it is a regulated market, not a free one and the government has put into place a series of measures that controls the complete cannabis trade, from the seed to cultivation, possession and finally, the use of it. Under the new law, smoking marihuana in public places is forbidden and cultivation is restricted to registered users. Anyone over the age of 18 can apply for a licence, and for a very small fee, they are then free to cultivate up to 6 plants, producing no more than 480 grams a year.

Groups of people can form clubs, by joining together to produce all the plants in one place. A club with ten registered users, is allowed to grow 60 plants, providing the harvest does not exceed 4.8 kilos, which gives each member their permissible annual quota of 480 grams.

Those who don't want to cultivate their own, are allowed to purchase up to 40 grams a month from pharmacies, which are supplied by special, government licenced growers.

Only approved strains can be grown, thus eliminating many of the problems associated with the new, super strains of skunk, which under Uruguayan law, are prohibited. Any marihuana that is cultivated outside of the regulations, is deemed to be illegal and as well as being destroyed, those responsible are liable to prosecution. When Uruguay announced their decision, the INCB reacted very strongly and its President, Raymond Yans, made his feelings very clear when he addressed the United Nations General Assembly shortly after, saying;

"A chain is no stronger than its weakest link. If the chain of drug control is broken in one country or region, and I am thinking now of certain projects in Uruguay, the entire international drug control system may be undermined".

When he openly accused Uruguay of negligence in respect of public health and taking a piratical approach towards U.N Conventions, Milton Romani, the Uruguayan Ambassador to the Organisation of American States, demanded his resignation, saying that he had no right to insult sovereign states, who were well within their right to interpret the treaty as they saw fit.

In an attempt to clarify Uruguay's position, Vice-Minister Luis Porto travelled to Vienna in February 2014, where he addressed the main committee, informing them that;

"Uruguay believes that production and sale in the manner prescribed in the new law may be the best way, on the one hand to combat drug trafficking, and on the other, to defend the constitutionally protected right to freedom of our fellow citizens. The spirit as well as the regulations of Law Number 19.172, follows the philosophy of the Single Convention on Narcotic Drugs of 1961 as amended by the 1972 Protocol, and incorporates the basis established by it".

The United Nations were extremely unhappy with Uruguay's interpretation, but they responded by demanding an open and honest debate, about the complete U.N drug control system. Diego Cánepa, told a U.N committee;

"Today more than ever, we need the leadership and courage to enable us to discuss in the international community, if a revision and modernisation is required, of the international instruments that we have adopted in the last fifty years".

The Single Convention was put under even more pressure, when Canada announced their intentions to legalise cannabis, which in turn, has led to others following a similar example.

Portugal introduced legislation that prohibits the prosecution of anyone caught in possession of any drug. They are focusing their efforts on education, and rehabilitation of heroin addicts and Jamaica introduced new laws which no longer treats possession of ganja as a criminal offence.

South Africa has recently introduced similar legislation, but this is only the first step, because they are only one of a number of African countries who have identified the commercial aspects of cannabis pharmaceuticals.

The African Cannabis Report, published in 2019, estimated that the African cannabis market could be worth over $7 billion a year by 2023. Clearly, major pharmaceutical companies have already carried out feasibility studies, complied their spreadsheets, done the figures and have already come up with a plan.

The offices of the Single Convention's administrative department must be overloaded with paperwork, as Article 14 (A) states;

"If the board has objective reasons to believe that the aims of this Convention are being seriously endangered by reason of the failure of any Party, country or territory to carry out the provisions of this Convention, the Board shall have the right to propose to the government concerned, the opening of consultations or to request it to furnish explanations".

Article 14 (B)

"The Board, if satisfied that it is necessary to do so, may call upon the Government concerned, to adopt such remedial measures as shall seem under the circumstances to be necessary for the execution of the provisions of this Convention".

Although the INCB take great pride when they announce their success, their failures are less publicised. Morocco is an excellent example of poorly managed, badly thought out schemes, which failed to take into account the geographical and climatic conditions of the Rif valley, as well as the rights and needs of the indigenous population.

MOROCCO – AN INTERNATIONAL FIASCO

Arab invasions from the 7th century onwards were probably responsible for the introduction of cannabis to Morocco, but its history really begins in the 18th century, when Berbers, living high up in the Rif mountains, began to grow it commercially. In an area that was not suitable for conventional agriculture, the cannabis plant thrived and many of the tribes living there, grew it as their principle cash crop.

The trade was officially recognised at the end of the 19th century, when the King of Morocco, Sultan Moulay Hassan, granted 5 groups of villages in the Senhaja district, a royal permit to cultivate, trade and smoke what was commonly known as kif, an Arabic word meaning "supreme happiness". Kif is a mixture of finely chopped tobacco and ground dried cannabis, and the smoking of it, in small clay pipes called sebsis, became a popular recreational custom for many Moroccans.

Cultivation centred around the village of Ketama, a rugged, mountainous region of the Rif valley, known as the "land of insolence". It was the Sultan's way of appeasing the wild Berber tribes, who had continuously fought against any form of authority. The Berbers, originally of Caucasian descent, were there long before the Arabs arrived and even the Romans failed to tame them, as a result, it was an area that was largely ignored by the outside world.

Under the Treaty of Algeciras in 1906, a French owned multi-national company, the Régie Marocaine des Kif et Tabacs, operating from Tangier, was given the monopoly for the sale of kif throughout the kingdom. It was not a lucrative trade for the Berbers, but it did at least provide them with a small annual income, although the French company who purchased their produce and who then mixed it with tobacco, made far more money out of it, since it was sold in every tobacco shop in the country, in standard paper bags, containing 5-grams.

In 1912, the whole of what is now Morocco came under imperial rule, when France and Spain signed the Treaty of Fés.

This split the country into two zones and although the Sultan was allowed to remain, it was the Europeans who now governed the country. The Rif valley was controlled by the Spanish, although the Régie still had the monopoly of the kif trade, and in order to protect the company's interests, the Spanish gave the Berbers a permit to continue growing cannabis, provided that they sold their harvest to the French company. It was a compromise that seemed to keep everyone happy; the Berbers kept their trade, the Spanish earned money from the sale of permits and the French continued to reap the revenue generated from sales.

Nobody at the time considered it to be a problem and it was a common sight to see workers, who had finished their chores for the day, sitting around in groups drinking tea, filling their small clay pipes with kif, while they chatted about the issues of the day.

Things changed dramatically in the Rif valley in 1920, when a local Berber chief united the other tribes to rebel against the Spanish and for a few years, the region became the Rif Republic. It was a very bloody up rising which nearly defeated the colonial forces, but eventually French and Spanish coalition forces once again took control.

Although both France and Spain had signed the 1925 Geneva convention, neither were willing to prohibit the sale of kif, which was now the principle trade for most of the farmers in the Rif valley and as demand grew, so did production. It was heavily taxed of course, so naturally a black-market trade quickly flourished.

Official sales of kif in 1943 are given as 20 tons, which by 1949 had risen to over 48 tons.

Illicit seizures of pure cannabis, smuggled out of the Rif valley in 1949, amounted to nearly 7 tons. This was probably less than 10% of the actual illegal trade, which may have been as high as 70 tons, which, when mixed with tobacco would have resulted in more than 150 tons of kif.

Although any figures regarding the illicit trade are by its very nature, speculative, what is not in doubt is the widespread use of it, particularly in urban centres.

In 1956, Morocco finally won its independence and although King Mohammed V prohibited the cultivation of cannabis in the former Spanish and French zones, after an insurrection by the Berber tribes who were determined to keep their trade, the King once again permitted cultivation in the original 5 villages of the Ketama region.

A report published in 1957 by the UNODC, (United Nations Office on Drugs and Crime), makes interesting and at times, amusing reading;

"Many consumers are content to smoke a few pipes every evening while sipping coffee or a cup of tea, before going to bed. It can be said that cannabis has no serious effects on this type of person. Their health will not suffer, and they will be able to carry on their work without difficulty. The number of these careful smokers is fairly high in the towns among the artisans and small shopkeepers".

"Those over whom the drug has a greater hold meet in the evening in groups of five or six, in their favourite cafes or in a shop belonging to one of their number. Sometimes, if they can afford it, they hire premises, generally a single room".

"The furniture is scanty: mats or cushions on the ground or on benches, a few coloured prints on the walls, and a low table with a jar of basil, the perfume of which is much appreciated by the natives. They always bring with them either candied fruit or some pastries and sweets, including sometimes a kind of majun which they prepare by merely mixing powdered hemp with hot thick syrup. The mixture is poured out on to a marble slab, where it solidifies and then is cut into pieces, a clay stove is used for preparing coffee or tea: fresh mint leaves are often added to the latter".

Kif smoking had become a custom for more than a million Moroccans, but it was one which the UNODC viewed as a vice, which needed to be stamped out, as the report concluded;

"The meetings generally last a long time, as it is customary to attain complete intoxication. The smoking den is therefore left very late at night, if indeed, the stage of sleep which closes the cycle of the phenomena of intoxication, does not compel the smoker to stay all night. It is easy to imagine that nights thus passed, do not predispose to work on the morrow".

After further pressure from the international community, in 1958, the King once again tried to prohibit cultivation in the Rif valley. The Berbers rebelled and Moroccan troops, led by the Crown Prince, marched into the region, resulting in the deaths of more than 6,000 Berbers.

The King was forced to accept that the uprisings were due to economic hardship and realising that the Berbers were dependent on the kif trade, from that moment, it became a tolerated business, based on a system of bribes and unofficial taxes. There was no attempt to improve local infrastructure and the region was largely left alone, as the government focused its attention on developing the commercial and administrative centres of Tangier, Casablanca and Rabat.

Although the vast majority of the cannabis grown by the Berbers was used for the production of kif, shortly after the Second World War, they began to produce small amounts of hashish, which was mainly used in the manufacture of sweet confectionary.

In the late 1950's as the demand for cannabis resin grew in Europe, the Berbers began to produce more hashish, mainly for the French market, but it was the arrival of the hippies in the early 1960's, which marked the beginning of large-scale hashish production. This increased during the 1970's and due to the fall of the Shah in Iran, the Russian invasion of Afghanistan and political problems in Lebanon, by the early 1980's, Morocco was one of the largest producers of cannabis resin in the world.

Due to economic hardships and the lack of mechanisation, local agriculture was completely undeveloped and as a result, hashish became the main income for the vast majority of farmers and even though it was, in theory, illegal, it was grown everywhere. Attempts by the Moroccan government to put an end to the trade, only resulted in further uprisings in the 1980's and this lucrative trade continued to flourish.

National and international efforts to encourage the farmers to grow alternative crops and to develop an alternative economy, have been a complete failure. One such project, initiated by the United Nations in 1989, attempted to replace cannabis cultivation with apple orchards and goats. An enormous amount of money was spent developing new irrigation systems, but the orchards were a complete failure and the choice of French goats, which were completely unsuitable for the local terrain, was a total disaster.

During the 1990's, the Moroccan government intensified their efforts to eradicate cannabis cultivation and in 1997, a new 5-year project, aimed at turning the area into a huge fruit orchard was initiated by the United Nations at a cost of more than 4 million euros. Its failure was mainly due to the fact that it failed to provide the farmers with an income that was comparable to what they were earning before.

A French report, published in 2001 by the OFDT (Observatoire Français des Drogues et des Toxicomanies) stated;

"Even if a project of this type was a success, between half and two thirds of the population would leave the area. It would therefore be necessary for the European Union, and in particular Spain and France, to show a lot of imagination in order to channel a new flow of migrants, that would surely arrive on their territory".

As one Moroccan observer stated;

"The only way to eradicate cannabis, is to convince Europeans to smoke carrots".

The main problem is that the farmers in the Rif valley have been growing cannabis for so long, they don't really know how to do anything else. With more than a million people relying on the income they receive from its cultivation, finding a solution is now proving to be very difficult.

Although the United Nations has focused its efforts to eradicate cannabis cultivation, the European Union is primarily concerned about the increase of illegal refugees. Morocco has now become a major transit point for many looking to start a new life in Europe and the Moroccan economy and in particular, that of the Rif valley, is now heavily dependent on the money that these people send home.

In 2003, more than $3.6 billion was sent to Morocco by those who had successfully emigrated and found work in Spain, the vast majority of whom are from the Rif valley. This is now an important source of foreign currency for the Moroccan government, since it represents nearly 7% of the country's GNP (Gross National Product), 22% of the total imports and more than six times the amount of money that the country receives in the form of aid.

From a Moroccan point of view, there appears to be no financial incentive to curb either the cultivation of cannabis or the illegal emigration, since both generate a huge income for the country. The situation is made even more complicated by the fact that the European Union is not in favour of importing cheaper citrus fruit, olives and olive oil from Morocco, since this harms European producers.

Although it is in everyone's interest to resolve the economic crisis in the Rif valley, it is clear that the present situation is only making things worse, because further attempts to eradicate the illegal cultivation will only increase emigration. As the former Moroccan prime minister, Abbas El Fassi stated during a television interview;

"The government gives them a sheep and some olive trees so they can make a kind of alternative cultivation instead of cannabis. The question is: how can a sheep and some olives help Morocco get rid of hashish?".

Since cannabis cultivation is an illegal activity, corruption has become another key element in what can only be described as an international fiasco. Criminal organisations, the local mafia and the Moroccan government are the only winners, since the farmers themselves earn very little from the trade. A recent report published by the European Union Council stated;

"Unless major efforts are undertaken to do away with corruption and something is done in the production areas about the conditions which make cannabis production and cannabis trafficking the sole viable alternative for the local population, eliminating production and repressing drug trafficking alone will not suffice to resolve the problem".

A recent survey conducted by the INCB (International Narcotics Control Board), has estimated that Morocco is now exporting in excess of 3000 tons of cannabis resin a year, although this fails to take into account, the precarious position of the farmers.

According to Hamid Chabat of the Istiqlal Party, 80,000 growers in the Rif valley are currently on bail, their release only secured through the payment of bribes and unless the situation is resolved, this number will only increase, simply because the farmers are unable to make a living any other way. It is a ludicrous situation, but if a solution is not found, the economic stability of the region will become even more perilous for more than a million people who live there.

Cannabis cultivation has now become a major political issue in the country and since Uruguay and Canada have now legalised cannabis use, there are many in Morocco who feel that it should be legalised. During the election campaign in 2016, Ilyas El Omari, President of the Regional Council of Tangier, Tetouan and Al Hoceima, told a local newspaper that he believed local youths should be allowed to adopt a similar activity to that in Holland, stating they should be free to;

"Open cafes where they can legally sell cannabis to consumers in reasonable and specific amounts on a weekly basis".

If criminal activity, corruption and continued illegal emigration is to be prevented, legalisation appears to be the only viable solution. A legal, regulated market would enable growers to receive a much higher price for their crops, which would discourage emigration and provide a sustainable, prosperous local economy.

This would not only benefit those living in the Rif valley but also Morocco a whole, although of course, this would violate the Single Convention, which Morocco is part of.

India has only recently woken up to the fact that they are sitting on a gold mine, and one which can be harvested every year without fail. The Indian State of Himachal Pradesh is also capable of producing huge amounts of cannabis resin, rich in natural CBD. This could be put to very good use, by producing a natural, CBD cannabis-oil extract, providing a much cheaper alternative to Epidiolex.

In July 2017, Maneka Gandhi, Minister of Woman and Child Development, announced that marihuana should be legalised for medical purposes for the treatment of heroin addiction and to help cancer patients. The following week, the Union Government issued the first-ever licence to grow cannabis for research purposes, to the Council of Scientific and Industrial Research.

On December 12th, 2017 Viki Vaurora, founder of the Great Legalisation Movement of India, sent a letter to Prime Minister Narenda Modi, advocating the urgent need to legalise the cultivation of cannabis for medical use.

The Indian Prime Minister's office sent a notification to the Ministry of Health and Family Welfare, directing the ministry to examine the potential benefits associated with cannabis.

CANNABIS – A STUDY OF ITS HISTORY, PROHIBITION AND USE

On November 25th, 2018 the Central Council for Research in Ayurvedic Sciences, announced the results of the first clinical trial in India, on the use of cannabis as a restorative drug for cancer patients. The pilot study was conducted on patients receiving treatment at the Tata Memorial Hospital in Mumbai and Director General Vaidya Dhiman reported;

"In the pilot study conducted earlier this year, cannabis-based drugs have been found effective in alleviating pain and other symptoms in cancer patients, post-chemo and radiotherapy".

Following a conference held in Delhi at the end of 2018, hosted to promote the use of cannabis-based medicines, the Indian Institute of Integrative Medicine announced that it was developing three cannabis-based medications to treat cancer, epilepsy and sickle-cell anaemia.

In Himachal Pradesh, where same of the finest charas on planet earth grows wild, the state government is investigating the possibility of legalising it, not only for medical purposes, but also for recreational and religious use. Chief Minister Jai Ram Thakur said the government would consider legalising cannabis cultivation but only after examining the legal position.

At a recent meeting of local businessmen and hotel owners in the Parvati Valley, Mr Devan Khanna told the local community;

"We need to make policies about this substance because now, in 2018, we have data from other countries. The data shows how the amendments have helped improve different aspects of people's lives. One aspect is medicinal use, in some states of the U.S.A and Canada, clinics have been made for people suffering from medical conditions like cancer and epilepsy. We have one of the best varieties of the plant growing here, it is a natural resource which should be put to good use".

Similar clinics, if opened, would certainly rejuvenate the rural economy, especially during the spring and summer months when the weather is mild and pleasant. Stunning views over the valleys, combined with clean air, a wealth of fresh fruit and vegetables and the warm hospitality of the local people, would make it an ideal place to receive treatment.

The United Nations has been very slow to recognise the extensive medical research that is now taking place all over the world.

Under the Single Convention, cannabis is still classified as both a Schedule 1 and Schedule 4 substance, which according to their own interpretation, means that it is highly addictive, has no medical benefits and is unsafe even under clinical supervision.

On February 1st, 2019 the World Health Organisation finally issued a statement;

"There is increased interest from Member States in the use of cannabis for medical applications including for palliative care. Responding to that interest and increase in use, WHO has, in recent years, gathered more robust scientific evidence on therapeutic use and side effects of cannabis and cannabis components. Recent evidence from animal and human studies shows that its use could have some therapeutic value for seizures due to epilepsy and related conditions".

Doctor Ethan Russo, Director of Research and Development at the International Cannabis and Cannabinoids Institute said;

"It is gratifying that the World Health Organisation has recognised the scientific fact that cannabis and its derivatives have demonstrable therapeutic properties and can be the base for safe and effective medicines. It is now incumbent upon governments of the U.S.A and other nations to eliminate the barriers to research on cannabis and allow its free commerce across state lines and international frontiers".

I think it is amazing that it has taken them so long to admit something that doctors and medical practitioners all over the world have known for some time.

As Article 3 of the Single convention states;

"When a Party or the World Health Organisation has information which in its opinion may require an amendment to any of the Schedules, it shall notify the Secretary-General and furnish him with the information in support of the notification".

Their unwillingness to act earlier has more to do with internal politics, than health issues, but it is obvious looking at their recent report, that the provisions, classification and regulations in respect of cannabis, will alter dramatically, although of course, the final say rests with the Economic and Social Council of the United Nations, who are defined as, "The Council".

The Commission on Narcotic Drugs, will be the official body that will have to review the mountain of medical research, generated in the last 10-years. After deliberating at length, they will eventually submit their report, but it is interesting to note;

Article 3 (Section 8: (c);

"The Council may confirm, alter or reverse the decision of the Commission, and the decision of the Council shall be final. Notification of the council's decision shall be transmitted to all Member States of the United Nations, to non-member State Parties to this Convention, to the Commission, to the World Health Organisation and to the Board (International Narcotics Control Board)".

My interpretation of that is that the Council not only has the power to reject proposals, it can also issue its own ruling.

There is however another, far simpler solution for countries who wish to impose their own regulations in respect of cannabis, as Article 46 of the Single Convention states;

1: *"After the expiry of 2 years from the date of the coming into force of this convention, any Party may, on its own behalf or on behalf of a territory for which it has international responsibility, and which has withdrawn its consent, denounce this Convention by an instrument in writing deposited with the Secretary General".*

2: *"The denunciation, if received by the Secretary General on or before the first day of July in any year, shall take effect on January 1st in the succeeding year, and, if received after July 1st shall take effect as if it had been received on or before July 1st in the succeeding year".*

3: *"This Convention shall be terminated if, as a result of denunciations made in accordance with paragraph 1, the conditions of coming into force cease to exist".*

Countries who wish to adopt a more enlightened approach to the use of cannabis for medical, religious and recreational purposes, and who wish to regain their sovereign right to adopt legislation that is best suited to them, should denounce this Convention in writing, and submit it to the Secretary General of the United Nations without delay.

We should not forget, that the Single Convention formed the basis of Richard Nixon's draconian Controlled Substances Act of 1970, and the Misuse of Drugs Act that was introduced by the British Government in 1965 and later amended in 1971. Both of these Acts were responsible for ruining the lives of countless young people, who were persecuted and imprisoned for nothing more that the possession of cannabis.

Now that so many U.S States have legalised it for recreational purposes, there is a growing movement in America to legalise it nationally. On January 9th, 2019 Earl Blumenauer, the Democrat Representative for Oregon, introduced a tax bill to the House of Representatives, under the title; "Regulate Marihuana Like Alcohol Act".

Oregon is producing more marihuana than it can smoke, so if the bill was passed, it would allow growers to export it to other states, which would be a massive boost to the local economy. It is extremely unlikely that the bill will be passed, but it does illustrate a growing trend towards a more liberal approach. Speaking to the *Willamette Week*, Blumenauer said;

"Our federal marihuana laws are outdated, out of touch, and have negatively impacted countless lives. Congress cannot continue to be out of touch with a movement that a growing majority of Americans support. It's time to end this senseless prohibition".

The October 2018 Gallup poll indicated that 2 out of every 3 Americans are in favour of legalisation, and a survey carried out by the Quinnipiac University in April 2018 showed that 93% of Americans are in favour of medicinal cannabis.

All of this does not bode well for the Single Convention that is now facing the biggest crisis in its history.

With so much research being carried out on the medicinal benefits of cannabis, there is now a huge potential for countries that have a history of cannabis production. Countries like Morocco, Lebanon, Pakistan, India and Nepal are in an ideal position to become major suppliers of natural cannabidiol products, for a wide variety of illnesses. This would provide employment in rural areas as well as generating huge amounts of revenue, from exporting their products to the western world.

The Institute of Economic Affairs published an interesting discussion paper in June 2018.

Joint Venture – Estimating the Size and Potential of the UK Cannabis Market, was written by Christopher Snowdon, Head of Lifestyle Economics and it makes interesting reading. He estimated that the UK cannabis market is worth around £2.6 billion, which could provide the UK government with an annual revenue of around £557 million. This would require a controlled system, which would entail licensed cultivators, responsible for producing a product that would meet the government's requirements, in terms of safety and THC content, as well as licensed importers, wholesalers and vendors.

GW Pharmaceuticals, as one of the leading manufacturers of pharmaceutical cannabis-based medicines, would have an opportunity to reap even greater profits, than their present operation does.

Research has proved conclusively, that tobacco is a serious health hazard and some experts have estimated that in the 21st century, more than a billion people will die from smoking related diseases.

Tobacco is one of the most addictive drugs known to man, it has no medical benefits of any kind and it is not safe to use even under the most stringent medical supervision. Under the U.S Controlled Substances Act of 1971, tobacco meets all the requirements of a Schedule 1 drug and therefore, its use, possession, cultivation and transportation should be illegal.

Although laws have been passed in many countries which restrict its use in public places, it is still freely available all over the world. The only reason why it isn't, is due to the political and economic power of the American Tobacco Association, who donate huge sums of money to both the Democrats and Republicans, to ensure that their interests are looked after.

Such hypocrisy only serves to undermine public confidence in governments, international institutions and associations who play a major role in legislation around the world.

The United Nations is viewed by many as a neutral, impartial international organisation, but the reality is very different. Nations who contribute the most money, have the biggest say and since America is the biggest single contributor, it has the greatest influence. As an international body, responsible for monitoring world events from a political and environmental perspective, like its predecessor, the League of Nations, it has shown itself to be completely ineffective. The U.N Peace Force has been deployed in Africa on numerous occasions but due to its structure and mandate, it was unable to prevent large scale genocide that took place in Rwanda, Congo, Somalia and other countries. Allegations of sexual abuse by members of the U.N Peace Force have largely been ignored, which has damaged its reputation even more.

The U.N issues resolutions but is unable to enforce them, it condemns acts of aggression but is powerless to prevent them, and it makes recommendations that nobody pays any attention to, unless they suit the political agenda of its member states.

Israel is a prime example, the U.N has issued numerous resolutions in respect of Israel's continued occupation of the Golan Heights and its treatment of Palestinians living in the Gaza strip, but it changed nothing. President Donald Trump recently announced his decision to recognise the Golan Heights as part of Israel, the U.N denounced his decision, but it had no effect on Trump.

In a desperate attempt to justify its existence, it is now focusing its efforts on the war against drugs, and over the past 50 years, it has been slowly increasing its influence on drug legislation all over the world.

During the 2005 annual meeting of the United Nations Commission on Narcotic Drugs, which serves as a forum for nations to debate drug policy, France, Germany, Canada, Holland, Australia and Iran, all appealed against the United Nations zero tolerance approach to international drug policy, but their appeal was vetoed by America. It is ironic that they are now leading way by legalising its use in so many states.

We have an opportunity, perhaps our last one, to rectify the mistakes that were made by a generation, who left a legacy that has haunted us ever since. They knew what they were doing, although I still don't understand why they did what they did. Perhaps they were scared, perhaps they felt they had a right or perhaps they were so brainwashed themselves, they thought they were doing us a favour.

It doesn't matter, what matters is, that we now do everything in our power, to put an end to the Reefer Madness Mentality.

Medical science is on the verge of a new, exciting chapter, so far removed from the Prozac age, it will feel like a brave new world, but only if we play our part.

The Single Convention is a Treaty of Madness, which supports the big pharmaceutical companies who encourage doctors to prescribe drugs, that have turned our country into a nation of vegetables. In 2002, a report by the Canadian Senate Special Committee on Illegal Drugs, summarised the situation that had taken place in 1961;

"The international regime for the control of psychoactive substances, beyond any moral or even any racist roots it may initially have had, is first and foremost a system that reflects the geopolitics of North–South relations in the 20th century. Indeed, the strictest controls were placed on organic substances, the coca bush, the poppy and the cannabis plant, which are often part of the ancestral traditions of the countries where the plants originate, whereas the North's cultural products, tobacco and alcohol, were ignored and the synthetic substances produced by the North's pharmaceutical industry, were subject to regulation, rather than prohibition".

While the INCB (International Narcotics Control Board) continues to wage war against cannabis, their attempts to regulate and control addictive, dangerous pharmaceuticals appears to be a complete failure. Their 2018 report stated;

"The opioid overdose epidemic continued to worsen in the United States, with provisional data showing that over 70,000 drug overdose deaths had been reported in the country in 2017. In 2016, 63,632 died from drug overdoses, a 21.4% increase compared with 2015. According to the Centres for Disease Control and Prevention, opioids accounted for 66.4% (42,248) of those deaths, with increases across all age groups, racial and ethnic groups".

America is not the only country with an opioid problem, as the INCB report noted;

"According to government figures released in September 2018, there were nearly 4,000 apparent opioid-related deaths in 2017 in Canada, corresponding to an increase of 33%, compared to the number in 2016 (3,005). From January to March 2018, there were at least 1,000 apparent opioid-related deaths, 94% of which were accidental (unintentional); 73% of those accidental deaths involved fentanyl or fentanyl analogues".

"British Columbia remained the province hardest hit by the opioid crisis, with 1,399 deaths in 2017, an increase from the 974 reported in 2016".

With so many people dying every year in America from opioid overdoses, I am very surprised that the INCB continues to allow their use.

If 70,000 people had died in 2017 as a result of cannabis, I am certain it would have been headline news all around the world.

Canada's decision to legalise marihuana may have been due to their concern at the number of Canadians who are dying as a result of accidental overdoses. It is worth noting comments made in the 2017 report, by NASEM (National Academies of Science, Engineering and Medicines);

"Relief from chronic pain is by far the most common condition cited by patients for the medical use of cannabis. In addition, there is evidence that some individuals are replacing the use of conventional pain medications (e.g. opiates) with cannabis. For example, one recent study reported survey data from patrons of a Michigan medical marihuana dispensary, suggesting that medical cannabis use in pain patients was associated with a 64% reduction in opioid use".

"Similarly, the recent analysis of prescription data from Medicare Part D enrolees, in states with medical access to cannabis, suggest a significant reduction in the prescription of conventional pain medications. Combined with the survey data suggesting that pain is one of the primary reasons for the use of medical cannabis, these recent reports suggest that a number of pain patients are replacing the use of opioids with cannabis, despite the fact that cannabis has not been approved by the U.S. Food and Drug Administration for chronic pain".

However, it is blatantly obvious, that opioids are extremely dangerous, even though they have been approved by the FDA. This is the kind of illogical nonsense, that many people find unacceptable and yet, the INCB seems unwilling to budge.

In Chapter IV of their 2018 report, they state;

a) *"Governments that wish to establish special-access schemes to allow for the medical use of cannabinoids, should do so only where there is evidence of efficacy and safety, should limit the use of such preparations to approved medicinal cannabinoids and should monitor their prescription and use to minimise any risk of diversion and abuse".*

b) *"Governments should ensure that such programmes do not result in the de facto legalisation of cannabis for non-medical purposes".*

c) *"Medical use of cannabinoids should be regulated and supervised in a manner that meets the requirements set out in the drug control treaties. The integrity of the pharmaceutical regulatory system must be maintained, in particular by ensuring that cannabinoids are used in medical practise only where there is evidence of their equal or superior effectiveness relative to other medicinal products, and evidence of their safety".*

With so many deaths reported as a result of the use of opioids, I would suggest that integrity is in short supply in the world of pharmaceuticals, where profit appears to be the most important factor;

  d) *"Governments that allow the medicinal use of cannabinoids should monitor and evaluate the medicinal effectiveness as well as any unintended impact of those programmes".*

Shortly after the UK government announced its intention to legalise the use of certain cannabis pharmaceuticals, the UPA (United Patients Alliance), published an interesting report. It was based on a survey of more than 1,500 people, who used cannabis to alleviate physical or mental health conditions. As Jonathon Liebling, Political Director of the UPA stated;

"This is a window on the reality of the torture of pain and anxiety of thousands, perhaps millions of people who have not only endured multiple conditions, agonising physical and mental hardship, but have also been forced, whether personally or with the help of friends and family, to live the nightmare of secretly sourcing their only relief on black markets, on the street and in dark alleys for years".

The patients that took part in the survey are in many respects, the silent majority, those who had secretly and silently, resorted to buying cannabis on the street, as a means of alleviating their symptoms. A fact that for many, only added additional stress to their condition, as the UPA reported stated;

"These patients are the case studies, and, in many cases, arguably the true experts, on the efficacy of cannabis as medication".

The report showed that cannabis provided a significant improvement in 77% of those that took part. 70% said that conventional prescription medication gave them significant or severe side-effects. It also showed that 42% used it to replace conventional, pharmaceutical analgesics, including opioids while 29% used it as a substitute for conventional anti-depressants.

As Jonathon Liebling, Political Director of the UPA (United Patients Alliance) stated in 2018;

"We should be more concerned with the dangerous and addictive opiate medications, for which we have a serious and growing problem".

In August 2018, the government of British Columbia, announced its intention of suing 40 companies who produced opioids, in order to recoup the Canadian healthcare costs, incurred as a result of the opioid epidemic.

Attorney General David Eby informed reporters;

"Opioid misuse and addiction has taken a terrible toll on thousands of families and individuals in British Columbia. These British Columbians deserve our determination and support to end this epidemic".

Provincial health officer, Dr Perry Kendall said;

"We are still in the midst of a persistent and continuing epidemic of unintentional and poisoning deaths. Clearly, we are going to need to think more broadly and think further outside both the box and comfort zones, if we are going to get out in front of and turn this epidemic around".

Canada's decision to legalise cannabis use was certainly, "out of the box" but if it reduces the use and damage inflicted by opioids, it may well prove to be the most effective remedy.

Early indications appear to be very positive, showing a reduction of fatal overdoses in British Columbia from 164 in December 2016, to 99 in December 2017. Dr Patricia Daly, Executive Director of the British Columbia Overdose Emergency Response Centre, told Canadian reporters;

"The good news is it is not increasing, there has been a significant decrease in the last four months of 2017 but so far I think it is too early to say this is an ongoing trend".

I am certain that it is a trend which will continue, if allowed, because recent reports from America are even more encouraging, as Jonathon Liebling recently announced;

"In all U.S states that have implemented a broad enough medical cannabis policy, there have been a 24% reduction in deaths and addiction relating to opiate prescription and illicit medication".

My own view is that pharmaceutical companies are already working on a whole range of cannabis derived products for the pain relief market, after all, it is the core of their business and one that they are keen to protect.

SKUNK – THE NEW KID ON THE BLOCK

In the early 1970's, the cannabis scene in the UK was very different to what it is today.

Most consumers smoked "hash" or cannabis resin, which consisted of more than 80% of the cannabis market. Marihuana or "grass", mostly imported from Africa, was regarded as inferior and with so many seeds and twigs, it was considered to be a bad deal, even though by weight, it was far cheaper.

There were of course exceptions. "Malawi Cobs", so called because their shape resembled corn cobs, was a strong, high-grade grass, grown in Malawi, which was wrapped in banana leaves after being dried, and then buried in the ground for several months to cure. "Durban Poison" was a potent variety from South Africa and in the early 1970's, "Thai Sticks" appeared. This was a pale green grass with very few seeds, that was wrapped around a stalk tied with fishing line, but its price made it more of a fashion item and a talking point than anything else.

The resin market was very vibrant, there were ample supplies of hash from Afghanistan and to a lesser extent, a wide-variety of "Temple Balls" and "Temple Sticks", a much prized, hand-rubbed form of resin, from Nepal.

Hash from Kashmir also appeared now and again but although it was very pungent, it was often covered in white mould, a result of the Kashmiri's unique way of using steam, to press the agglutinated mass into a solid lump.

Lebanese came in two forms, a blonde version known as "Gold Leb" and one that was reddish in colour, known as "Red Leb". Huge amounts were smuggled into the country by the PLO (Palestinian Liberation Organisation) who used the profits to purchase arms. The cotton sacks, containing anything from 250 grams, up to 2 kilos, always had an Arabic stamp on them, many containing military images of crossed rifles, daggers, tanks and of course, the PLO logo.

The cheapest cannabis resin available was "penny slate", named after the thinness of the bars and the way it separated when you cut it. This was a pale green, Moroccan hash, cheap, but not particularly good. There were other varieties of Moroccan like "primo", a yellow, resinous hashish which was very popular and "zero-zero", named after the size of mesh that was used to sieve it.

Hippies who were travelling to India on the overland route were responsible for importing small amounts of a much higher grade of resin from India, Turkey, Afghanistan, Pakistan and Nepal. This provided consumers with a huge choice, especially for those living in London, where squats became focal points for anyone looking to buy a quality product.

Hash at that time was very popular, it was unadulterated, easily available, reasonably priced and safe to use and I think it is fair to say that London had the best selection of cannabis resin available anywhere in the world.

LSD was also very cheap, very good and widely available, due to the fact that Wales was the largest producer of LSD in Europe. It all came to an end in 1977, when British Police carried out, "Operation Julie". They discovered a farmhouse in Wales, where an American chemist and others, had been producing millions of what were known as "micro-dots". It was the biggest operation ever uncovered, supplying not only the British market, but also much of Europe as well, particularly France, Spain, Belgium, Germany and Italy. Coupled with the fact that London also had, arguably the best music scene in the world, it is not surprising that it became a magnet for young, adventurous people.

By the end of the 1970's, British Customs began to arrest large numbers of travellers and small-scale smuggling became a very hazardous occupation. Heavy sentences were handed out for importation, even for relatively small amounts and prices went up. Many hippies were arrested at Heathrow Airport and imprisoned, including a large number of foreigners who were arrested in transit, on their way to Canada, Germany, Italy and other parts of the world.

England at that time was full of "bucket shops", which sold cut-price airline tickets to every corner of the globe and as a result, many foreigners bought their tickets there and British prisons soon acquired a new, international clientele. You can't compare importing cannabis with robbery or rape and I think it was a huge mistake on the part of the British government to put people like that in prison. The only thing it achieved was to introduce cannabis to the criminal fraternity, which ultimately had a disastrous effect for everyone.

The PLO's demise in Lebanon, coincided with the involvement of criminal gangs from South London, many of whom had holiday homes on the Costa del Sol in Spain. Moroccan producers, identifying a gap in the UK market, expanded production to meet the growing demand and in a short space of time, with the help of UK criminal organisations, Moroccan hash dominated the market and as a result, the quality of cannabis resin declined significantly.

The criminal fraternity gradually took over the UK distribution network and the cannabis trade in general, became a criminal activity. Traditional hippie dealers were often robbed at gunpoint and rip-offs in general, became a common factor in the world of cannabis. Those involved in the importation were not interested in providing a quality product, many of the gangsters didn't even smoke, and although Morocco produces high-quality resin, the commercial grade produced for the criminal gangs did not meet the expectations of consumers.

To make matters worse, in order to increase profit margins, much of it was mixed with tranquilisers, as a means of increasing its potency. This was often carried out in Amsterdam, where the "soap", a phrase coined to describe the shape of the bars which resembled a famous brand of coal-tar soap, was adulterated.

The bars were put through a shredder, mixed with powdered barbiturates and tranquilisers and then re-pressed. This became known as "Euro-rock", an expression coined by knowledgeable consumers, denoting that the bars had been made in Europe, not Morocco.

Even though traditional Moroccan was still available, it was poor quality and as a result, people became bored and many people of my generation gave up smoking and resorted once again to alcohol. Ecstasy arrived on the scene in the 1980's and this became the drug of choice for the younger generation. Rave music replaced rock music, and, in many ways, it was the end of an era.

Cannabis had initially been classified in the UK as a Class B substance, which carried less severe penalties than heroin, which had been classified as a Class A material.

In 2004, following the advice from the ACMD (Advisory Council on the Misuse of Drugs), the British Government re-classified cannabis as a Class C substance and for a time, many believed that cannabis would eventually be decriminalised in the UK.

During the early 1980's, specialist growers in California began to experiment with new strains, developed by breeding potent strains of Columbian and Mexican varieties of *Cannabis Sativa*, with Himalayan strains of *Cannabis Indica*. This produced plants that were much smaller, with a shorter growing season and a higher THC content, ideal for indoor growing under lights, in controlled conditions.

Ronald Reagan's zero-tolerance policy towards drugs, made life very difficult for American growers and due to Holland's liberal laws regarding cannabis and their horticultural expertise, Dutch growers began to research these new varieties.

Although skunk is now a generic term, local legend recalls that it began life as a variety that proved to have a particularly pungent smell and as a result, it was given the name Skunk#1.

One of the early popular strains developed in Holland was "Northern Lights", which was apparently bred especially for countries in the Northern Hemisphere.

These new strains of marihuana developed in Holland, began to appear in the UK in the early 1990's. It was very expensive, and availability was limited, due to the fact that it was all imported.

Skunk, as it was now called, was a new type of grass, it had no seeds, it was very strong, and it was cultivated indoors using a new type of growing process known as hydroponics. As the technology improved and the price of equipment fell, more and more people turned to growing their own, not only in Holland but in the UK too.

The emergence of "grow rooms" replaced the need for importation, which always carried a high risk. With the ability to produce high-grade marihuana within the UK, it no longer made sense to import it.

As a criminal activity, grow rooms offered a number of advantages, especially from a financial perspective. Smuggling requires an enormous financial outlay; the cannabis has to be paid for before leaving the country of origin and great care has to be taken to conceal it. People employed to transport it have to be paid and then there is the cost of transportation itself, whether by air, land or sea. All of this presents a huge financial risk, which many were not prepared to take.

Grow rooms are easy to operate, cultivation requires only a minimum level of knowledge and with the advancement in hydroponics, 3 to 4 crops a year can be obtained. Not only is skunk cheap to produce, it can also be grown almost anywhere and grow rooms began to spring up all over Europe.

Specialised growers continued to experiment with new strains, creating varieties that were a blend of Cannabis Sativa and Cannabis Indica, which increased the THC content even more. These new strains attracted a new generation of young smokers, however, not having grown up in a cannabis culture, they were prone to abuse it, rather than use it. This has caused enormous concerns, both in the UK and around the world, as more and more youngsters are being diagnosed with mental health problems.

This prompted a statement in 2002, by Philip O. Emafo, President of the INCB (International Narcotics Control Board);

"It is possible that the cannabis being used in Europe may not be the same species that is used in developing countries and that is causing untold health hazards to the young people who are finding themselves in hospitals for treatment. Therefore, the INCB's concern is that cannabis use should be restricted to medical and scientific purposes, if there are any. Countries who are party to the Single Convention need to respect the provisions of the conventions and restrict the use of drugs listed in Schedules I to IV to strictly medical and scientific purposes".

In light of public concern over the safety of the new super strains of marihuana, the British Government requested the Advisory Council on the Misuse of Drugs to carry out a study, in order to determine the appropriate classification of cannabis.

The ACMD report, *Cannabis: Classification and Public Health*, published in 2008, revealed some interesting facts regarding the UK cannabis market.

Their investigations showed that domestic production of skunk, was responsible for nearly 80% of all cannabis sold in the UK.

According to the ACMD report, "grow rooms" can produce profits of anything from £90,000 - £480,000 a year, although it should be said, that not all of them produce a profit.

Many regular smokers, unhappy with the exorbitant cost of skunk, realised it was far better if they grew their own. Others set them up in order to become self-sufficient, enabling them to supply friends and family with a product that was often far superior to what they could purchase on the street. Those who use cannabis purely for medicinal purposes have also turned to grow rooms, as a means of obtaining a constant, regular supply, as well as being able to produce a variety that is best suited to their condition.

It is not surprising that criminal organisations are now exploiting the cannabis market, and the ACMD report showed that large-scale "grow-farms" have increased dramatically.

The Association of Chief Police Officers in Scotland reported that in the year 2006, less than 10 industrial-scale farms had been discovered but the following year, this figure had jumped to 70. In London, the Metropolitan Police reported that they were uncovering 10 small-scale operations every week, but with the potential for so much profit, this is not really surprising.

What was surprising, is that according to investigations carried out by the ACMD, there has been a decline in the use of cannabis of around 25% over all age-groups, during the previous 5 years.

This leads me to suspect that while the number of users have dropped, those who do use it, are consuming more and that "binge-smoking", like "binge-drinking" is probably on the increase. For me, this reflects an increasing trend by the younger generation who use cannabis simply to get as inebriated as quickly as possible, unlike the 1960's and 1970's, when it was used to "open one's mind".

Many people of my generation, who predominantly smoked cannabis resin in the 1970's don't like skunk. It certainly produces a different high than traditional varieties grown in sunlight, and I am certain that this is due to the proportion of THC (tetrahydrocannabidiol) and CBD (cannabidiol).

One of the most interesting aspects, from a research point of view, are the results shown in the ACMD report, relating to potency, which for me, explains better than anything, the difference between cannabis resin and marihuana.

Over the past 20 years, the THC content of cannabis resin and traditional forms of marihuana, have remained constant, however, the THC content of skunk increased dramatically from 1995 – 2000. Although they remained unchanged up until 2007, I suspect that new strains developed since then, contain even higher amounts.

There is definitely a trend among growers, to create varieties with even higher concentrations of THC, and many websites that sell seeds appear to promote their products based on the perceived THC content of the strain.

According to the 2008 ACMD report, the average THC content of cannabis resin was 3.5% and 2.1% in traditional marihuana, however, the average THC content of skunk was 13.9%. This clearly demonstrates, that the objective of those responsible for creating these new strains, is to produce a plant with the highest THC content possible.

After recently reviewing a number of web sites devoted to selling seeds, I was shocked to see some strains being advertised as having a THC content of 33%. For my money this is madness, if Shiva wanted us to smoke ganja with a THC content of 33%, he would have put it in the ground on day one.

THC content is not the only difference between cannabis resin and marihuana, from my perspective, the main difference can be attributed to the CBD (cannabidiol) content.

Looking at the table in the ACMD report, cannabis resin has a much greater CBD content than traditional marihuana. Analysis of samples showed that cannabis resin which contained a THC content of 3.54% also contained 4.17% CBD. In contrast, traditional marihuana with a THC content of 2.14%, only contained 0.1% CBD. Skunk, with a THC content of 13.98% contained only 0.1% CBD. These were only average figures, some samples of cannabis resin showed a CBD content of 6.9% and other samples of traditional marihuana showed a CBD content of 1.9%, however, other samples of skunk showed a CBD content of only 0.56%.

Clearly, skunk contains less CBD than traditional marihuana and far less than cannabis resin. These figures for me, clearly demonstrate why UK cannabis smokers preferred cannabis resin, which was regarded as a pleasant, mellow high, in comparison to a more erratic, speed like sensation, when smoking marihuana.

Recent studies have shown that CBD (cannabidiol) is an anti-psychotic, which leads me to believe that cannabis resin, which contains more CBD than THC, is far safer than skunk, which contains virtually no CBD. If the THC content is important when determining the psychological and physical effects of the use of cannabis, it seems to me that the CBD content is even more critical.

This is an aspect which has been completely overlooked by the policy makers, who now appear to be so obsessed with the dangers of skunk, that they have completely ignored cannabis resin, by simply regarding it as the same, which of course, is completely incorrect.

It should be remembered, that previous studies carried out by the Le Dain Commission, the Shafer Commission and others, were based on marihuana that contained a much lower THC content than the skunk that is smoked today. They therefore have very little relevance to studies carried out using modern strains that are now used in the 21st century.

During the course of their investigations, the ACMD concluded;

"In some instances, acute cannabis intoxication appears to precipitate a psychotic state that may continue for some time and may require treatment with anti-psychotic drugs. This is similar to the psychotic states following the intoxication with cocaine or amphetamine".

This is a characteristic that was not identified in the studies carried out in the 1960's and 70's and is undoubtedly due to the extremely high THC content, as well as the lack of CBD, which has been shown to have anti-psychotic properties.

The ACMD clearly shared this view, stating;

"There is evidence to suggest that users of cannabis are now exposed to products with a higher THC content. This has occurred largely because of the substantial increase in the market share of sinsemilla (skunk). The council is therefore concerned at the dominance of sinsemilla in the market because of its greater potency and the virtual absence of CBD".

One of the recommendations of the ACMD, stated;

"There is also a need to continue to monitor the market share of cannabis products as well as to continue to monitor their potencies in relation to their THC and CBD content. The possible protective role of CBD needs to be fully evaluated in humans".

A more recent report, published in the Forensic Research & Criminal International Journal, in 2016, revealed a huge rise in domestic production. According to a survey carried out by Andrew O'Hagan and Amber Parker of Nottingham University, the number of commercial grow-rooms discovered by British police, had more than doubled in a four-year period from 2007-2011. The number of commercial grow-room operations that were seized as a result of police action, rose dramatically from 3,032 in 2008 to 7,865 in 2012.

Results concerning smaller operations showed an even greater increase, the average number of grow-rooms being discovered every month, rising from 252 to 656 in the same period.

In 2010, there were nearly 190,000 cannabis seizures, of which 145,000 were skunk, 40,000 were cannabis resin and the remaining 5,000 involved plants. Although total seizures dropped to 120,000 in 2015, 110,000 of those were skunk, and only 3,000 related to cannabis resin, the remainder relating to the seizures of plants. The report also highlighted the fall in seizures of cannabis resin, dropping from 50 tons in 2011, to less than 4 tons in 2015. In my view, the market share of skunk will only increase, to such an extent that cannabis resin may become virtually extinct in the UK. There is no incentive to import it, when skunk can be easily produced in the UK at a price that is competitive with the cost of cannabis in countries like Morocco, India, Lebanon, Pakistan and Nepal.

The emergence of skunk has, in my view, ruined any possibility of cannabis being legalised in the UK and I suspect, that a post-Trump U.S Government, may not be so lenient on those states that have already legalised it for recreational purposes. In 2017, the National Academies of Science, Engineering and Medicines, commissioned an impressive committee to investigate the health effects of marihuana. Its introduction stated;

"Over the past 20 years, significant changes have taken place in the policy landscape surrounding cannabis legalisation, production and use. To date, 28 states and the District of Columbia have legalised cannabis for the treatment of medical conditions. Eight of these and the District of Columbia have also legalised cannabis for recreational use. These landmark changes in policy have markedly changed cannabis use patterns and perceived levels of risk. Based on a recent nationwide survey, 22.2 million Americans (12 years of age and older) reported using cannabis in the past 30 days, and between 2002 and 2015 the percentage of past month cannabis users in this age range has steadily increased".

The association with 12-year old children sets the tone;

"The years since 2007 have seen steady year-over-year increases in general population past-month uses, rising from 5.8% to 8.4% in 2014 (a 45% increase). There is no single clear explanation for the post-2007 increases in use. Hypothesised causes include declining potency-adjusted prices on the illicit market; the proliferation of medical cannabis laws, especially those that allow for sale at brick-and-mortar dispensaries; and changing public perceptions about the harms of cannabis use".

The committee explained how the present situation has arisen;

"The federal government has not challenged these state laws by invoking the supremacy clause of the U.S Constitution. However, under the 10th Amendment, as reaffirmed by U.S jurisprudence, the federal government cannot force a state to criminalise an act under state law".

Apparently is was all because of a thing called democracy;

"When the voters of these states passed initiatives to legalise, regulate and tax recreational cannabis, they simultaneously repealed the penal provisions and sanctions, prohibiting and criminalising unauthorised cultivation, trafficking and possession of cannabis".

Like all politicians, they blamed the previous administration and when they do, it is a very clear indication that they intend to change the status quo.

"Under the Obama administration, the federal government seems to have opted for a more pragmatic solution which allows for a rules-based cannabis industry, as dictated by state regulations, while maintaining the future option to pre-empt".

A summary of their findings in respect of the effects of marihuana stated;

A) *"Cannabis use is likely to increase the risk of developing schizophrenia and other psychoses: the higher the use, the greater the risk".*

B) *"In individuals with schizophrenia and other psychoses, a history of cannabis use may be linked to better performance on learning and memory tasks".*

C) *"Cannabis use does not appear to increase the likelihood of developing depression, anxiety and post-traumatic stress disorder".*

D) *"For individuals diagnosed with bi-polar disorders, near daily cannabis use may be linked to greater symptoms of bi-polar disorder than for nonusers".*

E) *"Heavy cannabis users are more likely to report thoughts of suicide than are nonusers".*

F) *"Regular cannabis use is likely to increase the risk for developing social anxiety disorder".*

I find their summary extremely confusing. On one hand the committee states that marihuana use increases the risk of schizophrenia and in the next breath, its use may have been responsible for the improvement of memory and learning skills of long-term sufferers. Even more confusing; they say marihuana does not increase the risk of depression, but heavy cannabis users are more likely to consider suicide. They were less ambiguous in respect of its medical benefits;

"Despite this reported rapid rise in the use of cannabis, both for medical purposes and for recreational use, conclusive evidence regarding the short-and-long term health effects of cannabis use remains elusive".

"While a myriad of studies have examined cannabis use in all its various forms, often these research conclusions are not appropriately synthesised, translated for, or communicated to policy makers, health care providers, state health officials or other stakeholders, who have been charged with influencing and enacting policies, procedures and laws related to cannabis use".

The committee did acknowledge some medicinal benefits;

"Irrespective of the mechanism of action, there is evidence that CBD could potentially be exploited in the treatment and symptom relief of various neurological disorders such as epilepsy and seizures, psychosis, anxiety, movement disorders: (e.g., Huntington's disease and amyotrophic lateral sclerosis) and multiple sclerosis".

In light of the fact that the FDA had already approved Epidiolex, GW's gift to American epileptics, they were not in a position to say otherwise. This report is only the first, but I think there will be a lot more of these types of investigations over the next few years and I think each one will be a nail in the coffin of the legalise cannabis movement.

It would be a great pity to return to the dark days, where cannabis smokers were persecuted, especially for those who use it responsibly. Specialised growers should realise, that high THC content reduces the possibility of the legalisation of cannabis, although in all probability, the damage may have already been done.

OLD SCHOOL – A SAFE AND SENSIBLE OPTION

I think it's safe to say that the battle for medical cannabis is slowly being won, but the same cannot be said for recreational use or for those who have become accustomed to smoking it as a means of pain relief, often dismissed as "self-medication". As I have already said, I suspect that new studies carried out on the effects of these new, high THC strains, will result in a demand for tougher legislation. The UK Government has several options;

It can wage a new war against cannabis, by introducing legislation regarding the importation, distribution and sales of lighting systems and all the other equipment used, and by introducing longer prison sentences for offenders. For this to be effective, the British police force would require a substantial increase in resources, providing more officers, more equipment and a bigger budget.

This presents a major problem. In the previous war on cannabis in the 1970's and 1980's, all the cannabis was imported and therefore, by imposing stringent customs regulations and practises at airports, docks and all points of entry, as an island nation, H.M Customs and Excise were able to make life extremely difficult for smugglers.

In this new age of "Made in Britain" Cannabis, without an obvious point of entry the situation is much more difficult to control, since, in theory, every building in the country has the potential to be a grow-room. This does, in effect, drastically reduce the possibility of enforcing effective prohibition, irrespective of the amount of additional resources the government may allocate to the task.

If one accepts the fact that prohibition has failed, and it would be a foolish person who tried to argue otherwise, the only other option is to establish a regulated, taxed market, similar to tobacco and alcohol. This would result in products that met government standards, regarding THC and CBD content.

Before presenting the case for the Association of Old School Smokers, I think we should first reflect, once again, on the words of the Honourable D.R. Lyall, who, in 1894, while giving evidence to the Indian Hemp Drugs Commission, stated,

"Ganja and charas are really one, and in time, if the question be scientifically followed up, possibly charas will be the only form used".

I begin with these words, simply because we are now in a position to consider scientific evidence, that was unavailable in 1894.

Scientific, laboratory analysis of samples of skunk, traditional ganja and cannabis resin were subjected to clinical, chemical examination. Since cannabis contains both THC and CBD, it is interesting to note the different levels in the samples tested. Analysis revealed that skunk with a THC content of 23% contained less than 0.6% CBD, while samples of traditional ganja, with a THC content of 11% contained 1.9% CBD.

Cannabis resin on the other hand, is an entirely different case, because unlike any other form of cannabis, it contains nearly as much CBD than THC and in some cases, even more. Samples showed that cannabis resin with a THC content of 3.5% THC, contained 4.1% CBD. Analysis of various samples of resin, showed that as the THC content increased, so did the CBD content. Samples that contained 8% THC contained 7% CBD, demonstrating that charas is a far more balanced preparation than ganja.

The scientific results are very clear; ganja is predominantly a THC product, which contains small amounts of CBD, while charas contains equal amounts of THC and CBD. Skunk on the other hand, is even less balanced, since it contains the higher amounts of THC and the least amounts of CBD.

This subtle difference must be taken into account. All available evidence points to the fact that CBD has been shown to be an effective anti-psychotic, so the prohibition of cannabis resin, based on the effects of skunk, would be entirely unreasonable.

One of the major problems with the vast majority of the research being carried out today, is that it is not geared towards comparative studies, involving cannabis resin and skunk. From a chemical composition point of view, they are entirely different products and clinical trials need to be carried out to determine the difference in psychological and mental effects between the two, because clearly, they will not be the same.

If CBD is an effective anti-psychotic and the government is determined to reduce the number of skunk users, the legalisation of cannabis would probably be the most effective way of killing two birds with one stone.

One of the delights of cannabis resin, is that it offers far more variations in terms of flavour, texture and effect. High quality Lebanese has a distinctly sweet taste, Moroccan has a more flowery flavour, while Himalayan varieties of hashish and charas can be either extremely fruity or exceptionally pungent.

A connoisseur of charas for instance, can distinguish subtle differences in both taste and aroma, which identifies the characteristics of the region or valley where it was produced. The same principles are used by wine connoisseurs, who are able, even on a blind tasting, to differentiate between a Meursault and a Corton Charlemagne and in some cases, even identify the vineyard where it was made.

If UK consumers had access to a wide variety of cannabis resin, I am certain that a fashionable, high value, connoisseur market would quickly develop. I am sure that many of the old forms of cannabis, that were so much adored in the 1960's and 70's, would become fashionable among the younger generation, who have never had the opportunity to try them before.

At present, they have very little choice, skunk or no skunk and that cannot be a good thing. The younger generation would be far better off smoking cannabis resin and I am sure that given the choice and a financial incentive, many would switch from skunk to resin.

For those who would prefer to smoke grass, traditional varieties of ganja, which contain less THC and a lot more CBD should be made available.

A legalised market would give them access to prime Jamaican "lamb's breath", a particularly sweet form of Jamaican ganja, which would certainly benefit the Rastafari community, and the former British colony would be only too happy to allow them to produce it, as an export product bound for the regulated British market.

Alternatively, they may enjoy some prime Colombian Gold, which would offer the farmers a legal alternative to growing coca for the Colombian drug cartels.

Durban Poison would stimulate dagga production in South Africa and the production of Acapulco Gold would certainly provide much needed work for rural communities in Mexico.

It would be very simple to regulate it, particularly in the case of cannabis resin, since it is often produced in large amounts and each batch is of a similar general consistency. Each shipment could easily be analysed, and although there would be slight fluctuations, most batches coming from the same area, would show consistent levels of both THC and CBD.

Morocco is not only the biggest producer of cannabis resin in the world, it is also the most adaptable. Recent studies suggest that Moroccan farmers are in the process of replacing traditional strains of cannabis, with new hybrid varieties, enabling them to produce a resin that has a much higher THC content. This has been done in order to make their product more competitive, in an attempt to win back a larger share of the market, as well as increasing production.

This demonstrates that cultivators are capable of producing a product of almost any criteria and there is no doubt that Lebanon, Pakistan, Afghanistan, Nepal and India, could all do the same thing. In a legalised market, cannabis producers would have to adapt their manufacturing methods, in order to meet government requirements, which obviously would be a good thing.

I think it is reasonable to say, that the most harmful effects are caused as a result of legislation, that treats users as criminals and, which punishes them accordingly. Unlike the effects of cannabis, which fade after a few hours, the subsequent criminal conviction, resulting from that legislation, lasts a lifetime.

Cannabis convictions, even from 40 years ago, can cause immense problems when applying for jobs which require a full background check. It also damages the prospects of obtaining a visa to visit countries like Canada, America, Australia and Japan, which can have a dramatic effect on families living apart.

It would be nice if all previous cannabis convictions were deleted and people were no longer arrested and imprisoned for smoking it but considering the controversy that has surrounded this plant over the last 100 years, that is probably too much to hope for.

Rupert Simmington

This is Rupert Simmington's second book. His first, The Politics of Failure – A History of Greed, Hypocrisy and Exploitation, examined the influence of capitalism and how it helped to shape the world we live in today. Cannabis – A Study of its History, Prohibition and Use, examines the controversy surrounding this remarkable plant and its use in 21st century medicine.

Printed in Dunstable, United Kingdom

71832390R00106